TELEVISED MORALITY

The Case of Buffy the Vampire Slayer

Gregory Stevenson

Hamilton Books
an imprint of
University Press of America,® Inc.
Dallas · Lanham · Boulder · New York · Oxford

Copyright © 2003 by
Hamilton Books
4501 Forbes Boulevard
Suite 200
Lanham, Maryland 20706
UPA Acquisitions Department (301) 459-3366

PO Box 317
Oxford
OX2 9RU, UK

All rights reserved
Printed in the United States of America
British Library Cataloging in Publication Information Available

Library of Congress Control Number: 2003116659
ISBN 0-7618-2833-8 (paperback : alk. ppr.)

♾™ The paper used in this publication meets the minimum
requirements of American National Standard for Information
Sciences—Permanence of Paper for Printed Library Materials,
ANSI Z39.48—1984

To Saysavad
whose many sacrifices made this book possible

Contents

Preface		vii
Acknowledgments		ix
Introduction		xi
Chapter 1	Taking *Buffy* Seriously	1
Chapter 2	The Moral Battleground	9
Chapter 3	Storytellers	23
Chapter 4	Buffy's Story	43
Chapter 5	Buffy's World	61
Chapter 6	Human Nature	81
Chapter 7	Identity and the Quest for Self	91
Chapter 8	A Tale of Two Slayers: Identity, Sacrifice, and Salvation	105
Chapter 9	Systems of Power: Technology, Magic, and Institutional Authority	125
Chapter 10	Together or Alone? The Dynamics of Community and Family	139

Chapter 11	The End as Moral Guidepost	159
Chapter 12	Morals and Consequences	173
Chapter 13	Sexuality	189
Chapter 14	Violence and Vengeance	203
Chapter 15	Guilt and Forgiveness	215
Chapter 16	The Vampire, The Witch, and the Warlock: Patterns of Redemption	235
Conclusion	*Buffy* and Moral Discourse	259
Notes		263
Episode Guide		273
Bibliography		279
Index		291
About the Author		301

Preface

I have always been fascinated by vampire stories, whether the grotesque horror of Stephen King's *Salem's Lot*, the dark romanticism of Anne Rice's Louis and Lestat, or the sheer camp of *Love at First Bite*. As a teenager, I could never explain this fascination, but now, as a theologian in his mid-thirties, I can hide behind the excuse that they tap into my interest in the dialogue between good and evil. So on a Saturday afternoon in March of 1997, I sat down to watch the series premiere of a new show on the WB network called *Buffy the Vampire Slayer*. I did so with great intrigue tempered with low expectations conditioned by the underwhelming 1992 movie of the same name. I was immediately hooked. This show combined in one package all of the elements of vampire stories (the horror, the humor, the romanticism) that I had long appreciated.

Yet I was also troubled. My conservative Christian background clashed with the occult elements of the show and the increasing sexual activity over the course of the seasons made me at times uncomfortable. On an instinctual level, however, I knew that *Buffy the Vampire Slayer* was much more than it seemed. The incoherence between the moral messages I was taking from the show and the seemingly immoral form in which they were sometimes cast captivated my imagination and set me on a journey of discovery.

This journey was further influenced by three other factors. First, was my growing belief that there is an ongoing conversation in American culture about theology and morality that Christians have oddly failed to join. Creators of film and television increasingly address moral issues in their art, yet many Christians have opted for surface evaluations of those works based on the level of sex, violence, and profanity, thus failing to engage the deeper conversation. My analysis of *Buffy the Vampire Slayer* is an attempt to draw people into that deeper conversation.

The second factor was my students in the class on "Hollywood and Religion in American Culture" that I teach at Rochester College. I witnessed in them the same desire I saw in myself of eagerly wanting to engage popular culture, but in a theologically and morally responsible way. Because *Buffy the Vampire Slayer* has sparked such wide debate and oddly divergent reactions to its message, it seemed like the perfect case study for testing the nature of moral discourse in popular culture. The third factor was conversations held with colleagues in the Communication, English, and Religion departments at Rochester College whose insights into this show were the catalyst for many of my own thoughts and ideas.

I write this book unapologetically as a fan of *Buffy the Vampire Slayer*, but also, I hope, as a responsible theological critic. For me, this book is part of a personal journey that is ongoing. I hope you will come along for this part of the ride.

Acknowledgments

I must especially thank Ronald Cox, Jennifer Hamilton, and Andrew Kronenwetter, my colleagues at Rochester College who are both scholars and fellow *Buffy* fans. Their support has been invaluable. Ronald and Jennifer read the manuscript and offered many insightful comments that have made this book better than it would have been without them. Jeanette MacAdam and the staff at the Rochester College library acquired for me many hard to find resources. I thank Rex Hamilton both for his playful mockery and for helping me with one difficult portion of the book. I thank Keith Huey for the Pez. I thank Luke Timothy Johnson for his support of this project and David Lavery and Rhonda Wilcox for their words of encouragement. Rodney Clapp deserves my gratitude for seeing value in this project early on. My gratitude is also due to Heather Anderson Haynes and her colleagues at Twentieth Century Fox who helped me traverse the minefield of legal issues. This book is an independent analysis of *Buffy the Vampire Slayer* and as such is neither authorized by nor officially associated with the show or with Twentieth Century Fox. Finally, I thank the people at Hamilton Books and University Press of America, particularly Nicole Caddigan and Stephen Ryan, for all their assistance and support.

Introduction

Film and television have captured the attention of the American public to a degree greater than any previous form of media, yet they still suffer from the common misconception of being "merely entertainment." Consequently, the general populace often expresses amazement when academics undertake scholarly analysis of popular movies and television shows. The *X-Files*, *Star Wars*, and *The Simpsons* are fine for Saturday evening recreation, it is argued, but not Monday morning debate and reflection. *Buffy the Vampire Slayer* is media junk food for teenage viewers, not fodder for doctoral dissertations and academic essays.

Film and television, however, deal in stories and stories shape how we understand ourselves and the world in which we live. Because stories often communicate indirectly, they can have tremendous impact on how we think and the decisions we make in ways that may not be immediately obvious. Joss Whedon, the creator of *Buffy the Vampire Slayer*, argues that his creation in particular (and popular culture in general) is a necessary topic of study for the academic community.

> I think it's great that the academic community has taken an interest in the show. I think it's always important for academics to study popular culture, even if the thing they are studying is idiotic. If it's successful or made a dent in culture, then it is worthy of study to find out why. 'Buffy,' on the other hand is, I hope, not idiotic. We think very carefully about what we're trying to say emotionally, politically, and even philosophically while we're writing it . . . I do believe that there is plenty to study and there are plenty of things going on in it, as there are in me that I am completely unaware of. People used to laugh that academics would study Disney movies. There's nothing more important for academics to study, because they shape the minds

of our children possibly more than any single thing.[1]

In this book I analyze *Buffy the Vampire Slayer* in the context of moral discourse. Whether explicitly or implicitly, intentionally or unintentionally, for good or ill, virtually every aspect of popular culture impinges upon the topic of morality to one degree or another.

For the purpose of this book, I operate with an understanding of morality as the categorization of life experiences and behavioral choices with respect to categories of good and evil, right and wrong. As definitions go, that is fairly straightforward, yet the application of this categorization to specific contexts is far from simple. Where precisely should the line between right and wrong be drawn? How does one decide where specific actions fall on the continuum? If, as I suggest, morality is an exploration of life and the attempt to order experience according to a specific system of values, then a discussion of morality should encompass more than traditional moralisms such as dishonesty, sex, violence, and the like. It should engage the variety of life experiences that create meaning and order in the world.

How works of art (including film and television as a form of artistic expression) relate to morality is a topic of much debate. On one side are moralists who view art as a vehicle for moral instruction. Thus, moralist critiques of television, for instance, evaluate a show on the basis of its success or failure at openly communicating specific moral perspectives, such as attitudes towards sexuality or violence. On the other side are those who wish to divorce art from morality altogether, seeing them as completely separate spheres of discourse. R. W. Beardsmore rejects both of these views because they "fail to see that what an artist reveals about morality cannot be distinguished from the manner in which he does so."[2] Beardsmore argues that art functions indirectly by facilitating a better understanding of life that then allows us to make more informed moral decisions.[3] Of course, if art can impact moral decisions, that impact can be for better or worse.

Building off the idea that art can provide a fuller moral understanding through an examination of life, I have chosen *Buffy the Vampire Slayer* as a case study for analyzing how a work of popular culture may engage in moral discourse. An accurate moral evaluation of a television show like *Buffy the Vampire Slayer* must transcend simplistic tallies of sex and violence and instead contextualize those acts within a larger moral vision that encompasses not only the content of what is presented (the "what") but also the manner by which it is presented (the "how").

My approach in this book is largely descriptive rather than evaluative. I offer a description of this show's moral vision and the manner in which that vision is communicated. Although I will make evaluative judgments throughout, it is not my intention to dictate for the reader what their moral evaluation of this show should be because such an ultimate decision relies on a variety of personal factors in the life of each individual to which I have no access. I hope to demonstrate that what constitutes a show's morality is far more complex and multi-layered than is often appreciated and that the determination of an adequate critique must engage the show in all its moral complexity. I offer my *interpretation* of the moral vision of *Buffy the Vampire Slayer*. The reader should understand that to appreciate the overall moral vision of a television show does not mean that one must agree with every aspect of that vision. I certainly do not. It is true that *Buffy the Vampire Slayer* has received criticism from Christians, yet they are not alone. Despite the show's obvious feminist agenda, some feminist scholars have criticized its portrayal of a feminist heroine for being too traditionally feminine. Modern practitioners of Wicca have criticized the show's portrayal of witchcraft. Homosexual advocacy groups have vocally complained about how the lesbian relationship between two characters ultimately played out. The goal is not to agree with everything communicated in the show, but to understand and appreciate its larger moral program.

Buffy the Vampire Slayer ended its seven season run in March of 2003, a sad occurrence for fans but in some ways a boon to scholars as it means we now possess a completed "text" for analysis. The danger of commenting on a show currently in production is that subsequent episodes could nullify earlier observations. Anyone who reads up on scholarly essays produced during the earlier seasons of this show can find numerous examples of this. On the upside, with a completed narrative interpreters can offer more informed and holistic analysis. On the downside, we can no longer appeal to our lack of prophetic foresight for some of the absurd things we say.

Some may wonder what value there is in studying a television show that is now off the air. With shows increasingly appearing in syndication and on DVD, they are becoming more like novels in the sense of being a completed story that continues to exist and can be revisited. Due to this extended existence, these shows continue to impact culture. Also, learning what *Buffy* accomplishes in the arena of moral discourse provides a foundation for analyzing other television shows currently on the air.

My own methodology for this study involved watching the episodes and reading selected transcripts,[4] from which I developed my interpretation of the series. I have also attempted to read as much of the scholarly literature on *Buffy the Vampire Slayer* as I had access to, both in traditionally published form and available over the Internet, and I dialogue with that material where relevant. I have sought out comments by Joss Whedon and his staff of writers who have been quite vocal over the years about their creation. The narrative goals of the creative voices behind this work is integral to understanding the moral vision of *Buffy the Vampire Slayer*; yet, it is the nature of a narrative to spark interpretations that may go beyond anything intended by the writer. More than one interpretation of the same text may be equally valid because many factors aside from authorial intent impact meaning.

My primary audience for this book is college students who are studying the debate over television and morality. In part, the origin of this project came from the realization that most of my students had little or no idea of how to determine the moral worth of the television shows they were watching on a regular basis. Because of my target audience, I cannot assume that all who read this book were or are regular watchers of *Buffy the Vampire Slayer*. In fact, I intend for this book to be accessible to those who are unfamiliar with the show. Consequently, I provide content information about the series whenever relevant to the discussion. Although the scholarly community is not the primary audience, they are a secondary audience for this book, and I frequently engage scholarly discussion and analysis throughout. These dual audiences present a challenge because the student and non-academic may at times find the discussion to be too technical, while the scholar may at other times find the discussion to be too general. This is unavoidable given the nature of this book, but I have worked hard to make those moments as rare as possible so that all readers of this book may find it beneficial.

My analysis unfolds over sixteen chapters and a conclusion. The first three chapters lay the theoretical groundwork that informs my reading of *Buffy the Vampire Slayer* (hereafter also referred to as *Buffy*). Chapter four is an introduction to and summary of the seven seasons of *Buffy*. This chapter functions for the benefit of those who may not be familiar with the show so that I can assume a certain level of knowledge in my subsequent analysis. Chapters five through sixteen explore a variety of topics and themes that illustrate aspects of moral discourse in *Buffy*. The variety of topics is matched by the variety of analysis, which includes thematic studies, character studies, and analysis of individual episodes. Throughout the book, specific episodes of *Buffy* are referred to by season number and episode number. These numbers correspond to the episode guide at the end of the book that provides further information. The concluding section summarizes the results of this study by highlighting significant features of *Buffy*'s moral discourse and by identifying certain analytical methods for determining the moral value of a television show.

Chapter 1

Taking *Buffy* Seriously

It's nighttime at Sunnydale High School. As the camera moves slowly through darkened hallways and empty classrooms, a hand suddenly punches in through a window in the biology lab. A teenage boy and blond girl climb in through the window. They walk together down the hallway but she starts to protest, unsure if she should go further. He responds by moving in to kiss her, but she is startled by a noise and pulls away, looking around anxiously. He attempts to comfort her by assuring her that no one else is there. Convinced that they are alone, the blond girl then turns to him with her face distorted in a demonic visage and sinks her bared fangs into his neck.

From this opening scene of the very first episode of *Buffy the Vampire Slayer* one thing is clear: nothing is going to be what it seems. As the blond girl/vampire turns on her "date," we quickly learn to expect the unexpected: the roles of the traditional prey (teenage girl) and the traditional predator (teenage boy) have been reversed.

The television show *Buffy the Vampire Slayer* is the brainchild of Joss Whedon, a third generation television writer whose father and grandfather wrote for such shows as *The Andy Griffith Show*, *The Donna Reed Show*, *Alice*, *Benson*, and *The Golden Girls*. Joss Whedon, who studied Film and feminist theory at Wesleyan University, began his career by working as a writer and script doctor for films such as *Toy Story*, *Speed*, and *Twister*. Whedon eventually wrote a screenplay that became the 1992 film *Buffy the Vampire Slayer*. The movie was a tragedy. The director had taken a film that Whedon intended as an equal mixture of horror, action, and comedy and had turned it into camp by essentially removing the horror.[1] When Whedon was later asked to create a television version of his screenplay, he jumped at the chance to return to his original vision. According to Whedon, that original vision was grounded in the idea of subverting standard conventions of the horror genre. In a commentary on the first episode of the series, Whedon declares that the mission statement of *Buffy* can be summarized as "Nothing is as it seems."[2] He says the idea for *Buffy* came from watching too many horror movies where the attractive blond girl is an unwitting victim lured into dark places and easily dispatched. He envisioned a narrative world in which the little blond girl became the thing that the monsters and demons feared the most.[3] And so Buffy was born — a sixteen-year-old California valley girl who by day obsesses over boys, clothes, and biology exams, while by night prowls cemeteries seeking vampires and monsters to slay.

Although on the surface, *Buffy the Vampire Slayer* is about a teenage girl pummeling monsters of the night all the while tossing off clever puns and maintaining a killer fashion sense, the show is not quite what it seems. In actuality, *Buffy* is a show about growth; in particular about traversing the dangerous terrain that makes up the journey from adolescence into adulthood. The various monsters and vampires that populate Sunnydale function as metaphorical representations of the inner demons that plague us and the emotional forces that we fight against in our struggle to grow up and to learn how to live in a complex world.

Throughout the series Whedon has maintained his mission of genre subversion by unexpectedly killing off major characters, turning "good" characters evil, and setting evil characters on the path towards redemption. Yet this subversion is not an attempt to transcend the boundaries of the genre but to play creatively within those boundaries. The rules of a genre are designed to court audience expectation. To subvert those same rules while remaining within the boundaries requires a sophisticated understanding of their function and a vision of the genre's potentiality that transforms expectation into surprise. An example of this is the first season episode "The Puppet Show" (1.9), which features a ventriloquist's dummy. Anyone familiar with the horror genre immediately develops expectations of how the story will unfold. In this genre, a ventriloquist's dummy is always self-aware and secretly evil, wielding influence over his ventriloquist, and setting out on a path of destruction and murder. In "The Puppet Show," however, the episode unfolds according to expectation until it is suddenly revealed that the dummy is in fact a fellow demon hunter trapped in his wooden prison by a curse. The expectations inherent in the genre have been subverted without violating the genre itself.

Whedon has deftly maneuvered this terrain in such a way that he has created a show that embraces genre yet is difficult to categorize according to genre. *Buffy the Vampire Slayer* is — sometimes independently, sometimes all at once — a horror show, a comedy, a drama, a satire and an action adventure. Joss Whedon reveals that the show's title, with its juxtaposition of the silliness of the name "Buffy" with the horror staple of "Vampire," is itself a nod to the cross-genre aspect of *Buffy*[4] and that a recognition of this cross-genre approach is essential to full appreciation of the series, or, to let Whedon state it more simply, "I believe that anyone who isn't open to a show with this title isn't invited to the party."[5]

DUMB TV?

The popular attitude towards *Buffy* confirms the mission of the show that "Nothing is as it seems." Most people, including many academics,[6] refuse to believe a show called *Buffy the Vampire Slayer* deserves to be taken seriously. Emmy voters have agreed, refusing to honor the show for episodes that many critics believed were far more worthy than those that actually won, although part of the difficulty for Emmy voters has been the problem of how to categorize the show. Throughout its seven seasons, *Buffy* struggled to attract viewers, in large part due to the public misconception of it as a campy diversion.

Joss Whedon disagrees. "I hate camp," he says. "I don't enjoy dumb TV. I believe Aaron Spelling has single-handedly lowered SAT scores."[7] *Buffy* is anything but dumb TV. The title *Buffy the Vampire Slayer* is a deliberate nod to the refrain that "nothing is as it seems." What sounds campy and corny is in fact a satirical and often serious examination of life, societal conventions, folklore, and religious mythology. Beyond virtually any other television show, *Buffy* functions on multiple levels. It is at the same time literal and metaphorical, text and subtext.

Testimony to the underlying seriousness of *Buffy* is the incredible interest it has generated among academics in institutions of higher learning. There have been numerous articles on *Buffy* written in academic journals, book collections of academic essays, and academic conferences held in the United Kingdom, Australia, and the United States. The show's fan base includes philosophers, linguists, theologians, literary scholars, psychiatrists, rhetoricians, and sociologists, all of which find value in the show for their respective disciplines. Robert Hanks says that even though the idea of academics addressing popular culture is not new, "nothing has generated the quantity of commentary that *Buffy* has, and in a comparatively short time."[8] Andy Sawyer, from the University of Liverpool, adds "academics all over the world are tuning in to get their weekly fix of semiotics and postmodernism."[9]

Not only is the sheer amount of academic analysis of *Buffy* quite telling, but also the tremendous variety of that analysis speaks volumes about the show's ability to communicate to different spheres of reference. Feminist scholars argue that the show subverts entrenched societal attitudes towards patriarchal authority structures and gender roles.[10] Classical scholars examine the show's use of the writings of Sappho and parallels to the myths of Orpheus and Eurydice, while calling special attention to Whedon's acknowledged reliance on the mythological "Hero's Journey" as expressed by Joseph Campbell.[11] Scholars analyze *Buffy*'s use of language,[12] humor,[13] and music.[14] One psychiatrist writes of *Buffy*'s impact on adolescent therapy.[15] *Buffy* has been read as a philosophical critique of technology[16] and of institutions.[17] It has been featured in the Templeton Lectures at Harvard in a symposium on the topic of "Expanding Concepts of God."[18] Perhaps most intriguing is a study done for the "Center for Strategic and International Studies" (CSIS) that works out of Washington on issues of homeland defense. The author takes on the issue of biological warfare and proposes that the government approach the threat of biological weapons in terms of what he calls the "Buffy Paradigm." Using the show as a basis for evaluating traditional methods of dealing with biological threats, he argues that Buffy's response to various apocalyptic crises offers the best model for dealing with biological attacks.[19] Even professional librarians have gotten into the game, discussing *Buffy*'s portrayal of research methodology and debating the show's effect on the cultural stereotypes of librarians.[20]

Much of academia's engagement with *Buffy* is due to Whedon's injection of his own academic interests into the narrative. In addition to his avowed investment in feminism, Whedon has shown an interest in history and classical mythology. Whedon's influences flow from both high and popular culture. After all, this is a man who loves comic books and science fiction movies, yet also held regular Shakespeare readings at his house for his cast and crew. It is thus no wonder that *Buffy* shares a similar variety of influences. The influx of ideas and perspectives from Whedon and his staff of writers results in a series that in Whedon's own words is "deeply layered textually episode by episode."[21]

If anything, this brief and limited survey illustrates that *Buffy the Vampire Slayer* is more than it seems. More than a simple television show, it is a cultural phenomenon and a visual text capable of sparking endless debate. What allows for these varying levels of engagement and widely differing perspectives on the show is the manner by which *Buffy* communicates.

OF TEXTS AND SUBTEXTS

Buffy's fictional town of Sunnydale, California functions as a metaphor for the show's own communicative methodology in that it exists on two levels. Most citizens of Sunnydale live on the surface world where their lives are characterized by the normality of jobs, families, and schools, blissfully unaware that another world lies beneath, a subterranean world of sewers and caverns, a world where the monsters reside. Although these two worlds coexist within the same town, Buffy and her friends are typically the only humans who inhabit both worlds and are thus truly aware of the nature of their town.

This visual dichotomy between the surface world of Sunnydale and the subterranean world below represents metaphorically the narrative world of *Buffy the Vampire Slayer*, which is composed of surface text and subtext. The surface text is the visual story presented on screen with Buffy and her pals fighting the various forces of darkness that align against them. It is a world of witches, vampires, demons, monsters and those who hunt them. But below that surface text lies another, the subtext. The subtext is the meaning that lurks beneath, unspoken but ever present. Although the surface text communicates the narrative events of *Buffy*, the subtext is where the real meaning lies for those who, like Buffy and her gang, are aware of it.

Whedon and his fellow writers are intentional about their use of subtext. He even jokes that the "watchword" at the show is "BYOSubtext" (Bring Your Own Subtext).[22] An example of the subtext at work is the heterosexual Willow's friendship with Tara during seasons four and five. Both are novice witches who strike up a friendship over their mutual interest. On the "textual" level of the show they share an interest in magic and practice spells together. However, on the subtextual level Willow's growing proficiency in magic signals her growing awareness of her own homosexuality. Indeed, Whedon once commented on the Willow/Tara relationship by stating that "ALL the relationships on the show are sort of romantic (Hence the BYOSubtext principle)."[23]

In one early episode titled "Ted" (2.11), the subtext principle becomes part of the plot. Buffy is frustrated over her mother's dating of a new suitor, Ted, and over her friends' growing fondness for the man, exemplified by their love of his mini-pizzas. Obviously insecure about her place in this new relationship, Buffy throws herself into her slayer duties with abandon, repeatedly pummeling a vampire before slaying it. The incessant beating of this vampire functions metaphorically as a representation of Buffy's battle against her own insecurities. On the subtextual level, one could substitute "Ted" for "vampire" in this scene. Afterwards she sits in the cemetery with her Watcher and mentor, Giles, and engages him in a conversation in which Buffy's own textual narration becomes increasingly transparent.

> BUFFY: Vampires are creeps.
> GILES: Yes, that's why one slays them.
> BUFFY (Speaking rapidly): I mean, people are perfectly happy getting along and then vampires come and they run around and they kill people and they take over your whole house, they start making these stupid little mini-pizzas and everyone's like 'I like the mini-pizza' but I'm telling you I have . . .
> GILES: Buffy! . . . I believe the subtext here is rapidly becoming text.[24]

This scene is a winking acknowledgment of *Buffy*'s tendency to play with the boundaries between text and subtext and its willingness to move deftly between the two.

Joss Whedon's desire to create a "juxtaposition of something very frivolous versus something very serious" often finds fulfillment in the dialectic of text and subtext.[25] Executive producer, writer, and sometime director Marti Noxon identifies the surface silliness of *Buffy* as a type of textual diversion that engages the attention of the audience, allowing for a more resonant subtextual message to sneak in. She says, "You can get to the emotional truth of things almost by sleight of hand, while people aren't really looking. It's sort of like, 'Here, look at the shiny vampire,' and behind that, there's something really raw going on."[26]

Another way of coming at the relationship between text and subtext in *Buffy* is to explore the idea of the "incoherent text." Film theorist Robin Wood (it is likely not a coincidence that a major character in the seventh season of *Buffy* is named Robin Wood) writes about the incoherent texts of the 1970's in which the attempt to give order to experience is defeated by aspects of incoherence in the narrative.[27] One way of understanding the incoherent text is to view it as a narrative in which the text and subtext are at odds, as in action movies that glorify graphic violence on the screen, while maintaining an underlying message of peace. Although the focus of Wood's study is on films that are unintentionally incoherent, he also refers to those films that use incoherence deliberately as "a structuring principle, resulting in works that reveal themselves as perfectly coherent once one has mastered their rules."[28]

I suggest that *Buffy the Vampire Slayer* is just such a text. Whedon himself has expressed interest in the kind of structure that incoherence can provide to a narrative. While discussing Wood's theory, Whedon concludes that "the best texts are incoherent."[29] In the case of *Buffy*, the incoherence between text and subtext structures the narrative and creates meaning. *Buffy* is a show whose narrative appears to glorify violence, but whose underlying (subtextual) message preaches peace; whose narrative appears to glorify sexual irresponsibility, but whose underlying message is that of sexual responsibility; whose narrative appears to glorify the occult and the demonic, but whose underlying message resonates spiritual and moral themes. Once one masters the rules of *Buffy*'s narrative world, the perceived incoherence gives way to a tightly structured coherence that ultimately brings the text and subtext into a harmony of meaning.

The issue to be explored in this book is how the "incoherence" of *Buffy the Vampire Slayer* and an accompanying failure to learn the show's narrative rules has resulted in misperceptions about *Buffy*'s moral agenda. Is it possible that a show called *Buffy the Vampire Slayer* that is about vampires, demons, and witches and that offers envelope pushing portrayals of sexuality and violence could actually be one of the more insightful and sophisticated purveyors of morality ever aired on television? After all, in *Buffy*'s world, nothing is as it seems.

Chapter 2

The Moral Battleground

WHAT'S AT STAKE?

Television is a battleground for wars over morality and societal values. As a technological medium of communication, however, television is morally neutral. It is neither inherently evil and intrinsically designed for the corruption of society nor is it a divine microphone intended for the propagation of a particular religious point of view. Nevertheless, as a cultural force, television is anything but neutral.[1] Recognition of this latter point has brought the church and conservative media watchdog groups into sharp contention with the institution of television, although the primary adversary is not the technology itself but the various individuals and groups who use the technological medium of television to push a competing moral and cultural agenda.

That television has the capacity to change as well as reflect cultural values and attitudes is a given within pop cultural studies. At issue here is the extent to which television has claimed ground that was previously under the purview of religion. One cultural function of religion is to give order to experience and to make sense out of the chaos of life. This is accomplished through the presentation and maintenance of mythology. In the sense that I use the terms here, "mythology" and "myth" have no particular reference to truth or falsity but denote that set of stories through which a people or culture express the truths and values that construct meaning and identity. For instance, the stories of George Washington chopping down a cherry tree and Benjamin Franklin flying a kite are cultural myths that define

American self-identity. Religion has played a vital role in the shaping of American cultural and moral values by the way that it has defined our shared cultural experiences. In this sense religion is not just a sacred activity but also "that part of culture that persuasively presents a plausible myth of the ordering of existence."[2]

The advent of television and film, however, has brought with it an important shift in the cultural landscape as religion is no longer the undisputed arbiter of moral values. Television is also a mythmaker.[3] Through the stories it tells, television perpetuates and promotes various worldviews that attempt to make sense of life. Andrew Greeley suggests that both religion and popular culture are imaginative ventures because they both experience and reflect on life. This may explain why they are inherently attracted to the same territory. He says that because popular culture is imaginative, it has the potential to be a "theological place" where paradigms of meaning are expressed and explored.[4] By dealing in the meaning and purpose of life, television has thus usurped some of the cultural authority that has traditionally been the province of religion and become a direct competitor for the moral voice of the nation.[5]

At the root of the attack on television from certain segments of the religious community is an awareness of what is ultimately at stake, and that is the American cultural and religious identity.[6] The battle over morality on television is a battle to determine which worldview will be most influential in shaping our cultural values, and which institution will provide the foundation for moral responsibility.[7] It would be a vast oversimplification to suggest that Christians are interested in morality, while the creators, producers, and writers of television are not. The issue is not interest in morality, but differing approaches to moral reasoning and different methods of moral discourse.

Without a doubt, religious critics of television do have cause for concern. The media is certainly to blame for foisting upon the American public large heaps of televised refuse in the name of profit and religious critics provide a valuable public service by calling attention to the moral laxity of such programs. Too typically, however, the response of religious and media watchdog groups suffers from an overly narrow and simplistic assessment of the nature of moral discourse on television.

The problem of morality on television from the perspective of conservative religious critics and media watchdog groups is that television's propensity to glorify immorality contributes to the breakdown of societal values.[8] Michael Medved, who refers to Hollywood as a "poison factory," views the entertainment media as "an all-powerful enemy, an alien force that assaults our most cherished values and corrupts our children."[9] The primary focus of criticism among moral conservatives is on the media's portrayal of the moral trifecta of sex, violence, and profanity, which typically becomes the sole measurement of a show's moral value.[10] The solutions proposed by many moralist critics of television include the use of economic pressure on advertisers through attention-grabbing campaigns and boycotts and attempts to encourage more Christian artists, producers, and writers to infiltrate Hollywood. The assumption is that what is needed is a medium that portrays a distinctly Judeo-Christian worldview, with the result being that evaluations of morality on television are often measured against a narrow conception of what constitutes morality.

A reductionist approach that defines the moral value of a television show solely on the basis of how much sex, violence, and profanity is present is both simplistic and dangerous. It is simplistic because the dominant focus on this moral trifecta obscures other moral issues of equal or even greater significance. For instance, a show might be fairly pristine in terms of its portrayal of sex, violence, and profanity, while implicitly glorifying materialism, pride, gossip, racism, misogyny, and self-interest.[11] The understanding of what fits under the definition of morality needs expansion in the vocabularies of many religious critics of the media. This approach is also dangerous because the tendency to overlook other moral issues in favor of the moral trifecta can lead to an uncritical acceptance of a show's worldview that is all the more threatening because of its subtlety.[12] Another result of a reductionist approach is that Christians effectively remove themselves from the real cultural conversation on morality, settling for a type of name calling rather than true dialogue.

Essentially, the larger moral vision is lost in the quest to purge television of immoral presentations of sex, violence, and profanity. Most religious critics of television want morality painted in black and white strokes with no shades of gray. Complexity and ambiguity are deemed inconsistent with presentations of morality. Their focus tends to be on a show's *portrayal* of morality rather than on its *perspective* of morality.[13] A show may present a very graphic portrayal of violence, while offering a perspective on violence that is critical of it. The overall moral vision of a show transcends portrayal in favor of perspective. This moral vision is the larger system of morality that is embedded in the narrative and that provides structure and meaning to that narrative world. To link back to our previous discussion, one could say that portrayal functions on the "textual" level of the show, while perspective involves interaction between the "textual" and "subtextual" levels. When perspective is allowed into the discussion, the issue becomes not how a show portrays violence visually, but what that show is ultimately saying about violence. Sexuality and violence are rampant in the Old Testament, yet careful readers know that one cannot confuse the Bible's portrayal of those acts with its moral perspective on them.

To say that there is a war going on between the television industry and religious critics of television is misleading. Yes, there is an ongoing battle for the hearts and souls of people and for the determination of the American moral agenda; yet, to characterize this struggle as a war, though true to some extent, implies an intentionality to defeat the other that is grounded in antagonism. When Hollywood is portrayed as a "poison factory" and an assaulting alien force, the clear message is that Hollywood is intentional about destroying society's moral foundation. Such arguments oversimplify the issue and suggest that the television industry is opposed to morality and dedicated to the degradation of Judeo-Christian values, when, in fact, the real cause of conflict may instead be differing definitions of morality and different methods of moral discourse. To illustrate this, let's turn to the case of *Buffy the Vampire Slayer*.

THE MORAL PROBLEM OF *BUFFY THE VAMPIRE SLAYER*

In 2002, the Parents Television Council ranked *Buffy the Vampire Slayer* number one on their list of the top ten worst shows on television from a moral standpoint.[14] This capped off previous years' rankings as the fourth and third worst show on television. The basis for this judgment is the show's portrayal of "offensive sexual content," offensive language, and violence that is "not only frequent, but also very graphic." Illustrative of this evaluation is the comment given on behalf of *Buffy*'s earlier ranking as the fourth worst show on television.

Bloody violence, dark occult themes, and bizarre and scary sex scenes permeated the family hour in this show intended for teen audiences . . . Episodes this season regularly included one-night stands, heavy doses of sexual innuendo, sexualized violence, and dark, occultist elements. Violent scenes including vampires, demons, werewolves, and other creatures make this dark fantasy series a nightmare for parents.

The Parents Television Council is representative of attacks on the moral character of *Buffy*. Those who would respond to such attacks must first face the moral problem of *Buffy* squarely.

There are valid reasons for questioning this show's moral character and its attitude towards Christianity. *Buffy* is indeed replete with sexual references and portrayals of sexuality that are at times graphic and disturbing. Violence is an integral part of every single episode of the series; in fact, the very premise of the show is grounded in violence as the title itself indicates ("Slayer"). Although not as pervasive as on other television shows, profanity does have its place. Occult elements of magic and witchcraft permeate *Buffy*. If one chooses to play the numbers game, the results are telling. Over 85% of the episodes contain profanity, about 50% feature witchcraft or occult elements, and around 42% contain overt sexuality or strong sexual innuendo. By contrast, God or Jesus is mentioned in a substantive way in about 16% of the episodes, while places of worship (churches, monasteries) occur in roughly 13%.[15] Vampires, demons, werewolves, and witches have all at one time or another functioned as positive, even heroic, characters on the show. For two seasons the show featured a lesbian relationship between two witches that lasted longer and was treated more positively than almost any other relationship on *Buffy*. These reasons alone account for why many evangelical Christians reject, ignore, or attack *Buffy*.

Buffy's cosmology and spiritual perspective is also problematic. *Buffy's* world is polytheistic, populated by a smorgasbord of demons, demigods, and spirits. Curiously, despite this polytheistic cosmology, God is largely absent. It is not that God is rejected or his existence overtly denied; he is simply not mentioned in any way that implies an active role. Although churches do make occasional appearances, they are almost always abandoned or empty. In a way, the abandoned churches on *Buffy* are a metaphorical comment on the spiritual *zeitgeist* of America at the end of the twentieth and the dawn of the twenty-first century. Christianity in America has become increasingly anti-institutional. People embrace spirituality, the teachings of Christianity, and the idea of God, but have little interest in organized religion. *Buffy* is a reflection of this trend.

The spiritual focus of *Buffy* is more immanent than transcendent. The lack of overt acknowledgment of God results in a world in which the protagonists rely on themselves and each other in their battles against the forces of evil rather than on divine aid. This immanent cosmology locates the divine all around us in a generic sense. Thus, Jenny Calendar, Sunnydale High's computer teacher, can say to Giles in relation to his distrust of the Internet: "The divine exists in cyber space same as out here" (1.8). An episode of *Buffy* from season four provides an analogy of the show's attitude towards transcendence. In the episode titled "Beer Bad" (4.5), college freshman Buffy is in a bar and is hit on by four older college guys. In their attempt to impress her, they engage in heated intellectual discussion. Buffy's offhand suggestion that beer might be evil launches them into a debate on moral absolutism in which one of the students attempts to bring Thomas Aquinas into the conversation. The reply to this by the other students is swift: "There'll be no Thomas Aquinas at this table!" Another adds, "Keep your theology of providence to yourself." It is not that *Buffy* avoids any sense of fate or of the predetermination of events by forces outside normal human control, but the association of such with divine providence is muted at best.

The Godless cosmology of *Buffy* can perhaps be explained in light of Joss Whedon's own theological outlook: "I'm a very hard-line, angry atheist," he says.[16] Certainly the shows' treatment of Christianity is at times derogatory. In one episode ("The Harvest"; 1.2), Giles gives an account of the world's origin that is "contrary to popular mythology." In his commentary track on this episode, Whedon notes that he expected to receive complaints about this "dig on Christianity."[17] Vampires use religious language and engage in religious rituals that almost parody Christian practice. In one instance, Buffy and Giles discover a reliquary of an ancient saint excommunicated by the Vatican. When Giles informs Buffy that a reliquary houses significant religious items like "a finger or some other body part from a saint," Buffy replies, "Note to self: Religion freaky" (2.9). The book of Isaiah gets quoted (1.12), but is given no more weight than all the other various texts of ancient prophecy used on the show. When Buffy's mother researches alternate schooling options for her expelled daughter, Buffy asks, "What about home schooling? You know, it's not just for scary religious people anymore" (3.2). In another episode, a religiously oriented homeless shelter turns out to be a gateway to a hell dimension (3.1). In "The Freshman" (4.1), Buffy replies to the question "Have you accepted Jesus Christ as your personal savior?" with "You know, I meant to and then I just got really busy." In another episode, vampires take hostages in a church building and one of the vampires comments: "It's hard to believe. I've been avoiding this place for so many years, and it's nothing. It's nice. It's got the pretty windows, the pillars . . . lots of folks to eat. Where's the thing I was so afraid of? You know, the Lord?" (4.16). One of the last episodes of the series features a fallen priest named Caleb who has become a serial killer of young girls and, in one scene, mockingly comments on the act of communion by questioning what would have happened at the Last Supper if someone had ordered white wine instead of red ("Dirty Girls"; 7.18). This episode in particular raised the ire of the Parents Television Council and the Dove Foundation (another Christian media watchdog organization), leading them to decry *Buffy* as anti-Christian bigotry and evidence of Hollywood's moral decline.[18]

Defenders of the morality of *Buffy the Vampire Slayer* have their work cut out for them. Yet there is another side to this story. In direct response to the Parents Television Councils' 2001 ranking of *Buffy* as the third worst show on television, Buffy herself, Sarah Michelle Gellar, responded vehemently by claiming, "We're like the most religious show out there! We're more religious than *7th Heaven* . . . We answer the big questions!"[19] Others concur. *Christianity Today* has defended *Buffy*'s moral perspective and argued that it is a valuable show for Christians to watch, even addressing the sexuality and occult elements by noting that they are dealt with "honestly and without glorification."[20] The conservative *National Review Online* praises *Buffy* as one of TV's "most morally serious" shows.[21] *The Door Magazine*, a satiric Christian publication, named Buffy its "Theologian of the Year" in 2002 because "we need someone who can not only deconstruct the problem of evil, but kick its hiney."[22] Robert Hanks writes that "four or five episodes of *Buffy* would be on my list of the 10 best pieces of television drama ever made."[23] In 1998, David Graeber, professor of anthropology at Yale, wrote that *Buffy* was "quite possibly the best show on television" and that, despite its Godless cosmology, it contains a very healthy moral premise and underlying ethic.[24] *Buffy* also receives praise for its realistic depiction of moral and ethical issues. In 2000, Mim Udovitch called this fantasy tale about vampires "the most realistic show on the air" for its portrayal of the inner struggles that people face.[25] *Buffy* has also been recognized with the "Seal of Quality" by the organization Viewers for Quality Television and has been honored with its "Founder's Award."[26]

Buffy's attitude towards religious imagery and themes is also less clear-cut than often recognized. Crosses and Holy Water retain an efficacy in Buffy's world, striking fear in vampires and burning them on contact. The reality of the Crucifixion is acknowledged as in one scene where a vampire brags about having been present at the Crucifixion, and the vampire Spike replies: "You were there? Oh, please! If every vampire who said he was at the Crucifixion was actually there, it would have been like Woodstock" ("School Hard"; 2.3). Buffy herself typically wears a silver cross around her neck that symbolizes her calling. In fact, christological imagery runs throughout the series with Buffy often functioning as a Christ-like figure, complete with sacrificial death and resurrection. Much of the criticism of *Buffy* derives from a failure to pay due attention to context. For instance, the Parents Television Council criticized *Buffy* for portraying a suicide in the 2001 season finale, ignoring the fact that Buffy's "suicide" was an intentional Christ-like sacrifice of herself in order to save the world! ("The Gift"; 5.22). Likewise, although it is true that churches are often portrayed as abandoned or empty, it is also true that significant moments of redemption often take place in these very same churches.

One can certainly argue that *Buffy*'s cosmology is a Godless one; yet it is also a cosmology in which the reality of the spiritual realm is never doubted and the impact of that spiritual realm upon the physical is a given. Buffy's world is a place where religious and moral topics such as redemption, eschatology, honesty, violence, guilt, forgiveness, and sacrifice are dealt with regularly and seriously. The dichotomous response to this series may be represented by an assignment I gave to my sophomore students in a religion and popular culture class at Rochester College. After viewing selected episodes of *Buffy*, they were to write their own theological critique of the show. The results spanned a spectrum from those who thought the show was blasphemous to those who argued that it was a highly moral show that parents should encourage their teenagers to watch.

This is the moral problem of *Buffy the Vampire Slayer*. That this show can be the catalyst for such widely opposing views of its moral foundation and agenda screams for an explanation. It is an incoherent text in the best tradition. These divergent responses to *Buffy* reveal clearly that people are evaluating *Buffy* on the basis of different models of moral discourse. Does one have to be a Christian in order to address morality? Can an avowed atheist reveal spiritual and moral truth through his art and, if so, what then is the source for his moral reasoning? To properly evaluate the nature of moral discourse on television, we need to move beyond surface portrayals and understand *how* such media communicate morality, and we need to evaluate that discourse in light of the larger cultural project within which a particular show operates.[27] It is an approach that requires a greater understanding of a show's moral vision.

THE MORAL VISION OF *BUFFY THE VAMPIRE SLAYER*

Although any attempt to describe the moral vision of a television show is open to the objection that television shows are typically written by teams of writers and therefore do not represent a single person's point of view, this objection holds less weight with a show like *Buffy*. Despite its contingent of writers, *Buffy* is ultimately the product of Joss Whedon. As creator, executive producer, and frequent writer and director, he employs an approach that is extremely hands-on. He helps "break" every story and reads and edits virtually every script produced by his writing team.[28]

Whedon had a purpose in creating *Buffy* that transcended simple entertainment. He wanted *Buffy* to be a cultural force. He says:

> I designed *Buffy* to be an icon, to be an emotional experience, to be loved in a way that other shows can't be loved. Because it's about adolescence, which is the most important thing people go through in their development, becoming an adult. And it mythologizes it in such a way, such a romantic way — it basically says, 'Everybody who made it through adolescence is a hero' . . . I wanted people to embrace it in a way that exists beyond, 'Oh, that was a wonderful show about lawyers, let's have dinner.' I wanted people to internalize it, and make up fantasies where they were in the story, to take it home with them, for it to exist beyond the TV show. And we've done exactly that.[29]

Elsewhere Whedon states, "The idea of changing culture is important to me, and it can only be done in a popular medium."[30] Through popular culture, Whedon envisions *Buffy* impacting cultural values and attitudes towards morality. For Whedon, *Buffy* represents his vision of what is true and important in the world and to that end "every single one of those [144] episodes had a message and a meaning and a very specific purpose."[31]

Buffy is by no means neutral in its presentation of moral issues. An example of Whedon's cultural agenda is *Buffy*'s obvious feminist stance. The theme of female empowerment serves a desire to influence positively cultural attitudes towards women. Whedon has always been up front about *Buffy*'s feminist outlook, although some scholarly treatments ascribe to Whedon a higher degree of intentionality in how the issue is dealt with than he himself will cop to. He tells *Rolling Stone* that part of his attraction to feminism is grounded in his personal belief that the concept of a woman warrior is "extraordinarily sexy." He adds, "If I wasn't compelled on a very base level by that archetype, I wouldn't have created that character. I mean, yes, I have a feminist agenda, but it's not like I made a chart."[32]

Whedon's desire to say something meaningful and influential about culture feeds into his moral vision, which is essentially a reality-based vision. Rather than rely on clear cut moral guidelines, Whedon suggests that an accurate understanding of morality can only be accomplished by exploring life's full complexity and messiness. If the creation of mythology through narrative is about making sense of life, one cannot accomplish that by ignoring the reality of life. R. W. Beardsmore says of the relationship between art and morality that art is not designed for the clear communication of moral propositions. Its moral message, if any, is implicit rather than explicit in that the moral function of art is to grant insight into the human condition, thus allowing people to make moral and ethical choices that are influenced by a greater understanding of reality.[33]

Anthropology is also theology. Speaking about humanity is a way of speaking about God, just as the analysis of any created thing gives insight into its creator. We could say that *Buffy* operates with a related principle in mind, that anthropology is morality. By this I mean that we gain a greater understanding of right and wrong, good and evil, by exploring the reality of the human condition with all its virtue and vice, its potential and failure.

The perception of *Buffy* as immoral is due in part to an uneasiness with the nature of reality portrayed in the show, but a moral system that fails to account for the dark impulses of humanity and face them squarely is ultimately ineffectual because it embraces a pristine vision of the world that is illusory. What media watchdog groups often desire is a wholesome portrayal of religion and life that lacks any complexity, ambiguity or unresolved conflict.[34] Several Christian scholars, however, counter that it is by engaging works that confront the reality of evil, the depth of human failings, and the complexity of moral choices within a framework that also embraces redemption, forgiveness, and mercy that we gain greater understanding of ourselves and the world in which we live.[35]

For Joss Whedon, one cannot effectively talk about morality without embracing the dark side of reality. In answer to a question about whether he feels a responsibility to society in his writing, he says:

> I've always been . . . very careful about my responsibility in narrative. How much do I put what I want to put, and how much do I put what I feel is correct? People say, 'After Columbine, do you feel a responsibility about the way you portray violence?' And I'm like, 'No, I felt a responsibility about the way I portrayed violence the first time I picked up a pen' . . . But . . . at the same time . . . a writer has a responsibility to tell stories that are dark and sexy and violent, where characters that you love do stupid, wrong things and get away with it, that we explore these parts of people's lives, because that's what makes stories into fairy tales instead of polemics. That's what makes stories resonate, that thing, that dark place that we all want to go to on some level or another. It's very important . . . I feel that we're showing something that is true, that people can relate to and say, 'Oh, I made that bad choice,' or 'Oh, there's a better way to do that.' But as long as its real, then however politically correct, or incorrect, or whatever, bizarre, or dark, or funny, or stupid — anything you can get, as long as it's real, I don't mind.[36]

Of course where to draw the line is always a difficult question. When does the portrayal of reality become destructive rather than illuminative? Whedon is very much aware of the difficulty of navigating that line. He says, "What is my responsibility? How dark should I get, how much should every one of my characters represent an ideal or reality? How far can you delve into evil before you are actually propagating it? . . . These are questions that must be confronted every time out to bat, and every time the decision is different."[37]

This concern for reality may seem odd in the context of a show that is about vampires and vampire slayers, yet the focus is not on a realistic portrayal of the physical world we all inhabit but on a realistic portrayal of the *emotional* world we all inhabit. The focus is not "what is a true depiction of life," but "what is true about life." This is why much of *Buffy*'s message is presented metaphorically (more on this in the next chapter).

Given Whedon's atheistic beliefs and his emphasis on the depiction of truth in the form of what is "real," what can we say about the source of his moral vision? For Whedon, it is found in mythology and narrative — in the power of stories to expose truth. Mythic stories bring clarity and order to life, allowing people to understand themselves and their situation better, and thus enabling them to make better choices. Whedon states that *Buffy* operates on two levels: the mythic and the personal.[38] The show's perspective on truth and morality is found in the intersection between the two. That *Buffy* is a show about demons and vampires and the one chosen to fight them places it within the mythic context of the eternal battle between good and evil; yet this eternal, even spiritual, battle plays out as a personal drama in which characters negotiate what is good and evil, right and wrong, in the context of their daily lives.

Some critics of *Buffy* point to the show's moral ambiguity and its lack of references to God as evidence of an anti-religious stance. Nothing could be further from the truth. Atheist though he may be, Joss Whedon embraces the stories and mythology of Christianity as foundational for his moral understanding. The cosmology of *Buffy* is not an outright denial of the existence of God in Buffy's world, but rather an attempt to avoid the specificity of description that would lead to confinement of moral discourse within one religious perspective. Marti Noxon responded to a question about whether *Buffy*'s writers would ever introduce Satan as a character by saying that they would never name him as such because they prefer to keep their mythology "murky" and their cosmology "inter-denominational." She says, "We've indicated that there might be a heaven and various levels of hell, but then you don't want to don the cast of biblical characters because then it takes it to a place that is very specific."[39]

Whedon has commented that there is justification for providing Christian interpretations of his narrative creations. The *Buffy* spin-off *Angel* is more overt in its cosmology by identifying a transcendent source of guidance as "The Powers That Be." Whedon's explanation is that vagueness is intentional to allow for diversity of interpretation. He says,

> I would not say the Powers That Be is God, but I would say that some people would interpret it as God. That's just as valid as whatever interpretation they can come up with. We keep it vague for a reason. If people want to believe it's God, we're not going to say it's not any more than we're going to say it is.[40]

In a Christmas episode titled "Amends" (3.10), the character of Angel (a vampire with a soul) is literally haunted by the sins of his past. At the end of the episode, as Angel achieves a form of absolution for his guilt, it miraculously begins to snow (in southern California!). Whedon addressed the question of whether the snow represented God.

> Well, I'm an atheist, but it's hard to ignore the idea of a 'Christmas miracle' here . . . The fact is, the Christian mythos has a powerful fascination to me, and it bleeds into my storytelling. Redemption, hope, purpose, Santa, these all are important to me, whether I believe in an afterlife or some universal structure or not.[41]

As Craig Simpson notes, "Whedon demonstrates the difference between taking myths literally and taking them seriously."[42] Although as an atheist, Whedon does not embrace the literal truth of the Christian story, he nonetheless takes the Christian story seriously as a narrative that can expose the truth of human nature and the quest for meaning in life. Consequently, Christian themes like redemption, sacrifice, and forgiveness resonate throughout the series.

I have explored the moral vision of *Buffy the Vampire Slayer*, including Whedon's desire to impact culture and his reliance on narrative and mythology as a way of ordering existence. This provides a window into the moral perspective of *Buffy*. In the next chapter, I look more closely at how *Buffy* communicates this moral vision through narrative and metaphor.

Chapter 3

Storytellers

Everyone loves a story. Our culture's fascination with film and television witnesses to the hold that the telling of stories has over us. Joss Whedon is a self-described "storyteller," a weaver of narratives. Understanding the moral fabric of *Buffy the Vampire Slayer* requires awareness of the supremacy of narrative for Whedon and his writers.

Andrew Greeley argues that fantasy stories are inherently theological, meaning that because they deal with the relationship of good and evil, death and resurrection, and the nature of true love, they are stories about religion.[1] Whedon takes this concept a step further suggesting that these stories are not simply about religion, but that, for him, they have a type of religious authority themselves. He says there is "a religion in narrative" with homage being paid to the story itself, not the teller of it.[2] He describes how he wants viewers to respond to his stories with the proverb, "Trust the tale, not the teller."[3] This is not to say that stories are infallible. The fluidity of narrative reveals itself in the numerous narrative adjustments and plot innovations that have characterized *Buffy*'s seven seasons. The geography of Sunnydale alone has undergone startling transformations when needed, such as the sudden appearance of a castle (5.1), and characters back-stories are at times progressively rewritten. Yet, the point is that these alterations occur because they serve the story. The centrality of the narrative is the key to understanding Whedon's use of sexuality and violence in *Buffy*. Whereas some shows use such tactics to push boundaries or to garner attention, *Buffy*'s use of sex and violence is story driven. One of the show's writers, Douglas Petrie, says that they never make narrative decisions with an eye towards publicity or scandal, but that all plot developments derive from "character and story."[4] Whedon himself adds that he has no interest in the pushing of boundaries because, "If you can just be sensational, then you don't have to tell the story right."[5] In Whedon's world, the story reigns supreme.

NARRATIVE AND THE DARK THINGS

Stories are not just entertainment. They are the lifeblood of experience. We tell stories to give order to the chaos of life, to make sense out of the senseless, to organize our experiences in a way that gives them meaning. They teach us to look at the world in a certain way. It is no surprise, therefore, that most major religions communicate through story. Ironically, Christians, for whom stories have played such a dominant role in the formation of their own identity and view of the world, have too often failed to recognize the power and function of stories within the larger culture.

Whedon's own interest in narrative seems connected to a desire to find meaning in the world. His childhood fascination with comic books and science fiction novels was due to his perception that "those worlds made a lot more sense to me than the one I lived in."[6] His atheistic outlook also contributed to a need for narrative. Whedon says, "There's no meaning to life. That's kind of depressing. There's no God. That's a bummer, too. You fill your days with creating worlds that have meaning and order because ours doesn't."[7]

How do these statements square with his desire to portray what is "real" through his narratives? The fantasy narrative of *Buffy the Vampire Slayer* is an attempt to represent the *emotional* reality of trying to live in this world because otherwise "it's just guys with horns running around and some good jokes, but it's not going to resonate."[8] That portrayal of how the world *is* emotionally, however, is juxtaposed in the narrative with a vision of how the world *ought* to be.

Fantasy stories are not merely escapism; nor are they reducible to imaginative retreats whereby one finds resolution for problems and fears that remain unresolved in the real world. Although both of those ideas play a role, they suffer from making too strong a disconnect between the story and the real world. Fantasy stories are not so much a way to escape the world as a means of dealing with the world.

The intrinsic relationship between narrative and mythology is due to their mutual functions as organizers of experience and communicators of meaning. Joseph Campbell says that we live today in a scientific and technological world that has been stripped of mythology, and so people hunger for it. They hunger for stories that give order to their existence, that help them come to terms with reality, and that teach them "how to live a human lifetime under any circumstances."[9] As if in answer to this call, Joss Whedon says that his desire is to tell "mythic stories."[10]

When Whedon says that the stories on *Buffy* are "fairy tales, not driving manuals,"[11] he is making a point about narrative. Fairy tales are a form of mythic stories we tell our children in order to teach them about life. They tap into true emotion and reveal truth about the world. Fairy tales are populated with monsters, giants, witches, and other dark creatures of fantasy because they function to explore the dark things in life as a way of helping children (and sometimes adults) deal with the harsh realities of life. In the episode "Lie to Me" (2.7), Angel comments on a group of teenagers who idolize vampires by saying "they're children making up bedtime stories of friendly vampires to comfort themselves in the dark." Willow's reply highlights the need for fairy tales when she says, "The dark can get pretty dark. Sometimes you need a story." Whedon's view is that we do indeed need a story, a story that doesn't shy away from the dark things in life, but that, in fact, faces them squarely. He says,

> Stories come from violence, they come from sex. They come from death. They come from the dark places that everybody has to go to, kind of wants to, or doesn't, but needs to deal with. If you raise a kid to think everything is sunshine and flowers, they're going to get into the real world and die. And ultimately, to access these base emotions, to go to these strange places, to deal with sexuality, to deal with horror and death, is what people need and it's the reason that we tell these stories. That's the reason fairy tales are so creepy, because we need to encapsulate these things, to inoculate ourselves against them, so that when we're confronted by the genuine horror that is day-to-day life we don't go insane.[12]

So he created *Buffy the Vampire Slayer*, a type of modern fairy tale that uses monsters and demons to represent the dark things that we face in life and a teenage girl with the power to defeat them. Or, to take Joseph Campbell's description of the function of myth: "Slaying monsters is slaying the dark things."[13]

NARRATIVE AND INDIRECTION

Many who desire to find morality taught on primetime television want straightforward moral propositions that are clear, unambiguous and not open to misinterpretation. What they want is a driving manual for life, not a fairy tale. Fairy tales and mythology can be messy and obscure, their message not always readily transparent. For the storyteller, however, this is their greatest asset. Stories communicate indirectly and inductively. They engage their audience in the world of the story so that the audience encounters the message in a moment of discovery. Although some stories and television shows attempt to be overtly moralistic, the most effective stories are those that communicate indirectly.[14] People will resist being preached at by their television set, but with a good story they will already have heard the message before realizing there was one. They unwittingly become part of the moral discourse of the narrative, all the while thinking they are watching mere entertainment. This may sound deceptive but is in fact simply being faithful to the modus operandi of narrative.

The indirection of narrative allows a storyteller to communicate a message in a way that is readily heard and persuasive. As with all subjects related to narrative, Joss Whedon has been vocal on this point as well. Motivating his creation of *Buffy* was a desire to affect the way people value women in American society. He is able to accomplish this through the indirection of narrative in a way that could not be done otherwise. He says that he could have turned *Buffy* into a series of lectures on PBS on the value of feminism but then no one would listen.[15] Instead he says, "If I can make teenage boys comfortable with a girl who takes charge of a situation without their knowing that's what's happening, it's better than sitting down and selling them on feminism."[16] Throughout the run of the series, Whedon frequently noted that there would never be "a Very Special Buffy,"[17] meaning that moral and political issues would grow out of the story rather than being forced upon it. They would be woven into the fabric of the narrative to be encountered indirectly, unlike other series where "very special" episodes serve to call attention to the treatment of a moral issue.

NARRATIVE AND *BUFFY*

Given that Joss Whedon and his cast of writers are highly self-aware of what they are attempting through narrative, it should not be surprising that certain episodes of *Buffy the Vampire Slayer* offer self-conscious commentary on *Buffy*'s own narrative world. Three episodes — "Superstar" (4.17), "Normal Again" (6.17), and the aptly titled "Storyteller" (7.16) — reflect on narrative in general and the narrative of *Buffy* in particular.

"Superstar" (4.17)

"Superstar" revolves around the quintessential high school nerd, Jonathan. Jonathan is a lonely outsider whose disillusionment with life moves him to attempt suicide towards the end of the third season until Buffy convinces him that life's problems must be faced and dealt with, not avoided. In "Superstar," however, Jonathan decides to resolve his problems through another means, an augmentation spell that transforms him into everyone's ideal person. Suddenly, in this new world Jonathan is attractive to women, a well-known author and singer, medical school graduate, star of *The Matrix*, coach of the U.S. women's soccer team, and has his own swimsuit calendar. In addition, he is a revered fighter who often comes to Buffy's aid.

Disillusioned with the story of his life, Jonathan created a new one. Highlighting this recasting of the show's narrative are the opening credits of the episode, which feature Jonathan as the star of the show rather than Buffy. Jonathan's alternate version of reality is a selfishly motivated retreat from life, designed to correct his problems through avoidance of them. It is only when Buffy convinces him (again) that one's life requires effort and perseverance, not quick fixes, that Jonathan abandons his false narrative.

The message that resonates throughout the episode is that narrative can be dangerous because narrative can be deceptive. As Jonathan explains in "Superstar," "People can't always see what's right in front of them." As if in illustration of this principle, Buffy and her friends are as much fooled by Jonathan's illusion as anyone. The only individual not deceived is Adam, a human/demon cyborg who sees through the illusion because, as he says, "I'm aware." Self-awareness exposes the lie. Adam's self-awareness derives from his "otherness." He does not belong in the world. Those who belong in the world lack the appropriate self-awareness and so are at the mercy of the false narrative. For instance, Xander remains so unaware that even when informed that Jonathan has cast a spell in order to make them all think he is cool, Xander continues to be fooled by the illusion and comments, "That is so cool!" Buffy, however, becomes increasingly suspicious as she recognizes the incongruities in Jonathan's narrative. Initially, she appears unaware of her own nature. When the vampire Spike calls her Betty, Buffy, who typically is quick with a witty pun or snide insult, can only muster, "It's Buffy, you big bleached . . . stupid guy." Her inability to marshal a clever response reveals her lack of self-awareness. As her self-awareness grows, however, so does her ability to pierce the illusion.

"Superstar" accents the importance of truth in narrative. When Jonathan creates his new narrative, Adam says, "These are lies. None of this is real. The world has been changed. It's intriguing but it's wrong." Jonathan's narrative is "wrong" because it conceals the truth rather than reveals it. In failing to resonate with truth, it remains only illusion and deception. The writers of *Buffy* thus appear to acknowledge through this episode their own responsibility to create narratives that enlighten, rather than deceive, by revealing what is real and true about life.

"Normal Again" (6.17)

"Normal Again" is a form of self-commentary on the act of creating narrative. The episode begins with Buffy battling a demon that injects her with a form of poison. Immediately she begins to experience hallucinations in which she is a patient in an insane asylum being treated for schizophrenia. In her hallucinations, a doctor informs Buffy that she has been in the asylum for the last six years (the length of the series to that point) and that she has created in her mind a fantastic world of demons and monsters where she is a superhero. We thus have a battle of competing narratives, Sunnydale versus the asylum. Which is the real world and which is the hallucination?

On one level, the question of which world is real is irrelevant because the point is that people use narratives to cope with life. Both worlds that Buffy inhabits in this episode function as escapism. One could interpret this episode along two different tracks. On one track, it is the asylum world that is real and Sunnydale is a fiction. Buffy thus created Sunnydale to escape from the hardness of her life, for her to be a hero and strong in that story when she was weak in her own. The doctor in the asylum even takes this a step further, noting that not only did Buffy retreat to the fantasy world when her life got hard, but now she has returned to the real world because her Sunnydale fantasy life has become unexpectedly difficult. The second interpretive track views Sunnydale as the real world and the asylum as the fiction. In this case, Buffy once again reacts to the harshness of her life. Her mother has died, her father is distant, her attempts at love have self-destructed, and she is working a dead end job. She goes through the motions of life but has effectively given up on it. Her mind thus creates the asylum so that she can become part of a different story. Dawn refers to the asylum world as Buffy's "ideal reality" for in it her mother is alive and her parents are together. One notices that when Buffy flashes to the asylum, it is typically at a moment when her life is coming apart: when the demon stabs her, while working at her fast food job, when her friends are fighting, and when Spike threatens to tell her friends about their relationship. The world of the asylum becomes her refuge from the entropy in her life.

Ultimately, Buffy must make a choice as to which story, which world, she desires to inhabit. Initially she chooses the asylum world because her life in Sunnydale is on a downward spiral. As she is about to cut herself off from the world of Sunnydale for good, Buffy's mother, Joyce, encourages her in the asylum by telling her to believe in herself. This advice strikes a chord with Buffy and in it she finds the strength within herself to say goodbye to her mother and return to the world of Sunnydale. Joyce's advice to Buffy echoes the same advice she herself gave to Jonathan in "Superstar," that one has within them the strength to face the harshness of life.

As self-commentary, "Normal Again" reminds us that *Buffy the Vampire Slayer* is a story, a fantasy. The episode reflects on the absurdity of its own narrative world. When Xander learns that Buffy thinks Sunnydale is a creation of her mind, he replies, "Oh, come on, that's ridiculous! What? You think this isn't real just because of all the vampires and demons and ex-vengeance demons and the sister that used to be a big ball of universe-destroying energy?" The issue, however, is not whether *Buffy* is a fantasy story, but whether it is a fantasy story that helps us confront the harshness of life. In "Superstar" Jonathan's story was wrong because it was an avoidance of his life. Buffy, however, rejects the escape offered by the asylum, instead finding in that story the strength to return to her life. Whereas Jonathan had chosen the easier story to live in, Buffy chose the harder one. In this self-aware look at the creation of a story, the writers of *Buffy* may be saying that just as Buffy entered the story of the asylum in order to find the strength to deal with the problems of her life, viewers may enter the story of *Buffy the Vampire Slayer* and find in it strength for their own lives.

Taken together, "Superstar" and "Normal Again" stress the value of creating stories, but creating stories only has value insofar as the story resonates with truth. In the case of "Normal Again" that truth is found in Joyce's advice that allows Buffy to find strength and to believe in herself. These two themes of creating stories and their relationship to truth come together in the last of these three episodes, "Storyteller."

"Storyteller" (7.16)

"Storyteller" focuses on another quintessential nerd, Andrew, a friend of Jonathan's — at least until Andrew murdered him. Andrew is a teller of stories who relates everything in life to popular culture. He describes his level of boredom by comparing it to watching *Episode One* of the *Star Wars* series (7.11). When danger threatens, he announces the tingling of his spider-sense (7.11); and when danger strikes, he can only muster the courage to shout "deflector shields up!" (7.11). He also comments on Dawn's possible future by comparing her to Luke Skywalker (7.12). Andrew views his own life as an extended narrative in which he is merely playing a role. Although, according to Andrew, Buffy sees him as "a super-villain" like Dr. Doom, Apocalypse, or The Riddler (7.10), by the time of "Storyteller," Andrew has cast himself in the role of a misunderstood bad guy on the path to redemption.

In "Storyteller," Andrew decides to narrate Buffy's story by filming her life and adventures with his camcorder. In doing so, he puts his own narrative spin on events. The episode opens with a Masterpiece Theater type of set, complete with Andrew sitting in a leather chair, adorned in a smoking jacket, and with pipe in hand. He speaks into the camera, addressing the audience as "gentle viewers" and extolling the virtues of getting "lost in a story." He calls his tale "Buffy, Slayer of the Vampyrs."

The bookshelf of this set features several volumes, but only one with a clearly legible title. It says "Nietzsche." Friedrich Nietzsche, in an essay titled "Truth and Falsity in an Ultramoral Sense," examines the relationship between language and truth. Arguing that people use language to construct the reality they want and so are "deeply immersed in illusions and dream fancies," he posits that the weak in particular allow falsity to creep into their narratives in order to preserve their sense of self.[18] So it is with Andrew. In fact, the Masterpiece Theater set quickly dissolves to Andrew sitting not in a leather chair, but on a toilet in Buffy's bathroom narrating his story to a camcorder set in front of him. Throughout the episode Andrew narrates Buffy's story through diagrams on his whiteboard, interviews with her friends, staged scenes of conflict, and his own glamorized commentary. For instance, he describes Buffy and Spike's run-of-the-mill entrance into the kitchen as a scene that would only be at home on the cover of a romance novel.

Andrew is a murderer who can only make sense of his experience and actions by telling stories. Yet, by frequently embellishing his own story and altering the facts, Andrew's stories become a form of self-deception designed to absolve himself of any responsibility for his own actions. It is only when Buffy forces him to abandon his stories and face the reality of what he did that he can move forward.

We will discuss "Storyteller" and its impact on Andrew's arc in more detail elsewhere. Here I want to focus on the apparent subtextual connection between Andrew and Joss Whedon himself. Aside from the murdering and super-villainy, comparisons are unavoidable. Whedon, a self-professed nerd and fan of comics and science fiction, claims to have watched mostly Masterpiece Theater as a young man.[19] He calls himself a "storyteller" and has at times referred to his audience as "gentle viewers." In his office is a whiteboard that he and the writers used to break stories for the show and he would reportedly explain his ideas to the writing staff by referencing movies.[20] So in "Storyteller" Andrew is a young man armed with a whiteboard and an arsenal of movie references telling the story of "Buffy, Slayer of the Vampyres." Art imitates life.

On the subtextual level of this episode, it serves as a self-reflection on the art of storytelling. The question, though, is what Whedon and company are trying to say about their own project. At the end of "Storyteller" Andrew learns the importance of truth in narrative. We all tell stories to make sense of life, but those stories only succeed if they ring true to life at their emotional core. We return to Whedon's statement that above all he wants what is presented in *Buffy* to be "real" in terms of the emotions portrayed. In contrast, Andrew's stories were deceptive because they did not ring true. Two episodes after "Storyteller," Andrew introduces the character of Faith by telling her story to some girls. When they remind him that he is not supposed to make up stories anymore, Andrew replies, "I'm not. This is true" (7.18). The telling of stories is indispensable to life but the storyteller bears a responsibility to the gentle viewers to weave a narrative that exposes truth. In *Buffy the Vampire Slayer*, one means of exposing truth is metaphor.

METAPHOR AND MORALITY

A metaphor is a means of understanding or gaining a perspective on one thing by comparing it to another. "John is a teddy bear" is a metaphor that creates insight into the personality of John. We use metaphors to express symbolically or figuratively what we cannot express literally, or at least what we cannot express as well through literal language. For many people, metaphors are merely figures of speech, a form of literary ornamentation that is ultimately unnecessary. Metaphor theorists, however, argue that metaphor is absolutely essential to our perception of reality because it adds a dimension to truth otherwise unattainable. We comprehend our reality by means of the symbols and language we use to describe it so that metaphor becomes a means of expressing "how things are."[21] Lakoff and Johnson argue that metaphors belong as much to the province of thought as to that of words. They are an inherent part of how we conceive of things and thus aid our "understanding of our world and ourselves."[22] Metaphors guide us in our perception and conceptualization of things. A metaphor is not simply a description of a pre-existing similarity between objects; rather, the metaphor *causes* us to experience two objects as similar.[23] For instance, there is no inherent similarity between John and a teddy bear that would necessitate comparing them, but through the metaphor "John is a teddy bear," we learn to perceive John in terms of a teddy bear.

A metaphor is a structuring device that allows us to categorize experience. Aiding this are some metaphors that create structure by producing a whole system of metaphors. A "root metaphor" is a foundational metaphor that gives rise to several "surface" metaphors. The root metaphor may often be unstated but can be identified by similarities between the surface metaphors. For instance, to use an example from Lakoff and Johnson, the metaphor "Time is money" functions as a root metaphor. It organizes our experience by getting us to perceive time in terms of financial dealings and so produces a variety of other metaphors that grow out of this concept. Consequently, we speak of wasting, saving, spending, investing, borrowing, and budgeting our time, all metaphors that owe their existence to the root metaphor of "Time is money."[24]

Ironically, even though the Bible communicates prominently through metaphors, Christians have long been nervous around them, preferring instead literal propositions that are more easily defended and proclaimed. This suspicion of the metaphorical is part of the reason why many Christians have misunderstood the moral vision of *Buffy the Vampire Slayer*. They have failed to recognize both its metaphorical character and how those metaphors function.

If what contemporary metaphor theorists claim about metaphor is true, then metaphor is integral to morality. In *Metaphor and Moral Experience*, A. E. Denham combines metaphor theory with moral philosophy to argue that metaphors allow us to make more informed moral judgments. Denham asserts that accurate moral judgments require an awareness of the "inner lives" of others by which we sympathize with them "as from their own point of view." To do this requires an act of imagination and is thus well served by metaphor which can provide us with understanding of the unfamiliar perspectives of others.[25] Denham adds that metaphorical discourse can open our eyes to moral perspectives of which we would otherwise be unaware and that this is best accomplished in fictional narratives.[26] The way we recognize the truth of a fictional narrative's perspective on morality is that "we recognize that the moral aspects of the possible worlds they construct are equally possible aspects of our own moral lives." Consequently, metaphor in fictional narratives offers greater understanding of how the world is and how it might be.[27]

Not only do metaphors provide increased understanding of others and of moral perspectives, but also they can affect moral action. Metaphors help us define reality and comprehend our world and ourselves. Since we act on the basis of our knowledge, the metaphors that we use to define our reality also serve as the basis for the moral choices we make.[28]

Any attempt to analyze the use of metaphor in a show like *Buffy the Vampire Slayer* shares one glaring problem — that all of the theory discussed above relates primarily to *literary* metaphor. Can we say that the same holds true for metaphor in film and television? I suggest we can. Metaphors in film and television are no doubt related to their literary cousins, yet possess distinct characteristics. If "seeing as" (in the sense, for instance, of seeing time as money) is central to the concept of metaphor, then in film and television that "seeing as" occurs visually. The metaphor of repressed anger as a beast within trying to break out visually comes to life in a movie like *The Hulk*.

Some scholars refer to this as metaphor made literal. With respect to a visual medium, however, it is perhaps best to speak of *embodied* metaphors. These metaphors take on flesh in a way that allows them to exist visually rather than in the more ethereal realm of ideas. This embodiment of metaphor has led to the objection that film images cannot be metaphorical because they offer a visual depiction of their object rather than the abstract and figurative connection that metaphor demands. Trevor Whittock offers a defense of metaphor in film, and he argues that such objections suffer from relying too heavily on metaphor as a linguistic phenomenon rather than as a category of thought.[29] The difficulty of metaphor in film is that the metaphors typically occur within a nonfigurative narrative structure so that the "metaphorical and literal levels of meaning are made to coexist to a far greater degree than is the case in literary modes" and this, in turn, raises the question of whether metaphors that are so heavily visualized can remain metaphors. Whittock says yes "so long as we can perceive figurative layers of meaning alongside the literal."[30] According to Whittock, the most powerful metaphors in film (and by extension television) are those that help shape the mythic structure of the film. He says, "Subordinate to the tale told, they yet seem central to its very conception. For it is by means of them the cinematic fable achieves its potency and resonance."[31] Such is the metaphorical world of *Buffy the Vampire Slayer*.

METAPHOR AND *BUFFY*

When a dying monk tells Buffy that his journey is at an end, she warns him, "Don't get metaphory on me" (5.5). That may have been good advice under the circumstances, but with respect to *Buffy the Vampire Slayer* it is impossible advice to keep because metaphor is integral to many of the very genres from which *Buffy* partakes. Horror and fantasy genres use various kinds of monsters and fantastical creatures to represent the fears and problems that afflict a society. A society's monsters aid in the construction of human identity by helping that society navigate the boundaries between the human and the monstrous.[32] Our monsters often represent the chaos and disorder that we fear in life, whether that be the chaos of science run amok (Frankenstein) or the uncontrollable beast within (Mr. Hyde). *Buffy* writer Jane Espenson comments on this metaphorical function of a society's monsters:

> Human beings love order. The world is full of disorder. Human beings are constantly trying to bring it into some semblance of order, and the world always fights back. Disorder became demonized, as if it were an actual entity against which we struggle. Entropy as demon. I think that's why so many of our demons have that function.[33]

Fighting against these monsters is an attempt to replace chaos with order. It is the eternal battle between our desire for a better world and the world's tendency to resist.

Vampire lore in particular has a long history of metaphorical usage. Nina Auerbach argues that each age creates the vampire it needs as a personification of its own struggles.[34] At different times, the vampire has represented aristocrats who live off the poor, cultural outsiders or marginalized ethnic groups, and mysterious health threats like plague or, more recently, AIDS.[35] Robin Wood says that most horror films use the monster to represent the Other, or the marginalized outsider.[36] This trend was certainly influential on Joss Whedon who claims that his interest in vampires was due to "the isolation they feel. They're in the world, but not of it. As a child I always felt the same way and 'Buffy' deals with that kind of alienation."[37]

So it should come as no surprise that *Buffy the Vampire Slayer* self-consciously deals in metaphor. *Buffy* writer Jane Espenson says, "Most of our episodes are driven by a metaphor."[38] Several *Buffy* writers have commented that they begin the process of creating story ideas by talking about the emotions and metaphors they want to deal with. These emotions are then exaggerated to demonic proportions and expanded into a horror story. Whedon has said, "When I get together with my writing team, I ask them, 'What is your favorite horror movie? What's the most embarrassing thing that ever happened to you? Now, how can we combine the two?'"[39] The metaphors on *Buffy* are the vehicle for delivering emotional resonance to the audience. One scene on *Buffy* illustrates the connection between metaphor and the emotional pain that often underlies it. After Xander breaks off his engagement with the literal-minded Anya, she is angry and desirous of revenge.

> ANYA: I wish your intestines were tied in knots and ripped apart inside your lousy gut!
> XANDER (sadly): They are.
> ANYA (hopeful): Really? (Xander nods) Right now? Does it hurt?
> XANDER: God, yes. It hurts so bad it's killing me. Anya . . . I love you, I want to make this work.
> ANYA (annoyed): Those are metaphor intestines! You're not in any real pain! (6.18)

Of course, Anya got it wrong. The intestines may be metaphorical, but they are no less painful. The emotional pain that Xander is feeling is just as real as any physical pain could be, and that emotional pain is communicated by means of a metaphor. Likewise on *Buffy*, the horned demons, gooey monsters, and apocalyptic scenarios may not be real, but the emotions and struggles they represent certainly are.

At the center of *Buffy*'s metaphorical world stands a root metaphor that is the foundation and source for all the other metaphorical constructions used on the show. That root metaphor is "High School is Hell." As with many root metaphors, it is left unstated in the series itself, yet governs the many surface metaphors populating the show from week to week. Sunnydale High School is built on a hellmouth, thus accounting for the demons, vampires, and beasts that never run in short supply, and providing what Whedon calls the "central myth" of the series that high school is a horror show.[40] Anyone who has been to high school knows the truth of that metaphor: the alienation, humiliation, challenges to one's identity, hormonal confusion and fear of impending adulthood characteristic of high school all contribute to an emotional experience that when exaggerated becomes virtually hellish.

The idea to do a show as a metaphor for the horrors of high school came from Joss Whedon's own high school experience. Noting that *Buffy* was designed to be "a metaphor for how lousy my high-school years were," Whedon says,

> I had a very painful adolescence, because it was all very strange to

me. It wasn't like I got beat up, but the humiliation and isolation, and the existential 'God, I exist, and nobody cares' of being a teenager were extremely pronounced for me . . . It's not like I think I had it worse than other people. But that's sort of the point of *Buffy*, that I'm talking about the stuff everybody goes through. Nobody gets out of here without some trauma.[41]

In fact, Joss Whedon's high school experiences sometimes inspire actual scenes, such as in the first episode ("Welcome to the Hellmouth") where Jesse asks Cordelia to dance and she replies, "With you?" Whedon claims that is the exact response he received the one time he asked a girl to dance in high school.[42] One of *Buffy*'s executive producers and writers, David Greenwalt, says of the impact Whedon's high school years had on the creation of *Buffy*, "If Joss Whedon even had one decent date in high school none of us would be here today."[43]

In "Doublemeat Palace" (6.12), Buffy gets a job working at a fast food restaurant. When she suspects that the disappearance of some workers is due to demonic activity, Xander offers a rebuttal: "I think you're seeing demons where there's just life." Xander's statement inadvertently reveals the show's approach towards metaphor, which is to set the ordinary and the fantastic side by side. On *Buffy* demons are exactly what one sees as a stand-in for life. The root metaphor of "High School is Hell" sets the mundane events of high school in the context of the demonic and monstrous, thus expanding everyday fears and anxieties into metaphorical representations of life.

Consider several examples. In the opening scene of "Ted" (2.11), Buffy comes home one night, and as she puts her key in the front door lock, the door pushes inward. Someone is inside. She walks into a dimly lit house as spooky music plays. She hears a glass break and her mother say "No." Buffy hurriedly rushes into the kitchen thinking her mother is in danger only to find her kissing a man. By presenting the discovery of a mother's new boyfriend with the trappings of traditional horror shows, *Buffy* argues that this seemingly mundane event can be a frightening thing (emotionally) for a teenager. The scene creates an expectation that Buffy will find a monster in the kitchen and in fact she does, as Ted turns out to be a robot incapable of love or emotion.

What about the ordinary, common occurrence of parents who try to relive their high school glory days through their children? On *Buffy*, this becomes a witch who magically switches bodies with her daughter so she can reclaim her cheerleading fame (1.3). The punishment of this witch (she gets magically trapped within her own cheerleading trophy) serves as a visual metaphor for how one's obsessive desire to reclaim lost glory can be enslaving. This episode also illustrates how the metaphorical character of *Buffy* gives rise to misunderstandings of its agenda. After it aired, some people were upset at the episode's stereotypical portrayal of witchcraft. Whedon says, "We got a lot of flak from witches and from people claiming to be witches, but what's really going on here is a story about mothers and daughters."[44]

The social problems of high school also receive metaphorical treatment. The peer pressure, social ostracism and predatory behavior of high school cliques find representation on *Buffy* as a group of students possessed by the spirit of a hyena. They consequently become an animal pack, preying on the weak ("The Pack"; 1.6). When Buffy realizes Xander is also possessed, she goes to Giles for advice.

>   GILES: Xander's taken to teasing the less fortunate?
>   BUFFY: Uh-huh.
>   GILES: And is there a noticeable change in both clothing and demeanor?
>   BUFFY: Yes.
>   GILES: And, well, otherwise all his spare time is spent lounging about with imbeciles?
>   BUFFY: It's bad isn't it?
>   GILES: It's devastating. He's turned into a sixteen-year-old boy. Of course, you'll have to kill him.

When Giles adds that teasing and preying on the weak represent "natural teen behavior pattern," he highlights the thin line between the metaphor of the animal pack and the reality of teen life. Likewise, the scary real-life problem of sexual predators on the Internet finds expression as Moloch the Corruptor, a demon that inhabits the Internet and preys on socially awkward students (1.8). The metaphor of "being unpopular is being invisible" comes true on *Buffy*, as a socially isolated student becomes physically invisible to parallel her social invisibility. This is another metaphor that found its genesis in the experience of Joss Whedon who says, "That was based on, when I was fifteen I actually drew a picture of myself becoming transparent . . . I felt myself feeling extraordinarily alienated."[45]

In the second season episode "Phases" (2.15), the werewolf serves as a metaphor for the hormonal changes of puberty that turn normally nice boys into animals. Willow's boyfriend, Oz, learns that he has become a werewolf and that three days out of the month, he will change into a beast driven solely by animalistic urges. The ordinary fear of a boyfriend suddenly changing into something unrecognizable gets exaggerated to monstrous extremes as Willow explains her discovery of Oz's nocturnal habits: "He said he was going through all these changes then he . . . went through all these . . . changes." At the conclusion of the episode, however, Willow explains to Oz why she wants to keep their relationship going despite his condition.

> WILLOW: Well, I like you. You're nice and you're funny, and you don't smoke. Yeah, okay, werewolf . . . but that's not all the time. I mean, three days out of the month I'm not much fun to be around either.

The hormonal changes of teenage girls are clearly not immune from metaphorical treatment as well.

The *Buffy* writers' intentionality in their use of metaphor sometimes manifests itself in a self-referential wink at the nature of their own show. As graduation day looms, Buffy's mother encourages Buffy to pursue a college education, telling her that she should be at college with keg parties and boys rather than in Sunnydale with hellmouths and vampires. Buffy replies, "Not really seeing the distinction" (3.8). Another time, when Buffy is hired by Principal Wood to serve as a guidance counselor for students, he tells her not to try and be their friend because "you open that door, and these students will eat you alive." Buffy responds, "You heard about Principal Flutie, right?" Flutie was Buffy's sophomore year principal who was indeed eaten alive by the hyena-possessed pack of students he had tried to befriend.

The metaphors on *Buffy* are distinct from literary metaphors in that they bear a higher degree of concreteness. The metaphors take visual form. It is not just that unpopularity equals invisibility in a figurative sense; the unpopular actually become invisible. When Xander tells Buffy, "You can't just bury stuff, Buffy. It'll come right back up to get you," we then see zombies as representatives of Buffy's buried emotions rise from their graves and try to kill her (3.2). In Buffy's world, people cannot simply claim metaphorically to be haunted by their dreams for there they truly are, as in the episode "Nightmares" where students actually show up for class naked and have their mothers come to school and kiss them in front of their friends. As the Master explains to Buffy, "Your nightmares are made flesh" (1.10). We could say the same about the show's metaphors. In the visual medium of television, metaphor becomes embodied.

On one level, these embodied metaphors have a greater power than their literary counterparts because they take visual form. Before our very eyes Buffy fights against the alienation and ostracism that threatens. There is a catharsis in witnessing our internal demons become external demons and then be dispatched. Yet on another level, the danger is that this embodiment of metaphor can obscure its figurative quality so that the metaphor is overlooked due to engagement with the visual image. Tracy Little demonstrates, for instance, that the line between metaphor and reality can become blurry on *Buffy*.[46] In "Lovers Walk" (3.8), the difficulty of distinguishing the metaphorical from the literal in *Buffy*'s world is acknowledged in Giles' and Buffy's conversation about test scores:

> BUFFY: She saw these scores and her head spun around and exploded.
> GILES: I've been on the Hellmouth too long. That was metaphorical, yes?

The key to maintaining the figurative power of the embodied metaphor is to not lose sight of what lies behind it. When Joss Whedon says that the scariest thing to him is not monsters but people,[47] he is getting at something very important. The real horror in life is not the witch who switches bodies with her daughter, but the real parents who deprive their children of their own future by their desire to dwell in the past. Invisible girls are fun, but the social isolation that many real girls feel is a genuine fright. Although Moloch the Corruptor may inhabit the Internet on *Buffy*, much scarier are the real corrupters of youth who seek out young girls in chat rooms. The emotional reality that generates the metaphor is what gives the metaphor its power and resonance; otherwise it's just people with horns running around.

This chapter has explored the means by which *Buffy the Vampire Slayer* communicates. Through the indirection of narrative and metaphor, it exposes the emotional and experiential realities of life, thereby creating a foundation for moral discourse. *Buffy the Vampire Slayer* operates from the premise that the more we understand the emotional realities of life and the more perspective we gain on the anxieties and fears we share in common with our neighbors, the better equipped we are to live. To this point, we have focused mainly on theory and method, believing that the moral content of a television show cannot or at least should not be divorced from the method by which that content is communicated. With this foundation laid, we now turn our attention to content.

Chapter 4

Buffy's Story

Above all else, *Buffy the Vampire Slayer* is a show about women. Buffy is a girl on the verge of womanhood struggling to come to terms with a power inside her that she does not fully understand and that others do not recognize. The idea of a vampire slayer plays out as a metaphor for all women who seek to find the strength that lies within them and who seek to battle the sexual predators inherent in the concept of "vampire." For Joss Whedon, this idea flows out of both an intellectual and emotional interest. He explains, "A lot of it is inherent and studied and strongly felt feminism, and a lot of it is just that chicks are cool."[1] That this theme of female empowerment is set in the context of the tempestuous years of adolescence and early adulthood means it is also a show about growth. Joseph Campbell says that most mythological stories are about "the stages of life" and the transition "from childhood to adult responsibilities."[2] The major characters on *Buffy* negotiate this transition together as they seek their place in the world and an understanding of themselves that allows them to live lives of quiet nobility. Claiming to be "a big fan of puberty and people who've been through it,"[3] Whedon has created a show that combines the themes of female empowerment and adolescent rites of passage in a tale about vampires.

THE NARRATIVE STRUCTURE OF *BUFFY*

The story of *Buffy the Vampire Slayer* unfolds over the course of seven seasons (from 1997-2003). Each season of twenty-two episodes corresponds roughly to one school year in Buffy's world or, as it is also known, the Buffyverse. The exception is the first season of twelve episodes, representing a partial school year. Events occur in relatively real time, meaning that when a new season starts in the Fall, we find the characters returning from summer break. Because *Buffy* deals with the process of growth and maturation, change is essential. Unlike shows where characters experience life-altering events only to return at the end of the episode to the exact point they were at the beginning, what happens on one episode of *Buffy* always carries over.

The story itself plays out on several levels. First is the macronarrative level. This is the overall, seven-year story of *Buffy* from beginning to end. Within the macronarrative, each season has its own story arc that furthers the overall story line, yet retains its own integrity. Each season features a major enemy, a "Big Bad" as it's called, which inevitably falls to defeat by the end of that season. On the smaller, micronarrative level are the individual episodes and stories that make up the larger arcs. Whereas each season has a dominant theme or themes that run throughout, each individual episode explores a particular theme or idea in a more self-contained form.

From the beginning, Joss Whedon knew where the general story was heading. Of course, the inherent fluidity of narrative means that plot lines change and the courses of characters are occasionally altered. Nevertheless, there is a distinct intentionality and foresight in the telling of this tale. Whedon would deliberately sow seeds in earlier episodes that might or might not sprout later on. He frequently mapped out individual episodes and larger story arcs years in advance. Kristine Sutherland, who plays Buffy's mom, says that she knew her character was going to die two years in advance, and Sarah Michelle Gellar claims to have known the ending of season five for about three years prior.[4]

The following sections introduce the story of *Buffy the Vampire Slayer* through a description of major characters and of the overall (macronarrative) plot lines.

THE SCOOBY GANG

Buffy does not fight alone. She is joined by a core group of three others: her Watcher Giles and best friends Willow and Xander. They are alternately dubbed the Slayerettes, the Superfriends, or most commonly the Scooby Gang in a knowing reference to that other group of youngsters who solved mysteries of a seemingly supernatural nature. Others come and go, at times becoming integral members of the group, yet these four form the heart and soul of the battle against evil.

Their informal base of operations is the Sunnydale High School library. This provides them a great deal of privacy as students rarely visit. That the library, which represents the source of knowledge in an educational institution, is consistently absent of students taps into *Buffy*'s sense of irony. With the library as their sole refuge, these four individuals bravely thwart apocalypses, outwit demons, and occasionally contemplate studying. Let's take a closer look at each of them.

Buffy Summers

Buffy Summers is a former cheerleader and Fiesta Queen who at the age of fifteen received an unsolicited calling to be savior of the world. Her life abruptly changed from pom poms to stakes and crosses, and from cheerleading on basketball courts to hunting in cemeteries. She became a Vampire Slayer. According to the legend, one girl is chosen in each generation and gifted with the strength and speed to fight vampires and demons. It is a dangerous job and the life expectancy of a Slayer is short. A new one is called only when the previous one dies.

Buffy is at times a walking contradiction: incredibly self-reliant yet desperate for companionship, fierce in combat yet gentle and insecure with her friends. She has no qualms beheading a vampire or skewering a demon, yet wears a tank top with a duck on it that says "Hug me," and after being briefly electrocuted, knows to get right to the important issue: "Tell me the truth. How's my hair?" (1.8). Buffy struggles constantly to balance the cheerleader and the Slayer within her, and the two do not always go together well, as when she tries to give a commanding speech about going out to kill demons while wearing "yummy sushi pajamas" (4.14). Buffy is kind and loving, sacrificial in spirit, generous to a fault, and an unrelenting foe to all that is evil in Sunnydale.

Rupert Giles

Rupert Giles, or just "Giles" as he is often called, is Buffy's Watcher. The Watchers are a secret organization that tracks and observes supernatural activity around the world. They view Vampire Slayers as the weapons they use to fight evil and so send a Watcher to train and guide each Slayer in her task. Giles is the brains to Buffy's brawn. He is British and thus extremely alien to these California teenagers who find his use of words like "anon" in normal conversation quite puzzling. He lists cross-referencing among his hobbies (2.6) and becomes positively giddy at the prospect of an afternoon spent researching werewolves, one of the "classics" (2.15). Giles is an old-school bibliophile who reveres the smell of books and declares, "Things involving the computer fill me with a child-like terror" (1.8).

Giles is a father figure to Buffy, providing her with the security and structure she lacks from her own absentee father. He is dependable and trustworthy with an unshakeable faith in Buffy and her friends. He is the adult voice in the group, wise and compassionate, yet willing to discipline when necessary. Without him, Buffy and her friends lose the compass that guides them into the adult world.

Willow Rosenberg

Willow is a shy, sweet, wearer of fuzzy pink slippers who has absolutely no idea of the strength within her. She is fiercely intelligent, bookish, and a whiz at computers. Willow is the overachieving student who gets excited at the prospect of a research party and who uses the time in between classes to re-copy her notes with a system of multi-colored pens (5.11). Willow's internal shyness manifests itself externally in her conservative and attention-deflecting clothing, which, as Cordelia points out, shows that Willow has "seen the softer side of Sears" (1.1). Her introverted nature also hinders the dating process, as she explains to Buffy: "Well, when I'm with a boy I like, it's hard for me to say anything cool, or witty, or at all. I can usually make a few vowel sounds, and then I have to go away" (1.1).

Willow is an innocent soul whose idea of injecting danger into a boring evening is for the gang to sneak their own tea bags into the Bronze (a teen dance club) and then request hot water (2.5). Her history of rebellion involves being lookout in the fifth grade for a girl who was smoking (2.3) and eating her banana well before the school lunch period (3.16). This innocence makes her later attempt to destroy the world all the more shocking.

Xander Harris

Xander is the consummate high school dork. This proud owner of *Babylon 5* commemorative plates sports a Tweety-Bird wristwatch and superhero posters on his wall. If Willow is the classic academic overachiever, Xander is the opposite. As he prepares to hand in his English paper, Xander excitedly proclaims to himself, "This time I'm ready for ya. No 'F' for Xander today. No, this baby's my ticket to a sweet D-minus" (2.16). Frequently Xander is shallow and insecure about his manliness and his usefulness to the group, and he uses humor as a defense mechanism to shield his vulnerability.

Although at times goofy and un-intellectual, Xander has the ability to put things into proper perspective when the minds of others are clouded by emotion or fear. He is "perspective guy" (2.21) and "the one who sees everything" (7.18). Because Buffy and Willow accepted him along with all his insecurities and fears, he has become to them the truest and most loyal friend anyone could have. He carries himself with a false bravado that masks an underlying cowardice. In his own words, "I laugh in the face of danger. Then I hide until it goes away" (1.3). Yet he repeatedly puts his life on the line without a second thought when those he cares about are endangered. He is the heart of the Scooby Gang.

THE SEVEN SEASONS OF *BUFFY*

Season One

During her sophomore year, Buffy Summers transfers from Hemery High School in Los Angeles to Sunnydale High School in the much smaller town of Sunnydale, CA. Joyce Summers was concerned about her daughter's increasingly destructive behavior (such as burning down the school gym). So Joyce brought Buffy to Sunnydale in the hope of a new beginning.

Buffy too hopes for a new beginning. As the new girl in an unfamiliar school, Buffy wants only to fit in and make friends, but instead quickly falls out of favor with the most popular girl in school, Cordelia Chase. The falling out occurs when Cordelia, who divides the world into "winners and losers," mercilessly picks on one of the "losers," Willow Rosenberg. Buffy opts instead to cast her lot with the "losers," Willow and her close friend Xander.

Complicating matters, however, is Buffy's secret identity as the Slayer, which turns out to be not much of a secret as both Willow and Xander soon discover it. With their newfound knowledge that Sunnydale sits on a hellmouth (most citizens are blissfully unaware), Willow and Xander vow to help Buffy in her fight against evil. Also on her side is her Watcher Giles, the school's new librarian, and Angel, a two hundred and forty-some year old vampire who for a hundred years "offered an ugly death to everyone I met. And I did it with a song in my heart" (1.7). Formerly known as Angelus, the vampire "with the angelic face," he now lives under a curse. Over eighty years ago, he killed a gypsy girl and her clan cursed him by restoring his soul to him, relegating him to an eternity in torment and guilt over his crimes. By the time Buffy learns the truth about Angel, it is too late. She is already in love and so is he.

Buffy's social problems are the least of her worries, however. She has a potential apocalypse on her hands led by the Master, an ancient and powerful vampire. Giles and Angel uncover an ancient prophecy, which says that on the following night Buffy will face the Master and will die, seriously complicating her plans to attend the Spring Fling dance that night. Wanting to leave town and hide, but knowing that to do so will bring harm to others, Buffy goes off to fight the Master alone — and he kills her. Xander quickly revives her with CPR, and Buffy resolutely sets off to face the Master again, this time emerging victorious . . . and just in time to attend the Spring Fling!

Running throughout season one are the themes of identity and destiny. The central characters of Buffy, Xander, Cordelia and Willow are all trying to find their place in the world as the turbulent experiences of high school continually alter their perceptions of life. For Buffy this quest is most pronounced for she must deal not only with the universal struggle of adolescence, but also the very particular duties of being a Slayer. This battle to reconcile the Slayer and the girl becomes even stronger in season two.

Season Two

The second season of *Buffy* revolves around the theme of love and relationships. Virtually every major character becomes embroiled in a romantic relationship and through that relationship learns the importance of trust and sacrifice. Buffy's relationship with Angel heats up. Giles begins to date Sunnydale High's computer teacher Jenny Calendar. Willow embarks on her first dating experience with Oz, the stoic, lead guitar player of the band *Dingoes Ate My Baby*. And Xander who heretofore was treasurer of the "We Hate Cordelia" club, inexplicably begins to date her.

During season two, a new threat arrives in town: Spike and Drusilla, the Sid and Nancy of the vampire set. Drusilla is slender with long black hair and an insane gleam in her eye that comes from, well, being insane. Now sick and frail as well, Spike has brought her to Sunnydale in the hope of finding a cure for her illness.

Spike is a bleached blond British vampire with a fondness for the Bloomin' Onion and daytime soap operas. With his rock star attitude and long black trenchcoat, he recalls Billy Idol (although we later learn that Billy Idol actually got his look from Spike). Also known as William the Bloody, he got the name Spike from torturing his victims with railroad spikes. Whereas the Master was all about structured religiosity, ancient prophecies, and tradition, Spike lives for rebellion and anarchy. He announces to the other vampires, "From now on we're gonna have a little less ritual and a little more fun around here" (2.3).

While Spike plots to kill Buffy and heal Drusilla, another surprise visitor arrives in Sunnydale: Kendra the Vampire Slayer. Buffy's short demise at the end of season one meant that another Slayer was immediately called and invested with the power. For the first time in history, two Slayers exist together.

Then on Buffy's seventeenth birthday, tragedy strikes. Angel loses his soul. The evil Angelus is back and bent on destruction. As Buffy struggles with whether killing Angel is a sacrifice she is able to make, others experience the pain of love and broken trust. Giles and Jenny deal with secrets from each other's past that come back to haunt them. Willow and Oz have to contend with his newly discovered werewolf nature, and Xander and Cordelia wrestle with carrying on a secret relationship of which both of them are ashamed. After all, Xander's hatred of Cordelia was legendary, and she can't face the social stigma that will result from dating "the lame, unpopular guy" (2.20).

Things rapidly fall apart for Buffy. Her boyfriend is a murderer bent on world destruction; Kendra is killed by Drusilla; Jenny is killed by Angel; and Buffy's mother, Joyce, who learns her daughter is a Slayer, does not take the news well. Ironically the only bit of good news for Buffy is that Spike shows up and offers his help. Buffy and

Spike strike a deal. He will betray Angel to her, and she will allow he and Drusilla to leave town.

Angel revives a demon named Acathla who has the power to suck the world into hell. The only way to stop Acathla once he wakes is with the lifeblood of the one who brought him forth. Yet, just as Buffy readies herself to kill Angel, Willow performs a magic spell that restores Angel's soul. But it is too late. Buffy kisses him, tells him she loves him, and then plunges her sword through his chest sending both he and Acathla to hell.

Season Three

It's senior year at Sunnydale High and the romantic relationships that dominated season two are all in disarray. Giles copes with the loss of Jenny while Buffy tries to move on without Angel. Initially Xander and Cordelia and Willow and Oz are doing well. Cordelia is even beginning to love Xander because "he kinda grows on you, like . . . a Chia pet" (3.5). But trouble lies ahead. Childhood friends Xander and Willow develop feelings for each other and are caught kissing by Cordelia and Oz.

Season three introduces two important new characters and offers the return of a third. Hurting from Xander's betrayal, Cordelia inadvertently enlists the aid of a vengeance demon named Anyanka, a patron saint of scorned women. Blaming Buffy for all her troubles, Cordelia wishes for a Buffy-less Sunnydale, and Anyanka grants her wish. Eventually, though, Anyanka's power source gets destroyed, nullifying the wish and resulting in her becoming human. As a human she goes by the name Anya. Being an 1120-year-old ex-demon has its downfalls as Anya struggles to adjust to mortal life. Anya is an extremely literal-minded person who speaks whatever is on her mind with neither guile nor tact. Through the adult but culturally ignorant Anya, *Buffy* is able to explore socialization and culture through the eyes of an outsider, as illustrated by her awkward attempt to ask Xander to the prom.

> ANYA: I have witnessed a millennium of treachery and oppression from the males of the species and I have nothing but contempt for the whole libidinous lot of them.
> XANDER: Then why are you talking to me?
> ANYA: (sighs) I don't have a date for the prom.

XANDER: Well gosh. I wonder why not. It couldn't possibly have
anything to do with your sales pitch?
ANYA: Men are evil. Will you go with me? (3.20)

The second new character is Faith, the new Vampire Slayer called at the death of Kendra. In many ways Faith is the polar opposite of Buffy. Highly sexual and rebellious, she appears to enjoy slaying a little too much. She arrives in town Watcher-less and throws her lot in with Buffy and her pals.

Returning is Angel who mysteriously shows up on the floor of an abandoned mansion, naked, mindless, and feral from the untold torture he suffered in hell. When Buffy discovers him, she conceals his presence from her friends and slowly nurses him back to health and sanity. After a long and hard struggle, Angel decides he was sent back for a reason — to seek atonement for his sins. With this new purpose in hand, and his growing belief that he can never give Buffy the life she deserves, he says goodbye to her and heads off to Los Angeles (and to his own spin-off show).

As senior year draws to a close, Buffy, Xander and Willow face graduation and the future. First, however, they must deal with the Big Bad of season three: Sunnydale Mayor Richard Wilkins. Mayor Wilkins is an upbeat, jovial fellow who says things like "That's swell" and whose most explicit exclamation is "gosh." Obsessed with cleanliness and propriety, he keeps a steady supply of moist towelettes on his desk and admonishes a gang of vampires he has sent out to kill with, "And boys? Let's watch the swearing" (3.22). But the Mayor has a dark agenda. He intends to transform himself into a giant demon during Sunnydale High's graduation ceremony.

Meanwhile, Buffy has another problem to deal with. While Buffy and Faith are out hunting vampires, Faith mistakes Deputy Mayor Allan Finch for a vampire and stakes him through the heart. The killing of a human being pushes Faith over the edge, and she turns her back on Buffy and aligns herself with the Mayor, choosing his brand of freedom from responsibility over Buffy's moral structure. To quote Andrew's later description of Faith, "Like so many tragic heroes, Faith was seduced by the lure of the dark side. She wrapped evil around her like a large, evil Mexican serape" (7.18). The eventual showdown between Buffy and Faith results in Faith hospitalized in a coma.

As graduation day arrives, Buffy prepares for her battle against the Mayor. After the Mayor ascends to demon form, Buffy lures him into the high school library and blows him up with a stockpile of explosives. Of course, this succeeds at blowing up the high school as well, a fitting metaphor for graduation. Buffy's high school career thus comes to a dramatic close. It was filled with heartbreak, loss, and change, but Buffy succeeded in giving the Class of '99 "the lowest mortality rate of any graduating class in Sunnydale history" (3.20).

The theme of betrayal runs throughout season three of *Buffy*. Buffy had betrayed her friends by running away (3.2). Xander, Willow, and Oz betray Buffy in her quest for Homecoming Queen by helping out rival Cordelia (3.5). Xander and Willow betray Cordelia and Oz with their hidden romance (3.8). Gwendolyn Post, Faith's initial Watcher, betrays everyone by seeking for her own gain the fabled Glove of Myhnegon (3.7). Buffy betrays her friends by lying to them about Angel's return, while Xander betrays Buffy by encouraging Faith to hunt down Angel (3.6). In "Gingerbread" (3.11), the parents of Sunnydale betray their children. In "Helpless" (3.12), Giles betrays Buffy by surreptitiously drugging her at the orders of the Watcher's Council and then betrays the Watcher's Council, leading to his being fired. Before being killed, Deputy Mayor Allan Finch was plotting to betray his boss. Finally, Faith betrays the Scooby Gang with her turn towards evil, but then, while appearing to Buffy in a coma-induced dream, betrays the Mayor (3.22).

All this betrayal highlights the change that the characters face during season three and their introduction to the complex realities of adult relationships. The graduation that caps off the season represents this theme of change and the transition to more adult responsibilities that will confront Buffy and her friends as they enter college and the work force.

Season Four

Season four has everyone adjusting to life after high school. Giles is unemployed. Xander, now sleeping in his parents' basement and paying rent, tries out a series of odd jobs. Buffy and Willow begin college, a whole different educational experience as illustrated by their first foray into the college library. With its huge expanse, countless volumes of books, and actual students, Willow announces to Buffy, "It's like a whole new world" (4.1). Indeed it is, and along with that new world comes new people and new relationships. After high school, those friendships that seemed as though they would last forever often weaken as people drift apart. Throughout season four Buffy, Xander, Willow and Giles find their bond challenged and their friendship strained, though never broken.

After the travails of season three, the gang's romantic lives get back on track . . . more or less. Buffy begins to date Psychology Professor Maggie Walsh's teaching assistant, Riley Finn, because she thinks the All-American Iowa boy can provide her the stable relationship she never had with Angel — like being able to go out together in daylight. Xander's wildly atypical relationship with Anya heats up. Willow, however, has the most trouble with romance. Her relationship with Oz hits a snag when Oz realizes that before he can truly be the man Willow needs, he must first tame the beast within him. So he leaves Sunnydale on a personal quest. Willow is crushed. The only solace she finds is when she meets Tara, a fellow practitioner of witchcraft. They quickly bond over their mutual love of magic, and that friendship eventually turns to romance.

Meanwhile, an old familiar foe returns. Spike shows up in Sunnydale without Drusilla, and announces himself as "the big bad" before being comically electrocuted. Yet the Big Bad of season four is not Spike. The danger of science and technology is a major theme this season, and the Big Bad falls in line accordingly. The Initiative is a secret, government organization located in a vast, underground facility. Their mission is to capture vampires and demons for study. Having electrocuted Spike, they take him into their possession and implant a computer chip in his brain that renders him unable to harm any human being without suffering intense neurological pain. Spike quickly escapes, however, only to find himself at a loss. No longer able to kill or feed off humans and with the Initiative hot on his trail, he has no recourse left but to go to Buffy and Giles for help. Giles takes him in, and Spike spends his time tied to a chair and watching "Passions" on the "telly." Spike is depressed until he discovers that though he may not be able to harm humans, he can harm demons. He then turns mercenary by occasionally helping out Buffy and her pals for money despite the intense hatred he still harbors for them.

Meanwhile, Riley is revealed as a high ranking soldier or demon-hunter in the Initiative, which is led by Professor Maggie Walsh. But she is wrong, for Maggie Walsh has her own agenda unknown to Riley. She has been harvesting demon parts and using them to construct a super-soldier: a part human, part demon, part machine cyborg appropriately named Adam. When he awakens, the ungrateful

Adam's first act is to kill his creator, Professor Walsh, and set off on his own path of destruction. Disillusioned, Riley leaves the Initiative to help Buffy. Buffy needs the help because Faith has unexpectedly revived from her coma, bent on revenge. When her attempt at revenge fails, Faith takes off for Los Angeles in a downward spiral of self-destruction. As Adam's plan begins execution, the Scooby Gang joins together (literally, in a magic spell that invokes the essence of the Slayer) to defeat Adam.

Season four continues the series' ongoing emphasis on growth as Buffy, Xander, and Willow begin their transition from high school into the adult world. Yet season four is also unique with its focused critique of science and technology. In season five *Buffy* returns more strongly to the supernatural elements that are its hallmark.

Season Five

This season opens with Buffy encountering a vampire of legend: Dracula. After defeating Dracula, Buffy returns home to her mother and sister. Yes, sister. Whedon and company ably pull off in season five what has killed other shows: the sudden introduction of a new family member into the preexisting dynamic. Buffy's fourteen-year-old sister Dawn simply shows up on the scene as though she has always been there and Buffy and her friends likewise behave as though Dawn has always been a part of their lives.

The mystery of Dawn is connected to this season's Big Bad. That would be Glorificus, a.k.a. Glory, a goddess who ruled over a hell dimension until being exiled to this world. She is imprisoned in the body of a human male, Ben. Ben and Glory share the same body, morphing back and forth between the two in both appearance and consciousness. Glory's goal is to get back to her own dimension and reclaim her divine throne. To do this she needs an ancient Key, a field of energy that when activated opens the gateways between all dimensions, thus causing them all to merge in chaos. Fortunately, the Key has long been in the possession of an order of monks dedicated to protecting it from Glory. To hide the key, they refashioned it as a human girl and sent her to the Slayer as a sister, even creating a spell that gave Buffy, Dawn and others the memories of a lifetime together. Upon learning the truth, Buffy claims Dawn as her true sister. Her mission is now to protect Dawn at all costs because the ritual shedding of Dawn's blood will activate the key.

While Buffy adapts to this new situation, Giles tries to build a life for himself. When the most recent owner of Sunnydale's Magic Shop is murdered (following the murders of the two previous owners), Giles decides to take it over as proprietor. Buffy questions his wisdom in this, noting that "most magic shop owners in Sunnydale have the life expectancy of a Spinal Tap drummer" (5.2).

Xander also appears to be getting his life together. He begins a steady career in the construction business and continues to date Anya, eventually getting engaged. Anya herself goes to work for Giles at the Magic Shop, discovering her love of money in the process. Willow's relationship with Tara continues to grow, but so does her proficiency in magic. In fact, her growing strength with respect to magic becomes a concern for Tara who thinks Willow is moving too fast and becoming too reckless.

Meanwhile Buffy's life takes a sudden turn for the worse. Riley breaks off their relationship and leaves town, joining up with a demon-hunting military operation in South America. On the home front, Buffy's mother dies unexpectedly from complications following brain surgery. Buffy now becomes not only sister but also de facto mother to Dawn. As if that were not enough, Buffy has an even more disturbing problem: Spike has fallen in love with her.

Eventually Glory learns that Dawn is the Key, so she captures her and ties her up at the top of a tower where the bloodletting ritual to open the dimensional gateways will occur. Buffy and the gang fight a fierce battle against Glory. As Glory is close to defeat, she morphs back into Ben, knowing that Buffy would never kill a human being. Giles, however, has no such compunction and kills the human Ben in order to destroy the evil goddess within him. Meanwhile Spike risks his life to rescue Dawn, but to no avail. Her blood has begun to flow. Since the only way to close the gateway once it has opened is with the blood of the one who opened it, Dawn intends to kill herself. Buffy, however, takes her place. Realizing that when the monks made Dawn, they did so out of the same blood that runs in her veins, Buffy sacrifices herself for Dawn and for the world, leaping off of the tower and into the gateway. Once the gateway is closed, her lifeless body falls to the ground at the feet of a weeping Spike. Once again Buffy has died, only this time without resuscitation.

Season Six

Joss Whedon has stated that the theme of season six of *Buffy* is "Oh, grow up!"[5] It represents that stage in life where young people suddenly realize that they must become the grown-ups. As adults, they need to learn to stand on their own. Along with that, however, come inevitable mistakes and bad decisions. Certainly season six is not lacking for bad decisions. Immaturity runs rampant throughout as characters do their best to avoid adulthood.

As season six begins, the gang, including Spike, attempt to keep the vampire population of Sunnydale down. Buffy has been dead for 147 days, by Spike's count, and they are all still grieving. Giles has returned to England and without his fatherly guidance, the gang is adrift. Willow continues to perform magic spells regularly; Xander is reluctant to tell anyone about his engagement to Anya; and Dawn, still trying to cope with her unusual background and the deaths of Buffy and Joyce, engages in frequent shoplifting.

Without Giles' knowledge, Willow, Xander, Tara and Anya make a more fateful decision. Convinced that Buffy is in hell and suffering, they perform a very dangerous resurrection spell to bring Buffy back from the dead. Their spell has an unexpected result: the newly resurrected Buffy appears disoriented, somber, and withdrawn. Eventually the reason for Buffy's mood comes out. She had not been in hell after all, but in heaven. Being torn from heaven has left her with severe depression.

In this state Buffy desperately seeks some kind of connection, something that will make her feel again. To her own confusion and dismay, she finds that connection with Spike. Subsequently Buffy and Spike engage in a disturbing relationship of sex, violence, and self-loathing. Buffy does not love Spike, in fact hates him, but becomes addicted to their self-destructive relationship. Continuing this theme of addiction, Willow's reliance on magic becomes more frequent and irresponsible and she finds herself unable to give it up.

While Buffy, Willow, and Dawn fight their respective addictions (to Spike, magic, and stealing), Xander and Anya prepare for their upcoming nuptials. Terrified at the prospect of a lifetime commitment and questioning whether he and Anya are right for each other, Xander breaks off the wedding at the last minute, leaving Anya to reconsider a career in vengeance.

In addition to these problems, Buffy also must contend with a trio of nerds. Jonathan, Warren, and Andrew join up in a quest to take over Sunnydale and proclaim themselves "super-villains." Together, in their quest to avoid anything resembling maturity, they invent a freeze ray and invisibility gun. Their moving base of operations is a black van whose horn plays the Star Wars theme song. On villainous missions they pass the time debating who was the best Bond, with Andrew getting justifiably slapped by Warren for suggesting Timothy Dalton (6.5).

This lack of a truly threatening villain in season six is noteworthy because the point is that Buffy and her friends have become their own worst enemies. There is little that a villain like the Master or Adam could do that they haven't already done to themselves. Essentially life itself is the Big Bad of this season. The poor decisions made in their clumsy transition to adulthood come back to haunt them. If the root metaphor of seasons one to three is "High School is Hell," then we could adapt that for season six as "Life is Hell."

Despite Spike's protestations of love, Buffy breaks off their warped relationship in an attempt to reclaim her dignity. Not taking rejection well, Spike resorts to his evil nature and tries (unsuccessfully) to rape her. Distraught and angry, Spike leaves town vowing to return.

After Buffy thwarts the Geek Trio's latest plot, Warren goes off the deep-end. Blaming Buffy for destroying his life, he goes to her house with a gun and shoots off several shots. Although one hits Buffy, a more fateful bullet strikes and kills Tara before Willow's eyes. Fueled by grief and anger, Willow draws on magic that turns her hair and eyes black. Bent on revenge she mercilessly hunts down and kills Warren. Willow then hunts Jonathan and Andrew while Buffy and friends try to protect them. The ensuing mayhem leaves Andrew convinced he and Jonathan are doomed. He announces to Buffy, Xander, and Anya: "She's a truck-driving Magic Mama! And we've got maybe seconds before Darth Rosenberg grinds everybody into Jawa-burgers, and not one of you bunch has the midichlorians to stop her" (6.21).

Willow's grief and anger reach such a fevered pitch that she cares little who she hurts, including her closest friends. Willow's sarcastic response, just before she attacks Giles, of "Daddy's home. I'm in wicked trouble now" (6.22) highlights the immaturity and bad decisions that have plagued Willow and the others this season. One of these bad decisions is Willow's subsequent attempt to destroy the world in order to end her, and everyone else's, misery. Before completing the act, Willow and the world are saved by an unlikely person (Xander), who in a display of unconditional love reaches the heart of the true Willow.

The world has been saved, and Buffy has regained her desire to live. Yet one more surprise lies in store. Spike's quest has taken him to a remote village in Africa where he undergoes a series of torturous challenges in a deal struck with a demon. When Spike emerges victorious, he demands that the demon give him what he seeks. The demon grasps Spike's chest, causing him to scream in agony, and says, "Very well. We will return . . . your soul" (6.22).

Season Seven

Season seven brings with it a Big Bad that exceeds all others: The First, as in the first, original Evil. It is the source of all evil and hatred in the world. A true spirit being, The First is incapable of taking corporeal form and can only appear in the guise of people who are already dead.

Season seven offers a return to the beginning in many ways. In addition to facing the originator of all evil, Buffy makes a return to high school. The show also returns to a prominent theme of season one, which is power, especially as it relates to female empowerment.

With Sunnydale High now open (rebuilt on the same spot as the old one, meaning it too is built over the hellmouth), Dawn begins the new school year and Buffy accepts a job as a high school counselor. Willow, meanwhile, has been in England with Giles. She is both learning to deal with the consequences of her murderous actions and studying about the magic power that is within her so that she can better control it. When news of the rising threat in Sunnydale reaches England, Willow returns and is gladly welcomed home.

Spike is also back in Sunnydale. Filled with disgust over his attempt to rape her, Buffy tries to keep him at a distance until learning that he now has a soul. Pity replaces the disgust (mostly) and she allows Spike to help her in her battle against The First.

The First's agenda is to destroy the line of the Slayer and open the hellmouth, thus allowing demons to overrun the earth with no formidable opposition. Consequently, through the aid of its minions known as Bringers, The First is killing off potential Slayers throughout the world. The Potentials, as they are called, are those girls who are born with the potential to be a Slayer, although only one of them would be called in the event of the Slayer's death. Buffy and her gang thereafter attempt to gather all the remaining Potentials that they can find.

As Buffy trains the Potentials into a fighting army, she and Spike grow closer. Convinced that his soul has made him a better man, Buffy slowly develops genuine feelings for him. However, Buffy has another potential romantic complication to deal with when the high school principal, Robin Wood, asks her out on a date. Buffy has been growing suspicious of Principal Wood, but has been unable to conclude whether he's one of the good guys or bad guys. She confesses to Willow that she is unsure of whether him asking her out on a date means he is romantically interested, wants to promote her, or wants to kill her. Willow replies, "Well, you'll have to dress for the ambiguity" (7.14).

Principal Robin Wood turns out, however, to be one of the good guys. He is the son of a former Slayer, raised by a Watcher after his mother's death. He now hunts vampires on a quest of vengeance in hopes of one day finding and killing the vampire that took his mother's life. The problem? That vampire is Spike. After Wood makes an ill-conceived attempt to take Spike out, they reach an accord of sorts, agreeing to set aside their personal animosity in view of the larger battle ahead.

Buffy prepares for battle against The First and Caleb, a fallen priest who has become the primary vessel of The First. Yet if Buffy has a new enemy, she also has a new ally. Willow returns from a brief visit to Los Angeles with another Slayer — the now rehabilitated Faith. In addition, Angel shows up with an ancient amulet on a chain that can be worn only by a champion, someone who is stronger than a human yet has a soul. To Angel's surprise, Buffy chooses to give the amulet to a shocked and humbled Spike.

The final battle arrives. On one side is The First with an underground army of countless super-vamps. On the other side are Buffy, her friends, and a small group of ill-equipped and unprepared girls. Buffy's gang gathers in the high school with plans to descend into the hellmouth for battle. Their only hope in this impossible battle is a rather daring plan Buffy has concocted. As Buffy, Faith, Spike and the Potentials face The First's overwhelming army, Willow performs a magic spell that changes history by imbuing every girl in the world who has the potential to be a Slayer with the Slayer's power. Buffy and Faith are now joined with thirty-some newly empowered Slayers, thus evening the odds.

Then as the tide seems to turn against Buffy's army, Spike's amulet begins to glow. A bright light shoots up out of him and through the roof. Sunlight now streams down into Spike and is channeled through the amulet with rays of light shooting out in all directions and destroying all vampires it touches. With the vampires dead, Buffy pleads with Spike to remove the amulet and save himself, but he refuses. The job is not yet done. He continues to channel the light until the hellmouth itself begins to crumble and Sunnydale above it. Laughing as the sunlight burns him to ashes, Spike destroys the hellmouth and all of Sunnydale, leaving only a giant crater behind.

Gathered at the edge of the crater, Buffy, Dawn, Faith, Xander, Willow, Giles and the other survivors look over the devastation. Xander says, "We saved the world." Willow corrects him, "We *changed* the world" (7.22).

Chapter 5

Buffy's World

In "Prophecy Girl" (1.12), Willow has a run-in with evil that leaves her truly shaken. A gang of vampires invades the student lounge and slaughters several students. This violent invasion of Willow's world makes her question whether any place is truly safe. She says, "It wasn't our world anymore. They made it theirs." A fundamental question that runs throughout *Buffy the Vampire Slayer* is: Whose world is this? Does this world belong to the demons or to the humans? Is this world the province of evil or of good?

Worldview determines action. We act on the basis of our knowledge. How people conceive of their world and of the nature of humanity affects the moral choices they make or whether they believe they have any choice at all. This is why virtually every major religion has a creation story. Because worldview affects moral choice, it is important to address the worldview of *Buffy the Vampire Slayer* and its function if we are to understand the nature of moral decision making in this show. I must stress that this chapter focuses on the worldview of *Buffy the Vampire Slayer* and not that of its creator and writers. Although their perspective may serve as commentary at times, the worldview of a show is not necessarily consistent with that of its creators and *Buffy* is a clear case in point. Joss Whedon is neither a devotee of neopaganism nor of Christianity, yet the worldview of *Buffy* reflects both. Whedon is an atheist, yet the worldview of *Buffy* is polytheistic. The soul is central to the conception of humanity in *Buffy*, yet Whedon himself does not believe in the soul. Our goal is to respect the integrity of the show and its message without necessarily assuming that what *Buffy* says about the world is always what Joss Whedon and his writers want to say about the world.

THE COSMOLOGY OF *BUFFY*

Creation

Buffy the Vampire Slayer has its own creation story. It is one that sidesteps both the biblical creation story and the secular creation story of evolution, although its emphasis on the struggle between good and evil bears stronger resemblance to the former. God is not denied a role in the creation of the world; he is simply not mentioned. Likewise, the origin of goodness is left unmentioned in favor of the origin of evil. The First is the original evil, predating both humans and demons and existing before creation. In "Lessons" (7.1), The First reveals its pre-creation existence to Spike: "And that's where we're going. Right back to the beginning. Not the bang . . . not the Word . . . the true beginning." The First functions much like Satan does in Christianity with its tendency to work through lies and deceit, yet Whedon and company intend it to be ambiguous, just as they do God, in order to allow the viewer room for interpretation. The closest the show comes to identifying Satan is when Caleb implies that Satan is subordinate to The First (7.18).

In *Buffy*'s creation story, the dominant species in the world was initially pure demons. They ruled over the world until humans drove them out and claimed the earth for themselves. These pure demons now inhabit other demon dimensions, but before they left one of them fed off of a human being and mixed their blood, thus creating the first vampire. So vampires and other lesser demons that were left behind roam the earth in conjunction with humans (1.2).[1]

The earth is therefore a place where the demonic and the human battle for territory. This parallels another territorial battle in Buffy's world: that of good and evil. Although the straightforward identification of demon with evil and human with good is not carried through in *Buffy*, the battle of good vs. evil is often set in the context of human vs. demon. To paraphrase Willow, is this our world or theirs? Moral choices are about deciding whose side one is on.

The battle between good and evil is a continual one and in *Buffy* this is represented through an emphasis on balance. For reasons unexplained, there are forces at work in the Buffyverse whose function is to maintain a balance between good and evil. When Jonathan performs the spell that turns him into everyone's ideal person, Willow explains that the drawback is that "to balance the new force of good the spell has to create the opposing force of evil" (4.17). In season two we meet Whistler who first sets Angel on the path of redemption because his job is to "even the score between good and evil" (2.22).

Persistence of Evil

This balance between good and evil means that evil is persistent. It never stops and is never fully defeated. Buffy thwarts one apocalypse only to encounter another. When it is said of The First that, "The First Evil has been and always will be" (7.11), it reveals that the fight against evil is always ongoing. In the mythology of *Buffy*, the Slayer was created as an instrument to fight against evil and maintain the balance. When Joyce asks Buffy if her efforts have made Sunnydale any better or whether they have run out of vampires (3.11), she forces Buffy to question the validity of her mission. If evil cannot be eradicated, why fight? Of course the truth is that Buffy's efforts have made Sunnydale better. No episode better represents this than "The Wish" in which we get to see what a Buffy-less Sunnydale would be like. Overrun by vampires, the people of Sunnydale live a depressing existence dominated by fear. Buffy has made the world of Sunnydale a better place. She may have to face apocalypses repeatedly, but should she ever fail, that world would end. Ultimately the fight against evil is not about eradicating it, but about the choice to fight.[2] In "Gingerbread" (3.11), the apparent murder of two children causes Buffy to lament the fact that they never completely win the fight. Angel says, "We never will. That's not why we fight. We do it 'cause there's things worth fighting for. Those kids. Their parents."

The persistence of evil is a theme that resonates strongly with certain aspects of Christian theology. Many wonder why God does not simply eliminate evil from the world. One response is that evil serves a function in the world. As binary opposites, good and evil define each other. Just as we could not comprehend light if there were no such entity as dark, we cannot comprehend good without evil. The Tree of the Knowledge of Good and Evil in the Garden of Eden pre-dates the first sin, indicating that evil is an entity that exists beyond human activity. In the biblical worldview, the battle against evil must continually be fought but it is a battle that will never be won by human activity alone. The war against evil is less about winning than it is about choosing which side to fight on.

On one level, the final episode of *Buffy* was disappointing in that Buffy never actually kills The First or directly faces it down in some grand climax. That lack of resolution is important, however, because it shows that evil will always persist and always need to be fought. Yet a vital shift also occurs. The First stated that the reason why it was making such an uncharacteristically direct attack against humanity was because "the whole good-versus-evil, balancing the scales thing — I'm over it" (7.7). The First sought to tip the balance permanently in the favor of evil. Since the Slayer is vital for the maintenance of that balance, the Slayer line had to be destroyed (7.10). When Buffy, however, shares the Slayer's power with other girls throughout the world, The First's goal is inverted. The balance of power has indeed shifted but in the favor of good. Consequently, Willow can say, "We changed the world" (7.22). Evil, in the form of The First, has not been eradicated but it has been weakened by the power of good.

Spirits and Dimensions

With respect to the spirit world, the Buffyverse is polytheistic. Populated with a smorgasbord of demons, spirits, and deities, it largely resembles and draws from the world of Greek mythology. As in Greek religion, these deities and demons are manipulated or placated by ritual and sacrifice. In contrast to a Christian worldview with its stark duality of a single heaven and a single hell, *Buffy*'s world matches its pluralistic view of the spirit world with a pluralism of dimensions and alternate universes. In "The Wish" and "Dopplegangland" we encounter an alternate universe in which Willow and Xander are vampires. Anya makes mention of others such as "the land of perpetual Wednesday," "the crazy melty land," and "the world without shrimp" (5.11).

Buffy acknowledges countless demon or hell dimensions. Buffy and Angel both spend time in hell dimensions that are places of torture or hard labor. Although these demon dimensions receive more frequent mention, heaven is a reality on *Buffy* as well. Buffy herself spent time in "heaven" after her death in "The Gift" (5.22) and the countless demon dimensions are balanced by "a zillion heavenly dimensions" (6.8). Whereas the Buffyverse is pluralistic in the makeup of its spiritual world, it is also dualistic in that all of the different dimensions are categorized in terms of hell dimensions as places of torment versus heavenly dimensions as places of peace.

The worldview of *Buffy the Vampire Slayer* is at odds with that of Christianity in several respects: one is monotheistic, the other polytheistic; one is strongly dualistic in its conception of heaven and hell, the other pluralistic. What place then does God and Christianity occupy in *Buffy*'s world?

GOD, CHRISTIANITY, AND FREE WILL

The portrayal of Christianity on *Buffy* is a topic of debate and the source of much misunderstanding. *Buffy the Vampire Slayer* is not a Christian show with a pagan veneer so that if we could only strip away the polytheistic coating we would find Christian theology neatly hiding underneath. Neither, however, is it an anti-Christian show with designs to undermine Christian belief. *Buffy* often engages in a satirical examination of life and consequently lampoons virtually all aspects of society, religion included. In doing so, *Buffy* is non-denominational in its satire. Christianity, Wicca, Judaism, New Age Religions, and Buddhism have all been lampooned at different times. Christianity likely receives greater attention because of its dominant role in western society, its pivotal role in the formation of American culture, and its historical connection to vampire legends.

Whereas Christian influence on *Buffy* is addressed at various points throughout this book, here I specifically address Christianity's place in *Buffy*'s world by examining three topics: the existence of God, the demonic appropriation of religious language and ritual, and the secularization of Christian artifacts and themes.

Existence of God

Joss Whedon has said that an interpretation that locates God within the Buffyverse is a potentially valid one. However, the primary focus of *Buffy* is the *human* struggle with evil, not the divine one. As such, the presence and involvement of God remains deliberately ambiguous.

That said, it is important to note that the existence of God is never denied nor is the reality of biblical characters and events. The Crucifixion is treated as a real event (2.3), as are Noah's Ark (1.6) and the reign of King Solomon (2.9). God's name is invoked during the funeral service of Buffy's mother (5.17). The fallen priest Caleb refers to both God and Jesus in a way that assumes their existence (7.18-19). In "Beneath You" (7.2), as Spike struggles to come to grips with his restored soul and the resulting guilt, he says, "God, please help me" in such a way that the address to God appears more than simple exclamation. Later in the same episode, while standing in a church Spike looks up towards heaven and says loudly (as if to God) of the acquiring of his soul, "It's what you wanted, right?"

The best expression of *Buffy*'s attitude towards the existence of God occurs in "Conversations With Dead People" (7.7) in the conversation between Buffy and the newly-risen vampire Holden:

HOLDEN: Oh, my God!
BUFFY: Oh, your God what?
HOLDEN: Oh, well you know, not my God because I defy him and all of his works, but — Does he exist? Is there word on that, by the way?
BUFFY: Nothing solid.

God remains a mystery in *Buffy*'s world, neither denied nor affirmed. Giles tells Buffy her duty as Slayer is a "sacred duty" (2.9), thus placing it firmly in the context of religion; yet, the role of God, if any, with respect to that duty is never made clear.

Demonic Appropriation of Religion

Buffy and her friends are not very religious. Giles knows the Bible well, but only as a resource. Xander is a non-practicing Episcopalian (6.16). Willow is Jewish, but not overtly so because she has to keep reminding her friends of it. Once, when asked what she's doing for Christmas, she replies, "Being Jewish. Remember, people? Not everybody worships Santa" (3.10). Despite such protestations, she does manage to sneak over to Xander's house every year to watch "A Charlie Brown Christmas" and to see Xander perform the Snoopy dance (2.17; 5.3). The exception to this trend is Riley, a regular churchgoer, although we do not actually see him going to church.

This lack of religiosity among the Scooby Gang contrasts with the frequent appropriation of religion by vampires and demons. The Master and his gang of vampires cloak themselves in religious language and ritual. Ken, the leader of a religiously-oriented homeless shelter, is a demon in disguise (3.1). Members of a college fraternity use religious ritual to summon a demon (2.5). The fallen priest Caleb spouts religious monologues even as he murders young women. These features have led to the conclusion that religion on *Buffy* is "not terribly effective at best, demonic and evil at worst."[3]

Such a conclusion may have value when limited to the portrayal of explicit religious practice, but overall it offers a judgment of religion in the Buffyverse that is too narrow. According to Joss Whedon, the dominant reason for the use of religious language and ritual by vampires is not a value judgment on Christianity or on religion, but is simply an organizational device for structuring the vampire community, defining their relationship with evil, and continuing with established vampire lore. He says of the vampires on *Buffy*:

> There are religions, there are religious leaders, different sects. What do they say in C. S. Lewis books, 'We all worship the same god, we just call it different names'? Well, they all worship evil, they just call it different names.[4]

Historically, the close association of Christianity with vampire legends also accounts for why the Master and other vampires in season one appropriate religion to the extent they do. They are vampires in the more traditional mold. Note that when the more modern vampire Spike arrives on the scene, he professes to leave the ritual behind. From that point on the use of religious language among vampires practically disappears.

If religiosity functions in *Buffy* to identify demons and vampires as worshippers of evil, it is noticeable that similar language does not identify an object of worship for Buffy and her friends. Nevertheless, they make no concession to the worship of demonic forces. When Ethan Rayne asks Giles when they stopped being friends, Giles states: "The same time you started to worship chaos." To which Ethan replies, "Oh, religious intolerance" (4.12). Indeed it is. Those who fight on the side of good on *Buffy* do not tolerate the worship of destructive and evil forces.

Much has been made of the idea that churches on *Buffy* are often abandoned or empty, as though this were a deliberate comment on Christianity. Perhaps, but the fact is that the use of churches on *Buffy* is also more complex than usually acknowledged. That the Master, for instance, is imprisoned within the ruins of a buried church has a dual function. It creates a fitting setting for the Master's religiosity, yet it also shows evil entombed and held captive within a church. Similarly, the confinement of the Master echoes the subterranean imprisonment of demonic forces in Jewish apocalyptic works like *1 Enoch*. Not all churches on *Buffy* are empty and those that are may be so as much for plot convenience as anything. Furthermore, significant moments in both Faith and Spike's journeys of redemption occur in churches, churches that appear fully functional. The forty-three churches in Sunnydale that show up on Willow's Internet check are apparently also fully operational. When Giles comments on how that number seems excessive, Willow responds, "It's the extra evil vibe from the hellmouth. Makes people pray harder" (2.10). Willow's comment identifies the link between good and evil and raises the question of whether there can be one without the other. The complexity of the portrayal of Christianity on *Buffy* also finds illustration in our next topic.

Secularization of Christian Objects and Themes

Those who study the portrayal of vampires in literature and film say that the traditional rendering of vampires as anti-Christ figures who operate within the cosmic battle of good and evil has given way in recent portrayals to a more secularized vampire. Along with this secularization of the vampire comes the loss of traditional folkloric attributes like the need to be invited over a threshold, the lack of reflection in mirrors, and reactions to crucifixes.[5] Several scholars have similarly argued that crucifixes have lost their Christian significance on *Buffy*, functioning as simply another weapon.[6]

The secularization of the vampire lore on *Buffy* is only partial. Without doubt, many of the vampires represent a modern take on the legends. Yet as a whole, *Buffy the Vampire Slayer* adopts a mixture of the traditional and the modern, the religious and the secular, in its portrayal of vampires. For instance, *Buffy* retains many of the traditional folkloric elements that most modern vampire tales reject: the crossing of the threshold, the lack of reflection, and aversion to garlic, Holy Water, and crosses. Whedon says that his use of the cross on *Buffy* is in part a simple desire to adhere to the traditional legend. Beyond that, he acknowledges that the cross on *Buffy* has specific Christian significance. He says, "I don't think vampires are affected by other religious symbols. It is not simply religiosity that offends them — I think there is old, bad blood between vampires and Christianity."[7] If so, then the ability of the cross to hurt and ward off vampires is distinctly due to its Christian association. *Functionally*, the cross may serve as just another weapon in the Slayer's arsenal, but *symbolically* its Christian significance is not lost. Willow acknowledges the Christian significance of this symbol when she nails crosses to the French doors in her bedroom in order to keep out Angel and expresses concern over how her Jewish father will react (2.17). Furthermore, the power that the cross has over vampires on *Buffy* does not come from the one who wields it, who need not believe, but the power is in the symbol itself and its effect on the demon within.

Similarly, themes like sacrifice and redemption are said to have lost their Christian connection on *Buffy* through the process of secularization.[8] There is truth to this. Although Whedon has stated that Christian teaching on themes like redemption and sacrifice has influenced his writing, the way these themes play out divorces them somewhat from a strictly Christian context. They are connected more closely to personal agency rather than transcendent agency. Yet it does not follow that their Christian significance is lost. First, Christian theological teaching on topics like sacrifice and redemption is so vast and multi-faceted that it encompasses a variety of perspectives. Often comments made about the secularization of Christian themes operate with a too narrow conception of Christian teaching on those themes. Second, that Buffy, Spike, and Xander at times serve as Christ-like figures with Christ-like sacrifices, that Buffy's cross in "Prophecy Girl" functions as a symbol of her sacrificial calling complete with death and resurrection, that an important stage in Angel's redemption occurs at Christmas and is marked by a miraculous snowfall (3.10), and that one of Spike's most significant moments of redemption occurs at a cross in a church (7.2) demonstrates that the Christian significance attached to themes of sacrifice and redemption has not been abandoned, even if it has at times been muted.

The reason why many Christians and theologians find value in *Buffy the Vampire Slayer* is not because it is a compendium of Christian belief. I believe it is a recognition that behind the demons, vampires and various deities that populate this show lies a serious attempt to explore emotional truth in which the treatment of themes like sacrifice, redemption, forgiveness, and community resonate strongly with Christian teaching. Now, this is not to suggest that all aspects of *Buffy* resonate so clearly. One area where the traditional

Christian worldview stands at odds with *Buffy*'s worldview is in the relationship between immanence and transcendence.

Immanence and Transcendence

Christian theology emphasizes both the transcendence of God (that he is beyond, or transcends, this physical world) and the immanence of God (that he is fully present, or immanent, in this world). There is a growing trend within segments of American Christianity, however, to seek spirituality and the divine in nature and in everyday life. Consequently, God becomes more of a subjective ideal rather than a transcendent reality. *Buffy the Vampire Slayer*'s worldview fits more comfortably within this trend than within traditional Christian notions of the divine.[9]

Buffy's worldview is clearly transcendent in many ways. The pervasiveness of the supernatural, the multitudes of spiritual dimensions, and even Buffy's occasional visions or consultations with the Slayer spirit guide are all manifestations of a transcendent reality existing beyond the mundane world. Yet the primary spiritual focus of *Buffy* is an immanent one that emphasizes human activity as opposed to divine activity. Rather than rely on miraculous or divine aid, human beings in *Buffy*'s world either find or fail to find the strength within themselves to fight evil, to forgive, or to achieve redemption.

This is an area of dissonance between the traditional Christian worldview and *Buffy*'s worldview, but it does not rise to the level of a contradiction for two reasons. First, Christian theology is as much about how to live in this world as it is about how to be redeemed from it. Although the power for salvation comes from God, the importance of human effort in the attempt to live lives of nobility and honor is never downplayed. Second, when *Buffy*'s immanent worldview is respected within its limited narrative context rather than expanded into a holistic philosophical system, its purpose appears not to be a denial of divine activity per se but an attempt to contextualize moral decisions and the exercise of power within day-to-day choices of how to live and act in this world.

Fate and Freewill

One aspect of transcendence in *Buffy*'s world is the belief that forces outside us predetermine certain events. When high school student Cassie Newton (full name Cassandra after the Greek prophetess) foretells her own death, Buffy fails to stop it from happening despite intense effort (7.4). The role of fate is especially tied to the Slayer. Prophecies surrounding the Slayer and her activities are common in the early seasons of *Buffy*. Giles notes that whereas some prophecies are mutable and can be thwarted, others are set in stone (1.12). Not only are there prophecies about Buffy, but Buffy herself has prophetic dreams where she glimpses a predetermined plan. Buffy even ascribes her calling as the Slayer to "fate" (2.22), and there is an assertion that some of her actions are destined. When Buffy first shows up in Sunnydale, Giles tells her, "There's a reason why you're here, and there's a reason why it's now" (1.1).

Despite these assertions, the role of fate in *Buffy*'s world is ultimately tempered by free will. Even seemingly immutable prophecies may be redefined by free will. In "Prophecy Girl" (1.12), one of those prophecies that Giles claims is set in stone states that Buffy will die at the hands of the Master. Indeed, she does. When Xander and Angel revive Buffy, however, they call into question the certainty of any interpretation of prophecy. This confounds the Master when he next encounters Buffy:

MASTER: You were destined to die. It was written.
BUFFY: What can I say? I flunked the written.

The exercise of free will on *Buffy* is most pronounced when addressing the choice between doing good or evil. In "Becoming, Part One" (2.21), we flashback to the days when Angel turned Drusilla into a vampire. He first encounters her when he kills a priest in the church confessional. Before he can leave the human Drusilla shows up for confession. Angel impersonates the priest and takes her confession. She says she wants to be pure and holy, but her mother tells her she is cursed because of her tendency to see visions. Angel tells Drusilla, "The Lord has a plan for all creatures," and that his plan for her is that she be evil. When she protests that she wants to be good, not evil, Angel says, "The world doesn't work that way." She is a puppet in the hands of a vengeful God and can only fulfill the plan God has for her. The irony is that Angel will himself learn through the later restoration of his soul that the world does not in fact work the way he assumes. In the voiceover that concludes the episode, Whistler says, "So what are we, helpless? Puppets? No." Angel learns that we all choose who we are to become.

Free will as moral choice continues as a theme throughout the series. When Adam says that Riley is essentially a machine that has been taught how to think and feel by Professor Walsh and that he has been fed chemicals to control his body, it raises the question of how environment affects choice. Are the paths we take in life predetermined by our biology, our education, or our family? When Riley replies, "I cannot be programmed! I'm a man!" he suggests that choice trumps all of those factors and then goes on to prove it by overcoming through sheer force of will the "programming" that the government did to him (4.14).

Can life's circumstances place us in a position where to do evil is the only acceptable option? When Tara is murdered, Willow fills herself with dark magic and pursues a path of vengeance. Her justification, given when Buffy and Xander suggest she should not use magic, is: "Sometimes you don't have a choice" (6.20). But she does, and in the end she chooses to abandon her magic and seek the path of goodness.

Buffy's attitude towards free will and moral culpability finds illustration in a comparison of Spike and Andrew. Spike, after regaining his soul, is brainwashed by The First and controlled through a memory trigger. The First sends him out to kill, actions that Spike does not remember afterwards. In the initial episode where we learn of The First's control over Spike, Aimee Mann performs at The Bronze and sings a song called "Pavlov's Bell," a reference to Pavlov's experiments in behavioral control. The question is raised: can Spike be held accountable for murderous acts committed unconsciously? The answer comes in a later episode when Andrew, who had previously murdered Jonathan, laments not being allowed to accompany Buffy and Spike on a mission.

> ANDREW: (whining) It's not fair. Spike just killed people, and he gets to go.
> BUFFY: Spike didn't have free will and you did.
> ANDREW: (sighs) I hate my free will.

As Andrew's response illustrates, free will is a double-edged sword. It gives us the power to choose good, but makes us accountable when we choose evil. The challenge lies in distinguishing between the two.

GOOD AND EVIL

The Good, The Bad, and the Not-So-Bad

Whenever I watch movies with my wife, I hear one question repeatedly: "Is he a good guy or a bad guy?" What frustrates my wife to no end is that half of the time, I don't know how to answer. The desire for moral simplicity, in which good and evil are easily distinguished and the bad guy always shows up with a scowl and black hat, is a powerful one. But the world doesn't work that way.

Buffy's perspective on good and evil is not a relativistic one in which the categories of good and evil are constantly redefined based on current circumstances, but neither is it an absolute one in which good and evil are always clearly defined. *Buffy* mocks the idea of an absolute moral structure when it is used as a club to manipulate the behavior of others. It does this by ascribing such an outlook to evil characters like Ted, who admonishes Buffy for innocently cheating at a game of miniature golf with "Right is right. Wrong is wrong. Why don't people see that?" (2.11). Likewise, Tara's abusive father justifies his behavior with the mantra "Evil is evil" (5.6). The fallen priest Caleb contrasts his own morally simplistic view of the world with the more complex view in the Bible when he says of the Bible, "Oh, it has its moments. Paul had some good stuff, for instance. But overall I find it a tad complicated. I like to keep things simple: good folk, bad folk, clean folk, dirty folk" (7.18).

Nevertheless, *Buffy*'s worldview is absolute in its conception of good and evil in the sense that both are categories that exist unequivocally. That true evil and true goodness exist is never doubted. Villains like the Master, the Judge, Adam, and the Mayor are absolutely evil. The Mayor is distinctly called "a Black Hat" (3.15). Giles describes The First as "Absolute evil" (3.10), and when Willow does a magic spell that inadvertently allows The First to pass through her, she describes it as "undiluted evil" so pure that she could taste it, further adding that pure evil tastes "A little chalky" (7.11).

Buffy operates with a clear moral imperative: it is her duty to fight evil in the service of good. So when The First rears up, Buffy declares war on it. By nature war is a dualistic entity that divides combatants into enemies and allies, good guys and bad guys. Buffy has staked her territory and identified her enemy. Buffy slays demons and vampires out of a sense of moral responsibility — it is the *right* thing to do. With her moral imperative comes also a strict moral structure centered on the rule that Slayers do not kill humans.

Although a form of moral absolutism exists in the assertion of good and evil as definitive categories, the real problem is differentiating between the two. How does one decide who is good and who is evil? What are the criteria for distinguishing right from wrong? Along with experience of this world comes an awareness that moral determinations often have a complexity that is not easily reducible to a "right is right, wrong is wrong" slogan. As a show about adolescence and the rites of passage into adulthood, *Buffy* emphasizes the moral ambiguity that attends many adult decisions. The clearest illustration of this comes from an episode titled "Lie to Me" (2.7). Buffy is visited by an old friend of hers from Los Angeles, Billy Fordham ("Ford"). After trusting him with her secret identity, she learns that he plans to betray her by turning her and some others over to vampires in exchange for immortality. As Buffy tries to convince Ford that what he is planning is wrong, he informs her that he is dying of a brain tumor, and only when she has experienced twenty-four hours of vomiting and intense pain can she lecture him on "the concept of right and wrong." Eventually, in order to save herself and others, Buffy is forced to abandon Ford to the vampires who will kill him. Afterward, as she struggles with how to feel about Ford and his deception, she learns that the moral choices we face in life are not always clear. This moment of growth comes in a graveyard (on *Buffy*, the most profound conversations tend to take place in graveyards) as Buffy discusses her feelings with Giles.

> BUFFY: Nothing's ever simple anymore. I'm constantly trying to work it out . . . who to love or hate . . . who to trust. Its just like the more I know, the more confused I get.
> GILES: I believe that's called growing up.
> BUFFY: I'd like to stop then, okay?
> GILES: I know the feeling.
> BUFFY: Does it ever get easy?
> GILES: You mean life?
> BUFFY: Yeah, does it get easy?
> GILES: What do you want me to say?
> BUFFY: Lie to me.
> GILES: Yes, it's terribly simple. The good guys are always stalwart and true. The bad guys are easily distinguished by their pointy horns or black hats, and, uh, we always defeat them

and save the day. No one ever dies and everybody lives happily ever after.
BUFFY: Liar.

On *Buffy* the boundaries between good and evil are often blurry, leading to confusion. Sometimes this is due to people's ability to mask their underlying nature. When Buffy and Faith discover that the Mayor is "a black hat," Buffy expresses surprise because he did not seem like a "bad guy" to her. Faith responds with a self-revealing lecture that "nine times out of ten, the face they're showing you is not the real one" (3.15). Other times self-deception can lead to a failure to recognize evil. After Willow returns Buffy from the dead, she is full of arrogant pride at what she accomplished and claims to have done what no one else could. Giles informs her that there are people in the world with the power to do what she did. Willow replies, "Well, they're the bad guys. I'm not a bad guy" (6.4). Her pride created self-deception, for the truth was that her actions were an important step towards her eventually becoming a "bad guy."

Buffy's willingness to blur the boundaries between good and evil is played for laughs in the scene where the formerly-evil-but-now-reformed Faith meets the formerly-evil-but-now-reformed Spike.

(Faith attacks Spike.)
SPIKE: I'm on your side.
FAITH: Yeah? Maybe you haven't heard. I've reformed. (She punches Spike.)
SPIKE: So have I. (He punches Faith.) I reformed way before you did. (Faith punches Spike.)
(Buffy shows up and protects Spike from Faith.)
FAITH: Are you protecting vampires? Are you the bad Slayer now? Am I the good Slayer now? (7.18)

In this respect, *Buffy* reflects life. The moral simplicity of good guys versus bad guys falters under the increasing weight of life experience in which one encounters degrees of good and evil and in which people live their lives as a journey where they, like Faith and Spike, may change from good to evil and vice versa. No character on *Buffy* better represents how experience can force a reevaluation of one's moral structure than Riley Finn.

When Riley first shows up on *Buffy* he operates with a strict moral code that views all moral decisions in unambiguous terms of good and evil. He suffers a moral crisis, however, when his experience calls that entire moral structure into question. A major part of Riley's moral code is the belief that demons are evil and those who fight demons are good. Yet upon learning that Professor Walsh and the Initiative have been exploiting demons for their own agenda, he begins to question who exactly the "bad guys" are, and whether he himself might be a "bad guy" (4.14). The title of this episode is "Goodbye Iowa," representing Iowa-born Riley having to abandon his childhood illusions about the nature of the world. Those illusions extend to Buffy herself. When Riley learns that Buffy has been harboring the vampire Spike, he questions whether she qualifies as a "good guy." His moral panic continues in the next episode where he claims to not be very good at dealing with the "whole gray-area thing" (4.15).

Riley finally reaches a turning point several episodes later, when Oz, in full werewolf mode, is captured by the Initiative. Riley's derogatory comments about Oz spark a debate with Buffy.

> BUFFY: You sounded like Mr. Initiative. Demons bad, people good.
> RILEY: Something wrong with that theorem?
> BUFFY: There's different degrees of -
> RILEY: Evil?
> BUFFY: It's just . . . different with different demons. There are creatures — vampires, for example — that aren't evil at all.
> (4.19)

As Riley watches doctors at the Initiative perform tests on Oz like any other animal, even when Oz is in human form, he realizes the truth of Buffy's words and helps Oz to escape.

The blurring of the line between good and evil is matched by the blurring of the line between demon and human. In the episode just discussed ("New Moon Rising"; 4.19), demons function as a metaphor for race relations. For instance, characters use the term "bigot" twice to describe Riley's attitude towards demons. One danger of a strict black (evil) and white (good) view of morality arises when those concepts are applied to race. Such a strict moral structure can easily lead to a deceptive self-righteousness whereby we identity ourselves as unequivocally "right" and anyone who is Other than us racially or culturally as "wrong."

One scene in particular in this episode reveals this show's attitude towards race. Riley is about to kill werewolf Oz until Oz suddenly morphs back into human form. Then, as Riley watches the doctors perform their tests on the human Oz, he pleads with them to stop because "I know him." The message is that only by recognizing our shared humanity and by working to understand and to "know" those who are different from us can we overcome the prejudice that leads to moral judgments about skin color and cultural difference.

The good guys and the bad guys are not always easily identifiable on *Buffy*. The show deliberately explores the middle ground of ambiguity "to keep pace with the metaphor of one's growing awareness of the complexities of the world in general."[10] *Buffy* explores the difficulty of making moral judgments about people by the way it addresses Buffy's duty as Slayer. Slayers have a strict moral code: she must slay demons but cannot kill humans. As the line between demon and human, evil and good, becomes increasingly blurred, however, the decision of who to slay or not to slay follows suit. Why does Buffy not kill Angel who is, after all, a vampire? For Kendra and Faith, the solution is initially clear: Angel is a vampire and therefore has to die (2.10; 3.7). But the moral structure of demons bad, people good is less clear-cut when one encounters a vampire with a soul. Mimi Marinucci argues that Buffy's moral decision-making with respect to the killing of demons is tied more closely to what they do rather than who they are; in other words it is about intent and ability to do harm.[11] Thus, Buffy does not kill Angel because he has no intent to harm others. She does not kill Oz because he is unaware and therefore unaccountable for what he does in his werewolf state. Likewise, Buffy spares Spike after he receives the chip implant and so becomes harmless to humans, as well as when he is under the mind control of The First.

Yet, in line with the difficulty of maintaining a set moral code when faced with the exigencies of life, Buffy does not follow this pattern consistently. When Angel loses his soul and reverts to the evil Angelus, she refuses to kill him for the longest time, despite his murderous actions. She spares the vampire Harmony and sends vampire Willow back to her own alternate universe knowing they will both attempt to kill again. The burden of making these life and death choices weighs heavily on Buffy, and she is not beyond questioning her own decisions. When a werewolf hunter tells Buffy that he hopes she can live with the responsibility should Oz ever kill a human, she says, "I live with that every day" (2.15). Later when a student is found mauled to death, she begins to question her choice.

The occasional inconsistency of Buffy's moral code does not go unnoticed in the series. After Anya reverts back to being a vengeance demon following her disastrous wedding attempt, her actions result in a mass slaughter of male students at a fraternity house (7.5). Yet when Buffy decides to kill Anya, Xander calls her on it. He points out the inconsistency of her not killing Willow when she turned evil, but now wanting to kill Anya. The issue here is how emotional attachments can cloud moral judgment. Xander, who never liked Angel and always wanted him dead, now pleads for the life of Anya whom he loves. Buffy tells Xander that he "can't see this for what it really is" because his mind is clouded by emotion. For Buffy, who never held any particular affection for Anya, the situation is clear: Anya is a demon. Xander replies, "And you're the Slayer. I see now how it's all very simple." Xander points out to Buffy that when she is the one with affection for a demon, like Spike or Angel, then suddenly "it's all gray area." Ultimately, though, Buffy recognizes the burden that comes with being the Slayer. She is the one who has to make life or death moral decisions and so is the one who must live with the consequences. She must constantly renegotiate the rule of "demons bad, people good" in the face of life's complexity. She firmly tells Xander when he protests that Anya's case is "different": "It is always different! It's always complicated. And at some point, someone has to draw the line, and that is always going to be me."

As a case in point, Buffy does, on extremely rare occasions, show a willingness to abandon the "do not kill humans" rule when humans, such as Faith, act like demons. Yet even here her moral reasoning can be clouded by emotion. She will try to kill Faith when doing so might save her beloved Angel's life (3.21), yet argues against killing Warren after he murders Tara simply because he is human (6.20).

The Greater Good

Adding another layer of complexity to the moral decisions people make is the concept of the greater good. Is it ever acceptable to commit evil or to cause pain to another person in service to a greater good? Identifying a greater good is fraught with uncertainty due to emotion and personal investment. This can lead to a manipulation of the concept in order to justify suspect acts. Professor Walsh attempts to kill Buffy when Buffy gets too close to uncovering the Initiative's secret agenda. Professor Walsh justifies her murder attempt by claiming it is "for the greater good" (4.13). Giles later kills the human Ben in order to destroy the evil goddess within him because it is for the greater good (5.22). Yet, what distinguishes Giles' act from that of Maggie Walsh? Both commit or attempt murder in the name of a greater good as conceived from their perspective. The uncertainty illustrates how the determination of a greater good is much more difficult when one is forced to make such moral judgments in the context of ever-changing circumstances.

Buffy's own growth into adulthood is accompanied by a growing awareness of the complex concept of the greater good. The most difficult moral decisions to make are those where someone will be hurt regardless of the choice. Early on in the series, Buffy's moral stance of protecting every individual human life was for her the greatest good. So when faced with the opportunity to kill Ben and thus stop Glory from destroying the world, she refuses to do so. She could not justify taking a human life, even to save others. Likewise, Buffy refuses to let her sister Dawn die, even though doing so would save the world.

In the final season, however, Buffy has acquired a different outlook. Giles and Robin Wood conspire together to kill Spike because Robin convinces him it is "for the greater good" (7.17). Robin Wood's determination of the greater good has been distorted by his emotion, however, as his real motivation is revenge against Spike for having killed his mother. Giles tries to justify this to Buffy by reminding her that there is a war going on against The First and as general in that war, she has to make decisions in light of the "big picture." This is a clear representation of the moral reasoning that goes on in warfare. In war, leaders often have to make decisions that will result in human death and the choices made are based on the concept of the greater good. Yet, as *Buffy* illustrates, the "greater good" is not a static concept but one defined differently by different people. When Robin Wood fails in his attempt to kill Spike, Buffy tells him that she is indeed interested in the greater good, but that the greater good in this instance is saving Spike, not killing him, because he is "the strongest warrior we have." In fact, she says if it comes down to a choice between Spike's life and his, she will choose Spike.

In contrast to earlier seasons, Buffy now shows herself willing to let a human being die in the service of a greater good, a concept unthinkable for her before. She acknowledges this in a conversation with Giles:

BUFFY: Giles, we had this conversation when I told you that I wouldn't sacrifice Dawn to stop Glory from destroying the world.
GILES: Ah, yes, but things are different, aren't they? After what you've been through, faced with the same choice now, (pauses) you'd let her die.
BUFFY: If I had to . . . to save the world. Yes. (7.17)

Buffy's moral code has not been compromised so much as complicated. The harsh realities of life and the demands of the battlefield have forced a reevaluation of her moral decision making. For Buffy, right and wrong, good and evil, have always remained definitive concepts, yet the longer she lives in her world, the more complex those concepts become.

Chapter 6

Human Nature

Does the duality of goodness and evil that exists in Buffy's world exist within human beings as well? Are human beings "good guys" or "bad guys"? The battle between good and evil plays out externally in Sunnydale as conflict between Buffy and the demonic forces. Yet the same struggle also takes place internally within each individual.

THE MONSTER WITHIN

The secularization of the modern vampire in literature and film blurs the line between the monstrous and the human. Contemporary vampires increasingly look, feel, and act like humans so that they have steadily moved away from their earlier function as "an objectification of metaphysical evil into simply another image of ourselves seen in a distorting mirror."[1] They have come to represent metaphorically the potential monster within us all.[2]

The duality of human nature, that is that each person bears within him or her the potential for good and evil, is a common theme on *Buffy the Vampire Slayer*. The episodes "Beauty and the Beasts" (3.4), a modern take on the Jekyll and Hyde story, and "Wild at Heart" (4.6), a werewolf tale, address our competing animal and human natures. The writer of both episodes, Marti Noxon, says, "The kind of metaphor that was working in that [episode] . . . was really resonant for me — the idea that most of us have a creature inside of us that makes us do things that we wish we didn't do."[3] Biblical theology represents this duality in terms of the flesh versus the spirit.

Vampires, especially, are appropriate metaphors for addressing human duality because they are liminal, or in-between, figures. Part human and part demon, they belong fully to neither world. On *Buffy* vampires are able to morph back and forth between a human face and a demonic face, representing this duality within them. This duality is most pronounced for Angel who has within him both a demon and a soul. He is both devil and angel. He desires to be part of the human world but can never fully fit in. The vampire Darla warns Angel that his desire to live in the human world is futile because, "You can only suppress your real nature for so long" (1.7). The question for Angel is which of his natures is more "real"? Later, when Angel returns from his time spent in hell, Buffy first sees him in human face but acting feral and with blood on his mouth. She thus wonders which aspect of his nature, the animal or the human, will dominate (3.4). After Spike regains his soul, he also becomes a fitting metaphor for the co-habitation of the human and monstrous. When Robin Wood seeks his revenge, he lures Spike into a shed whose walls are covered with crosses. Wood looks at Spike's human face and tells him that he does not want to kill Spike, but only "the monster who took my mother away from me." When Spike's face morphs into his demonic visage, Wood says, "There he is" (7.17).

The blurring of the line between monster and human on *Buffy* finds further expression in the concept of the human monster. The monsters on *Buffy* are make-believe, creatures of fantasy. The true horror is found by exploring the metaphorical value of these monsters, that is the potential for the monstrous that lies within human beings. In season two, Giles gives Buffy information on a pair of vampires she recently fought, telling her that they made their reputation by slaughtering an entire village in 1886. Buffy responds with, "Friendly little demons." Giles corrects her, "No, it was before they became vampires" (2.12). In "Gingerbread" (3.11), two young children are found dead by Buffy and her mother. When Giles suggests that a cult group committed the murders, Buffy is shocked: "A group of . . . human beings? Someone with a soul did this?" Joyce, however, concludes differently arguing that, "Anybody who could do this has to be a monster." The issue is whether the two are mutually exclusive. People hear reports on the news of children who are abducted and murdered and are then always shocked when the murderer is caught and turns out to look not like a monster, but very much like

themselves. This explains the emotional impact of Faith's turn to the dark side in season three. We knew her. We had seen her fight on the side of good, and then the monster in her came out before our very eyes.
The most startling transformation of all is Willow. The duality of human nature is a prominent theme in "Dopplegangland" (3.16). Willow and Anya perform a magic spell that accidentally transports an alternate Willow from an alternate universe to their world. The catch? In the alternate universe Willow is a vampire. Vamp Willow is the total opposite of Willow: provocatively dressed, assertive, sadistic, and violent. The thematic setup for this episode comes when Buffy and Willow discuss Faith's turn towards evil. Buffy wonders if the same thing would have happened to her had she been in Faith's situation. Willow's reply is adamant: "No way. Some people just don't have that in them." "Dopplegangland" is rich with irony and Willow's comment sets the tone because three seasons later it will turn out to be Willow who does have that in her. In fact after Vamp Willow is captured, the dialogue between Willow, Buffy, and Angel hints at as much.

> WILLOW: That's me as a vampire? I'm so evil and . . . skanky. And I think I'm kinda gay.
> BUFFY: Willow, just remember, a vampire's personality has nothing to do with the person it was.
> ANGEL: Well, actually . . . (gets a warning look from Buffy) That's a good point.

When they decide to send Vamp Willow back to her own universe, Willow, in her typically good-natured way, gives her a hug and some parting advice: "Good luck. Try not to kill people." Again the irony is that Willow will ultimately be the one who fails to heed that advice.

This episode is the first real hint in the series that sweet, innocent Willow has within her the potential for evil.[4] Vamp Willow is indeed Willow herself as seen in a distorting mirror. When Willow turns evil in season six, she both dresses and begins to act much like Vamp Willow, even using Vamp Willow's favorite phrase, "Bored now," just before committing her first murder (6.20). Vamp Willow's evil actions can be easily explained by the fact that she is absent a soul and has a demon residing within her. When Willow goes bad, however, she lacks that excuse. Her soul is intact and she is demon-free, thus making the point even stronger that the potential for evil lies within us all.

This is where the true terror lies. A couple of recent movies about Adolf Hitler have upset people because they portray the humanity of Hitler as well as his monstrousness. We are very uncomfortable with the idea of someone so evil sharing our humanity. When Buffy first learns that Angel is a vampire, she says to him, "I've killed a lot of vampires. I've never hated one before." He replies, "Feels good, doesn't it. Feels simple" (1.7). That is exactly how people want their monsters: simple, obvious, and devoid of humanity. The inability to distinguish between a monster and a man is frightening. Buffy's sister Dawn had been fond of Ben who, despite having to share his body with a hell-goddess, appeared to be a nice and decent person. Yet later, Ben betrays Dawn. So when Ben tries to comfort Dawn before her scheduled demise, she demands that he revert back to Glory so she doesn't have to look at his face. Dawn explains her reasoning to Glory: "He's a monster. At least you're up-front about it" (5.22). We are very uncomfortable with the concept of the hidden monster because the fear is that if we admit to the monster hiding within our neighbor, we may have to admit to the potential for the monstrous in ourselves.

In *Buffy*'s world, free will determines the realization of one's potential for good and evil. After Angel's soul is restored, he is faced with a choice between the soul and the demon within him. In "Becoming, Part One" (2.21), Whistler informs Angel that being a vampire does not mean he has to be evil.

> ANGEL: Whadaya mean, I can go either way?
> WHISTLER: I mean that you can become an even more useless rodent than you already are, or you can become someone. A person. Someone to be counted.

The resolution to the problem of our dual nature is not to ignore it by pretending that the capacity for evil belongs only to the truly monstrous, but to acknowledge the capacity for good and evil within ourselves and then choose who we are to become.

THE HUMAN SOUL

In one of his first encounters with Principal Wood, Spike informs the Principal of the change in his life: "Got myself a soul, whatever that means" (7.15). In *Buffy*'s world, what exactly does it mean to have a soul? In the early seasons of *Buffy*, the point is made that when a person becomes a vampire, their soul vacates their body and a demon takes its place (2.7). When Buffy asks Giles if a vampire can ever be a good person, he says "no" because even though the personality and memories of the individual may remain, the soul, and therefore the person, is gone (1.7).

As the series progresses, however, the connection between the vampire and the person he or she was before grows stronger, keeping pace with the growing tendency to blur the line between the human and the monstrous. On the one hand, having a soul clearly marks a distinction. With both Angel and Spike, their reception of a soul is said to have made them different or somehow new (2.3; 2.15; 7.6). On the other hand, the mere possession of a soul alone does not necessarily make one a good person, as the concept of the human monster makes abundantly clear. In "Amends" (3.10), The First torments Angel by reminding him of the pleasure he once found in doing evil. Angel responds that the monster that did those things was not the real him. The First then questions the distinction between the two by showing Angel a flashback of his life before he became a vampire. He is in a bar, drinking, womanizing and passing out. The First comments, "You were a worthless being before you were ever a monster." In "A New Man" (4.12), a magic spell transforms Giles into a Fyarl Demon. In this new persona, he feels an instinct to destroy. When Spike encourages him to embrace the rage, Giles says, "I refuse to become a monster because I look like a monster. I have a soul. I have a conscience. I am a human being." Yet, he then notices Maggie Walsh, whom he has come to despise, and so takes time out to chase her down the street, fully enjoying every minute of it. Clearly the having of a soul will only take him so far down the road of goodness.

What impact does the soul have on the duality of human nature? How does having a soul make one different from those without one? On *Buffy* these questions are most closely tied to the figure of Spike. The key moment in Spike's transformation from a fully monstrous being to a morally ambiguous figure occurs when the Initiative implants the chip in his brain. Unable to harm human beings makes Spike a less threatening character, which initially annoys him to no end. After the helpless Spike is stuck living in Xander's basement and helping out with the laundry, he laments, "Am I even remotely scary anymore?" (4.11). As he becomes gradually more involved with the Scooby Gang and thus more associated with goodness, Spike finds it necessary to remind people of his true nature. When Giles asks for Spike's help, Spike agrees only in exchange for money because, as he tells Giles, he's not going to do it "out of the evilness of my heart" (4.12). As he prepares to move out of Xander's basement, Spike packs Xander's radio in with his own belongings. When Xander catches him, Spike replies, "And you're what? Shocked and disappointed? I'm evil!" (4.12). Buffy explains to Riley that the reason why she lets Spike hang around her is because "he's not bad anymore." Notice that Buffy here defines badness simply in terms of ability to do harm. For Spike, however, that is not the issue. He replies to her statement with: "I'm bad! It's just . . . I can't bite anymore" (4.14). Spike defines his badness not in terms of action, but in terms of his nature. Thus, throughout seasons four and five, Spikes' very identity is called into question: is he good or evil, monster or man?[5]

The primary question addressed in Spike's narrative arc as it unfolds over seasons four through seven is whether one can truly be good without a soul. Spike has a chip in his brain that keeps him from doing harm, but is the absence of doing harm sufficient for goodness? Over the course of season five, Spike becomes increasingly humanized, even serving as a babysitter for Dawn. When Dawn develops a schoolgirl crush on Spike, Buffy has a sudden conversion in her view of him.

> BUFFY: He's a killer, Dawn. You cannot have a crush on something that is . . . dead, and, and evil, and a vampire.
> DAWN: Right, that's why you were never with Angel for three years.
> BUFFY: Angel's different. He has a soul.
> DAWN: Spike has a chip. Same diff. ("Crush"; 5.14)

Is it the same "diff"? Is moral behavior simply about programming? Is the chip's function, which is to prohibit harmful action, the same as that of a soul? Is goodness defined merely as the absence of evil action or does it involve intent? After Anya's canceled wedding, she and Spike console each other over their mutually failed romances. When Anya comments that she didn't ask to be human, Spike says, "And I didn't ask for this bloody chip in my head" (6.18). The question implied in that interchange is whether those two are the same. Does Spike's chip make him human?

The answer is unequivocally no. The chip and a soul are in no way the "same diff." Xander, the one who sees things others do not, recognizes this. Claiming never to have forgotten Spike's true nature, he tells Buffy: "He doesn't have a soul, Buffy. Just some leash they jammed in his head" (6.19).

Spike's crush on Buffy breeds confusion for him as his former insistence on the evilness of his heart gives way to a growing belief that he is becoming good. He claims as much to Buffy while trying to convince her to love him back.

> BUFFY: Please! Spike, you're a vampire.
> SPIKE: Angel was a vampire.
> BUFFY: Angel was good!
> SPIKE: And I can be too. I've changed, Buffy.
> BUFFY: What, that chip in your head? That's not change. Tha-that's just . . . holding you back. You're like a serial killer in prison!
> SPIKE: Women marry 'em all the time! (5.14)

In the same episode, Drusilla returns and tempts Spike to revert to his old ways by arguing that his chip is nothing more than electricity. She says, "It tells you you're not a bad dog, but you are" (5.14). Both Buffy and Drusilla point out an important truth — the inability to do harm does not qualify as goodness because there is no true element of choice.

The humanization of Spike over seasons four and five, combined with his growing popularity as a character, led many viewers to conclude that Spike had been redeemed. Because he could not physically harm others and because he began to act more and more like a human being, they assumed him to be a good man. The writers of *Buffy*, however, viewed that as a flawed assumption. David Fury stated: "I do feel strongly that Spike is evil."[6] Jane Espenson said, "As long as Spike hasn't a soul, he cannot be redeemed."[7] Later, Marti Noxon added, "A very vocal part of our audience thinks that Spike has fully redeemed himself, but to me and Joss, the issue of his core morality is not gone. He's a vampire."[8] Goodness on *Buffy* is not defined as the mere absence of evil. Rather, it is intrinsically tied to the presence of a soul.

Season six of *Buffy* served as a reminder of Spike's "core morality." Buffy's demented relationship with Spike in this season re-opened her eyes to the real Spike. In "Dead Things" (6.13), she tells him, "You don't . . . have a soul! There is nothing good or clean in you.

You are dead inside!" Later, when Buffy learns that Spike has secretly been engaged in a nefarious scheme, she shows no anger towards him because she realizes that is his nature" (6.15). The real reminder of Spike's evil nature comes in "Seeing Red" (6.19) when Spike, whose brain chip no longer works on Buffy, attempts to rape her. This act sparks a realization for Spike who comments afterwards, "Must still be a bit of the evil left in me after all." Yet what the chip did accomplish for Spike was a growing awareness of the duality of his own nature — that even he has the potential for goodness. After the rape attempt, Spike is torn between the monster and the man within him. When he says, "What have I done? Why *didn't* I do it?" his confusion stems from recognition of the battle within his dual nature.[9] What he learns is that the chip may have restrained his evil nature, but it could never fully overcome it. For that, he would need a soul.

Spike's retrieval of his soul marks a profound change. On *Buffy* the soul functions as a moral compass, allowing one to discern the difference between right and wrong and thus facilitating a choice between the two. It does not mean that one automatically becomes good because the option of making the wrong choice always remains. Dawn notes this when she says, "Xander had a soul when he stood Anya up at the altar" (7.6). What Spike's soul does that his chip could never do is give him the ability to overcome the evil within him. Buffy has Spike's chip removed because now he has the capacity to choose good or evil. In fact, for Buffy, refusing to remove Spike's chip would be immoral. She tells Giles that since Spike now has a soul, leaving his chip in would be "wrong" and that "You can't beat evil by doing evil" (7.14). Buffy clearly sees the hindering of Spike's free will as "doing evil" because it nullifies his ability to choose between right and wrong, which is itself the mark of humanity. The soul makes Spike, if not fully human, a person. So when Anya, who at this point is back in vengeance demon mode, sees Spike for the first time since his return from his soul-getting journey, she looks deep into his eyes and with astonishment says, "I can see you" (7.2). The real Spike, the human Spike, is now visible for the first time since he became a vampire.

With a soul, Spike's redemption is now possible. The culmination of his redemptive journey comes when he sacrifices his own life to save the world. Rhonda Wilcox notes that Spike's redemptive arc correlates with the metaphor of light and darkness.[10] A creature of darkness and confined to the night, Spike nonetheless flirts with the light. As his humanization unfolds, so does his association with the light. In the third season episode "Lover's Walk" (3.8), Spike exhibits human-like grief with his pining over the loss of Drusilla. After collapsing outside in a drunken stupor, he awakens in the shade with his hand extended out into the sunlight and burning. He has touched the light, but is not ready for it. Then, in "The Harsh Light of Day" (4.3) he finds a mystical ring that allows him to walk in the daylight unharmed. This, however, proves to be a fraudulent foray into the light as he is forced to retreat to the darkness when the ring is taken from him. As he becomes more human-like in seasons four through six, we see Spike venturing into the daylight with more frequency, whether under the cover of a blanket or sitting in the shade. In "Normal Again" (6.17), he stands in Buffy's bedroom during the day, flinching back only when getting too close to the sunlight streaming in through the window. By the time we come to the final episode and the completion of Spike's redemptive journey, the amulet he wears allows the sunlight to radiate through his entire body. He has now fully become the light. By triumphing over his evil nature with this final act of goodness, Spike becomes cognizant of the soul within him. As the sunlight streams through him, he says:

> SPIKE: (amazed) I can feel it, Buffy.
> BUFFY: What?
> SPIKE: My soul. It's really there. Kind of stings. (7.22)

With his soul intact, Spike is able to tap his potential for true goodness and to find a kind of peace and purpose that had eluded him in the darkness.

The importance of the soul in *Buffy*'s exploration of human nature is intriguing, given Joss Whedon's atheism. As with other religious concepts, Whedon takes the idea of the soul seriously while adapting it for his narrative creation. He comments:

> Spike was definitely kind of a soulful character before he had a soul, but we made it clear that there was a level on which he could not operate . . . With a soul comes a more adult understanding . . . Can I say that I believe in the soul? I don't know that I can. It's a beautiful concept, as is resurrection and a lot of other things we have on the show that I'm not really sure I can explain and I certainly don't believe in.[11]

For Whedon, Clem represents the distinction between having a soul and not having a soul. Clem is a very sweet, friendly demon with a fondness for kitten poker (kittens are apparently a tasty delicacy in the demon world). Because he is so harmless, Buffy befriends Clem, although she makes it clear that she does not condone the eating of kittens. During one encounter between them, Clem explains to Buffy how bad things are getting in Sunnydale: "You can't swing a cat without hitting some kind of demonic activity. Not that I swing cats, or eat — nope. Heh. Cuttin' way back. Cholesterol — morals! I mean, morals" (7.19). Despite his less-than-convincing insistence, Clem's choices in life are not based upon moral reasoning but upon pure pragmatism. For Whedon, this distinction is essential because the soul on *Buffy* "has consistently marked the real difference between somebody with a complex moral structure and someone who may be affable and even likable, but ultimately eats kittens."[12] Clem represents the consistent concept on *Buffy* that the lack of a soul hinders the ability to make profound moral judgments.

Chapter 7

Identity and the Quest for Self

Identity is a crucial component of moral reasoning. Morality is less about *what* one does than about *who* one is, for an individual's moral choices are motivated by how they see themselves in relation to the world around them. Identity and morality coexist in a symbiotic relationship. Our self-identity affects how we conceptualize right and wrong and why we make certain moral choices. On the other hand, the moral choices we make can also shape our identity either by affirming or calling into question our conception of self. In other words, we make moral choices based both on who we are and on who we wish to become.

The second season episodes "Becoming, Part One" and "Becoming, Part Two" are about defining moments of identity. Several characters (Buffy, Angel, and Willow) are in the throes of major life changes that force them to make decisions about who they will become. At the conclusion of part one, Whistler provides a voiceover that highlights the main theme of these episodes, a theme that characterizes the entire series of *Buffy* as well: "The big moments are gonna come. You can't help that. It's what you do afterwards that counts. That's when you find out who you are" (2.21). Those moments of crisis and challenge are when identity is both revealed and formed.

Identity formation is a continual process that is often messy and complex. This is the problem with stereotypes, not that they do not contain truth of a general nature, but that they reduce the components of identity to their most simplistic form. In real life, a person's identity is a complex web of genetics, environment, training, and life experiences. Part of the reason why some television shows fail at addressing moral issues competently is because they present one-dimensional, stereotypical characters, who consequently, and not surprisingly, engage in overly simplistic moral reasoning.

On *Buffy*, character development is a complex process in which characters grow, change, and sometimes regress over the course of several years. This evolution allows them to avoid stereotypical characterization. The one major character on *Buffy* who most closely falls prey to stereotypical categorization is Cordelia, the popularity-obsessed cheerleader; yet, by having Cordelia join up with the Scooby Gang, *Buffy* subverts the stereotype. According to Whedon, this was an attempt to show that identity boundaries are fluid and that we all are, like Cordelia, at times mean and at other times heroic.[1]

The theme of identity permeates *Buffy the Vampire Slayer* from beginning to end and a comprehensive treatment of it is certainly beyond the confines of this book. Also since identity is intertwined with moral reasoning, it is a theme that will pop up repeatedly in subsequent chapters. Consequently, this chapter focuses on two sub-themes that are frequently connected to identity issues in *Buffy*. One is power. Whereas people are typically identified by whether they have power or not, it is actually how they respond to that power or the lack of it that truly reveals who they are. The second is the sub-theme of change. Life never stands still. It is constantly changing around us and our identities change with it. What defines us is how we change along with it and what we do with those "big moments" that come our way. To explore these themes I examine particular identity issues related to three characters: Riley, Buffy, and Xander.

RILEY FINN: TRAINING VS. CHARACTER

Riley Finn is a good soldier. He has been trained to think and act in accordance with a particular philosophy and under the authority of a military organization. This training has been so comprehensive in his life that he is thoroughly defined by it. He is a follower of orders, taught never to question his superiors. Riley represents the individual whose identity is defined by an external power structure. The question for him is what happens when that external structure is suddenly removed?

In the early years, identity is shaped most prominently by family and by the organizations (school, church, etc.) that parents choose for their children. Parents create ideological and physical boundaries within which their children's identities are formed. They are trained to think a certain way. As a child grows and starts to explore outside of those boundaries, other ideas and organizations challenge his or her identity. When the structures that initially shape identity are removed, what remains is a person's core character. Out of that character a person chooses to take ownership of their own identity either by reaffirming their earlier beliefs on their own terms or forming new ones.

Riley represents the struggle between the various types of training that shape us and our core character. As Riley comes to question the morality of the Initiative and to realize that they deceived him, his entire system of belief begins to crumble. He disobeys orders for the first time and questions his own identity. Having always defined himself by his training as a soldier, he asks Buffy: "Take that away, what's left?" Buffy answers, "A good man" (4.15). For Buffy, Riley is not simply the sum of his training; rather, what defines him is his character. Beneath all of the training is a good man and that core character is ultimately what shapes him. Riley's fellow soldier, Forrest, shares the same training as Riley but lacks his character. So when the defining moment comes, Forrest is easily corrupted by the Initiative and eventually co-opted by Adam. Riley, on the other hand, combats that corruption, overcomes his training, and chooses the path that he himself determines to be the noble one. All people are trained by society in different ways, but the ultimate determinant of identity is not the behavior that is learned, but the moral character of the individual beneath.

BUFFY SUMMERS: SLAYER OR KILLER?

Buffy Summers is such a complex character that any discussion of her identity could take many forms. In this chapter, I focus on the nature of her power. In the next chapter, I address her sense of moral responsibility.

Although surrounded by friends and family, Buffy's power isolates her and makes her different. Her story is about young women learning to recognize their own strength, illustrating in fantastical form the normal obstacles young girls face on the journey from adolescence to adulthood. The very concept of "Vampire Slayer" is a metaphor for this journey. Buffy's first awareness of the power within her arrives during the midst of her turbulent teen years and her growth to adulthood coincides with a gradual acceptance and appreciation of that power.[2]

Throughout her high school years in Sunnydale, Buffy struggles with accepting her power, at times embracing it and at other times rejecting it. Through that process, she learns to appreciate her power and the importance of using it for good. On graduation day, the Mayor's speech focuses on change. Before attempting to devour the student body as a giant demon snake, he exhorts them by saying, "Graduation doesn't just mean your circumstances change; it means you do" (3.22). At the start of the next season, Buffy begins college, and it is a disaster (4.1). Feeling disoriented and overwhelmed, she returns to her traditional comfort spots, but they no longer comfort. She goes to Giles' apartment to recreate their high school research parties without success. She returns home only to find that her mother has stored art gallery crates in her room. Even the Bronze isn't the same. Her circumstances have changed, but the real issue is how she will change.

Up until the end of season four, Buffy operates with a fairly straightforward understanding of her power — she is chosen to fight evil. With the final episode of season four, the dream episode "Restless," the nature of her power comes into question. Buffy has always identified herself as the Slayer with great importance attached to that term. She *slays* vampires and demons, but she does not *kill* humans. For Buffy, that is a vital moral distinction. In "Restless," Buffy dreams of Riley and Adam seated together at a table. Twice Riley addresses her as "killer," while Adam implies that Buffy's power is not so different from his own. When Buffy protests that she is not a demon, Adam replies, "Is that a fact?" (4.22). In the first episode of season five, Buffy's encounter with Dracula hits the same note.

DRACULA: I came to meet the renowned . . . killer.
BUFFY: Yeah, I prefer the term slayer. You know, "killer" just sounds so . . .
DRACULA: Naked?
BUFFY: Like I . . . paint clowns or something. I'm the good guy, remember?
DRACULA: Perhaps, but your power is rooted in darkness (5.1).

Is Buffy a killer or a slayer? With this questioning of her power, she is being forced to redefine her identity and to choose who she will become.

During season six, Buffy's identity crisis becomes more pronounced. With her mother gone and Dawn to take care of, she has fully entered the adult world with all its responsibilities and is overwhelmed by it. The episode "Flooded" (6.4) provides a metaphor for Buffy's life. She tries to fix a leaky pipe in the basement but succeeds only at flooding the entire thing. The flooding of her basement represents the overwhelming flood of adult responsibility overtaking her. In the following episode, "Life Serial" (6.5), Buffy attempts to reconstruct her life, essentially by trying on different personas. The theme of the episode is revealed when Buffy attends a college sociology class with Willow, and the topic of discussion is the "Social Construction of Reality," which involves the idea that individuals play a role in the construction of their own identity. Buffy's attempt at life construction, however, is flawed because she tries to adopt the identity of others rather than find her own. She attends college classes with Willow, takes a construction job on Xander's crew, and then tries her hand at retail in Giles' shop. When all of these fail miserably, she tries on Spike's life, accompanying him to a back alley game of kitten poker. When Buffy protests that living in the demon world is not for her, Spike counters that she is simply denying the truth about herself. He tells her that she, like him, is "a creature of the darkness" and that her confusion will end only when she accepts that.

The writer of "Buffy vs. Dracula," Marti Noxon, says that Dracula wanted Buffy "to take her gift in a different direction."[3] That is the central issue here: not where Buffy's power comes from, but what she will choose to do with that power. Adam, Dracula and Spike pressure Buffy to give in to the animal side of her nature, with Spike even calling her an "animal" in a later episode (6.13). As Buffy's life crumbles around her, she finds the pull towards the darkness ever more tempting. Spike represents the primary source of this temptation, and Buffy is drawn to him like a magnet. Spike asks Buffy what her friends will think of her when they find out who she really is (6.13).

Who Buffy really is, however, is not an issue of her nature but of her choice. The protests of Adam, Dracula, and Spike aside, Buffy is the one who chooses her identity, whether she will be of the darkness or of the light. Buffy has always refused to be identified solely in terms of her power. Thus, when she meets the first Slayer in a dream vision, she tells her, "You're really gonna have to get over the whole primal power thing. You're *not* the source of me" (4.22). The real choice, though, comes when Buffy enters a dimensional portal and stands face to face with the tribal elders who imbued the first Slayer with her power. They tell Buffy that they used the energy of a demon to create the first Slayer, and they offer to give her more of that energy, which appears as black tendrils of smoke, so that she can become stronger and better equipped to fight against The First. Yet Buffy rejects the offer of more power because to accept it would be to accept the darkness, to embrace the monstrous over the human within her (7.15). She has been given a gift but will not allow that gift to consume her.

Buffy's Slayerhood functions as a metaphor for all those who have been gifted in life. She represents the charmed ones who possess a power that others lack, whether that be the power that comes from popularity, privilege, intellect, athleticism or attractiveness. Buffy is the Chosen One, the gifted one. Defining oneself in terms of one's gift, however, can lead to feelings of superiority ("I am smarter," "I am prettier"). Anya notes this when she says of Buffy's power, "But you didn't earn it. You didn't work for it. You've never had anybody come up to you and say you deserve these things more than anyone else. They were just handed to you. So that doesn't make you better than us. It makes you luckier than us" (7.19). Buffy's rejection of more power was a refusal to be defined by that power, a refusal to take her gift in a wrong direction. For those who have been blessed in life, it is a reminder that those blessings come with a moral responsibility that leads not to superiority but to service. To examine the flip side of this coin, we turn to another figure who does not possess obvious gifts: Xander Harris.

XANDER HARRIS: POWER AND WEAKNESS

Xander's primary identity issue is his profound sense of inadequacy. He is the person who has yet to find his place in the world, the one who lacks the gifts and obvious strengths that others enjoy. In contrast to Buffy, Xander represents all those who have not been "chosen" in life. If the Buffys of the world have to decide how to use their gifts, the Xanders of the world struggle with how to respond when one is not gifted, chosen, or blessed. The nature of that response is a moral issue, for some respond to their unfair lot in life with anger and resentment, lashing out at a society that did them wrong. Others, however, choose to rise above the unfairness of life and to become someone to be counted.

Xander comes from a highly dysfunctional family given to drinking and inappropriate social behavior. His Christmas Eve tradition is camping in the backyard in a sleeping bag to avoid the drunken quarrels inside (3.10). His lack of a strong home life leads him to seek a surrogate family in Willow, Buffy and Giles. But even there he feels inadequate. The Xander who gripes about the SAT test because "it discriminates against the uninformed" (3.6) lacks the intellect of Willow or Giles. The Xander who, after encountering a fish monster, "ran like a woman" (2.20), lacks the strength and fighting skills of Buffy. Out of shame, Cordelia refuses to tell her friends that she's dating Xander (2.13). Even when he tries to be the hero, like following Buffy to a frat house party in order to keep an eye on her, he gets hazed — forced to dress up in a wig and women's clothing to dance for the crowd.

Xander desperately wants to belong, wants to contribute to the group in a meaningful way, so Buffy's occasional refusal to allow him to accompany her on dangerous missions undermines his manliness. Xander's costume choices at parties and on Halloween reveal his longing for a macho reputation. At a school costume party, he comes as a rugged cowboy (2.4). In the episode "Halloween," Xander's manhood is upstaged by Buffy when she saves him from being pummeled by a student. Xander is incensed at Buffy for contributing to his reputation as a "sissy-man." So when the time comes to choose a costume for Halloween, Xander goes with a soldier outfit, which works out well when a magic spell turns everyone into their costumes (2.6). On another Halloween, Xander shows up to a fraternity party in a tuxedo, explaining his costume choice this way:

> XANDER: Bond. James Bond. Insurance, you know, in case we get turned into our costumes again. I'm going for cool, secret agent guy.
> BUFFY: I hate to break it to you, but you'll probably end up cool headwaiter guy.
> XANDER: As long as I'm cool and wield some kind of power. (4.4)

In season four, Xander's physical dislocation from Buffy and Willow, who have gone off to college, and his inability to find a meaningful job inflame his sense of uselessness. He drives an ice cream truck, lives in his parent's basement, and is even less help to Buffy than he was before. Xander's dream sequence in "Restless" (4.22) brings all of these identity issues to the surface. Xander's dream opens with he, Giles, Willow, and Buffy sitting on the couch in Buffy's house and watching *Apocalypse Now* on TV as Giles comments, "Oh, I'm beginning to understand this now. It's all about the journey, isn't it." It is for Xander who is on a journey of self-discovery, but who at the moment is lost in a sea of uncertainty. When Xander gets up from the couch to use the bathroom and Buffy asks him if he needs any help with that, it cuts to his sense of insecurity and powerlessness. His trip to the bathroom, though, represents his journey as he gets lost and becomes disoriented on the way. He walks through a door in Buffy's house only to find himself in his parent's basement. Then we see him driving his ice cream truck down the street but never actually getting anywhere. When Anya, who is in the truck with him, asks if he knows where he's going, it highlights the aimlessness of his journey. From the truck, Xander finds himself in the basement again. Then, with the rapid scene change that often comes in dreams, he is in army fatigues being interrogated. When asked where he is from, Xander replies, "Well, the basement, mostly." The dream concludes with him in the basement yet again. That Xander's dream journey continually takes him back to his parent's basement reflects his fear that his life will never get on track, that he will never amount to much. He fears that the words spoken by his military interrogator are true: he is not a soldier but "a whipping boy" who has been "set on a sacrificial stone." He is the weak one, the sacrifice, and the dispensable one.

Deep down Xander wants to be chosen like Buffy, not in the specific sense of being a Vampire Slayer, but in the sense of being taken account of and respected. He wants to be the savior of others rather than the one always in need of saving. In a moment of particular insecurity, he complains to Willow that his entire function in the group is to get in trouble and have Buffy save him. In a misguided attempt at comfort, Willow replies, "That's not true! Sometimes we all helped save you" (5.3). Xander stands by in the shadows watching as those around him grow more powerful: Buffy is the Slayer, Willow's a witch, Oz is a werewolf, and even his sometime girlfriend Anya has the experience of a thousand year old ex-demon. And Xander? Well, as he confesses, "I'm the guy who fixes the windows" (7.12). The critical issue for Xander is how he responds to his place in life. For those who are picked last in gym class, who will never be the star on stage or the athlete at center court, where do they find their value? Xander's journey is about discovering who he is. Is he going to be defined by his location in life or by his inner character? In "The Replacement" (5.3), we are given a glimpse into the complexity of Xander's character. The setup for "The Replacement" is a standard issue doppelganger plot in which a demon spell aimed at Buffy inadvertently hits Xander, creating a duplicate Xander. What one expects from such typical genre plotting is that one version is the real Xander, and the other an evil twin. Of course, in the Buffyverse things are never so simple. The two Xanders are polar opposites: one is insecure, dorky, and clumsy; the other is suave, confident, and commands respect. The catch is that both are the real Xander. The demon spell simply split Xander into two halves with his weaker personality traits in one body and the stronger traits in the other. These dual Xanders represent the duality in all of us: that we all are at times brave and cowardly, suave and dorky, competent and insecure. Within him is the power to be the man he wants to be. Ultimately Xander's identity derives not from his weaker personality traits that often bubble to the surface, but from the essence of his core character.

As Whistler said, a person finds out who they are when they face the big moments in life. How one acts at those moments is not a whim or a flip of a coin, but is born out of one's moral center. When those big moments come in Xander's life, he proves himself to be endlessly loyal to his friends and nobly self-sacrificing. The constantly terrified Xander displays a profound bravery whenever the chips are down. When evil Angel shows up at the hospital to come after an injured Buffy, Xander is the one who blocks the way and faces Angel down (2.18). When the Inca Mummy girl tries to suck the life out of Willow, Xander unhesitatingly offers his life instead (2.4). When Buffy prepares to face Angel for their final battle, Xander shows up with a rock in his hand and offers to fight with her to the end. He says, "Cavalry's here. Cavalry's a frightened guy with a rock, but it's here" (2.22). That's the essence of Xander. He is *always* there. Though terrified and powerless, and often with less than a rock in his hand, he never hesitates to stand and fight to the death for those he loves and for innocents who are in danger.

Two episodes, "The Zeppo" and "Grave," reveal Xander's moral center by how he responds to big moments. "The Zeppo" (3.13) deals with Xander's increasing sense of unimportance and expendability. The title refers to the fifth and virtually ignored member of the Marx Brothers. When Xander insists to Cordelia that he is an "integral" part of the group, she informs him that actually he is the "useless" part, the Zeppo. This is enforced in the opening scene where Xander is briefly knocked unconscious in a battle against fierce demons. When Buffy, concerned for Xander, tells him that in the future he should stay away from the fighting, her suggestion exposes his deep insecurity. He protests, "Excuse me? Who, at a crucial moment, distracted the lead demon by allowing her to pummel him about the head?" As Xander suggests, he has become Jimmy Olsen to Buffy's Superman. At school the next day, Cordelia, whose function in the episode is to repeatedly point out Xander's uselessness, witnesses Xander being thoroughly embarrassed by a bully named Jack O'Toole, and she takes the opportunity to further deride his manhood.

The unique aspect of "The Zeppo" is that it is told from Xander's perspective. Buffy, Willow, Giles and Angel are facing an upcoming apocalyptic battle that truly threatens to end the world, but we never learn the nature of that threat because it unfolds in the background while Xander's story plays out in the foreground. Xander frequently tries to join them in their struggle, but fearful for his safety, they continually push him away. Whenever Xander interacts with their story, the seriousness of the world-ending threat is blown up to maximum proportions and the emotions of Buffy and Angel are so exaggerated as to reach the level of parody. However, the point of this extreme depiction of the danger facing Buffy, Giles, Willow, and Angel is to set up a contrast with Xander's much smaller and seemingly insignificant problems.

Xander has run afoul once again of the bully Jack O'Toole. Through their interactions, he learns that Jack and his gang are plotting to blow up the high school. Xander decides to stop them. While Buffy and the others fight their apocalyptic battle in the high school library, O'Toole and his gang chase Xander into the high school. Xander's accompanying comment, "Where's a Slayer when you need one?" is revealing. At this moment, Xander does not need a Slayer, the Slayer needs him. Whereas Buffy fights to save the world, Xander fights to save the high school, but since Buffy's fight takes place in the high school, if he fails she fails. Thus Xander's much smaller battle has ultimate consequences. Eventually Xander corners Jack in the high school's boiler room where the bomb has been placed. (Notice Xander's moment of heroism takes place in a basement). As the timer on the bomb ticks down towards zero, Xander blocks Jack's exit from the room. Calm in the face of death, Xander stands up to the bully, vowing that they will both die in that room if Jack does not disarm the bomb. Xander saves the high school and, by extension, the world.

The message of this episode comes through the next day when Buffy, Willow, Oz and Giles are discussing the previous night's events and comment on how no one will ever know what they did and how they stopped the world from ending. The irony is that this is now true for them as well. They have no idea how close they came to dying and no clue of what Xander did because Xander doesn't tell them. They needed him, could not have survived without him, and yet they do not know it. That's okay with Xander once *he* knows it.

The integrity of moral actions does not require an audience for approval. At the conclusion of the episode, when Cordelia taunts Xander again, he does not retaliate as he had earlier, but instead smiles confidently and walks past her. Xander's quiet morality, his willingness to risk his life, with no desire for accolades or recognition, is a testimony to all those who toil nobly in anonymity.

Another defining moment for Xander comes in the final episode of the sixth season called "Grave" (6.22). Everything has fallen apart. Warren has shot Buffy, Tara is dead, and Willow has gone evil, threatening to destroy everything and everyone in her path. Throughout all of this, Xander again feels particularly useless, even blaming himself for not protecting Buffy and Tara. Willow has grown so powerful that no one, not even Buffy, can stop her as she heads to the site of an ancient temple in order to destroy the world. She cannot be defeated with power, so Xander defeats her with love.

That Xander functions as a Christ-like figure in this episode is unmistakable. As Willow begins channeling her power to destroy the world, Xander shows up referring to himself specifically as a "carpenter." He then places his body between Willow and the temple so that her power strikes him instead, thus becoming the one "set on a sacrificial stone" that his "Restless" dream foretold. He tells her that if she is going to end the world, she can begin with him. Willow seems okay with that but as she strikes Xander with her power, he repeatedly tells her that he loves her no matter what she does. Xander's sacrificial and unconditional display of love breaks through to Willow.

The sacrifice of Christ on the cross was not a victory accomplished by a display of power, but a victory that came through weakness. Christ the carpenter did not save the world through miraculous displays or by divine might, but through another kind of power — the power of weakness. Through self-sacrifice born out of unconditional love Christ demonstrated that the most powerful act imaginable looks like weakness to the world. Likewise, another carpenter, Xander, who according to the standards of the world is weak and inconsequential, saves the world by the power of unconditional love.

Xander has found his place. He is the heart of the Scooby Gang. He provides them the strength of conviction and unconditional support. When Buffy's sister Dawn arrives on the scene, she experiences many of the same insecurities as Xander. She lives in the shadow of an older sister who is a superhero. She has no super-powers to call her own and feels like no one notices her or appreciates her. That all seems to change in the episode titled "Potential" (7.12). As the battle with The First approaches, Buffy, Giles and Willow have been gathering all potential Slayers. Learning that a potential Slayer is in Sunnydale, Willow performs a spell to locate her that mistakenly leads to the conclusion that it is Dawn. Her head filled with a newfound pride and sense of self-importance, Dawn goes off to face down a vampire with a girl from school named Amanda. In the ensuing conflict, it becomes clear that Amanda, not Dawn, is the true potential Slayer. The next day as Dawn tries to readjust to being normal and unnoticed once again, Xander shares with her the wisdom he has gained from experience.

> XANDER: I saw what you did last night.
> DAWN: Yeah, I — (shakes her head embarrassed) I guess I kinda lost my head when I thought I was the Slayer.
> XANDER: You thought you were all special. Miss Sunnydale 2003. And the minute you found out you weren't, you handed the crown to Amanda without a moment's pause. You gave her your power.
> DAWN: (shrugs) The power wasn't mine.
> XANDER: They'll never know how tough it is, Dawnie, to be the one who isn't chosen. To live so near to the spotlight and never step in it. But I know. I see more than anybody realizes because nobody's watching me. I saw you last night. I see you working here today. You're not special. You're extraordinary.

Xander is the eternal supporter, the one who toils behind the scenes while others work in the spotlight. He demonstrates that not being chosen in life is not an excuse to become useless. Xander chooses to become someone to be counted. So many people in this world labor heroically in obscurity, never receiving the praise or notice due them; yet it is how one lives one's life when no one else is looking that is the true test of moral character.

Chapter 8

A Tale of Two Slayers: Identity, Sacrifice, and Salvation

What does it mean to have a power that sets you apart from others? What is the moral responsibility attached to Slayerhood? In this chapter, I explore these issues through a comparison of two Slayers: Buffy and Faith. Buffy and Faith are opposite sides of the same moral coin. Twins of a sort, they represent different attitudes towards power. A great comic book philosopher named Ben Parker once imparted the following nugget of wisdom to his young nephew Peter: "With great power comes great responsibility." There are many unmistakable similarities between young Peter Parker, a.k.a. Spider-Man, and Buffy Summers. (Indeed occasional references to the superhero crop up throughout the show). Both are unexceptional individuals gifted with enormous power. Both struggle to maintain their secret identity while also seeking a normal life. Both find that rather than solving their problems, their power only creates new ones. Both are fiercely driven by a sense of moral responsibility in the exercise of power. With Buffy, like Spider-Man, we witness an example of power with responsibility. With Faith, we witness power without it.

BUFFY SUMMERS: CHEERLEADER OR SLAYER?

A second season flashback reveals the moment when Buffy Summers learns she is a Vampire Slayer. As a high school freshman in Los Angeles, Buffy is a self-obsessed, fashion conscious, and ethically challenged cheerleader. In short, she is Cordelia. Her life, however, takes a sudden detour when a Watcher shows up and informs her that she is the "Chosen One." After defeating her first vampire, Buffy goes home to a scene that encapsulates the burden of her power. The formerly flighty, joyful, and shallow Buffy is clearly heavier of heart. As her parents fight about her in the background, Buffy tearfully stares in the mirror, wondering what she has become (2.21). Buffy's power does not bring her liberation but a kind of imprisonment. The responsibility hangs like a weight around her neck, and she begins to wonder if being the Slayer means she ceases to be Buffy Summers.

The Reluctant Slayer

As the first episode of *Buffy the Vampire Slayer* opens, Buffy has made a choice between the Slayer and Buffy Summers. With the transfer to Sunnydale comes a chance to start over so she has retired from being the Slayer. But responsibility is not so easily left behind. When a student is found murdered in a locker room, Buffy's strong sense of moral responsibility moves her back into action (1.1). She realizes she cannot ignore her duty, yet her desire for a normal life leads her into an identity struggle that dominates the first three seasons of the show. Representative of the struggle between her desire for normality and her duty is the following scene:

> GILES: This is madness! What could you have been thinking? You are the Slayer! Lives depend upon you! I make allowances for your youth, but I expect a certain amount of responsibility, instead of which you enslave yourself to this, this . . . cult!
>
> (We see Buffy standing in a cheerleading outfit)

When Buffy announces to Giles her intention of trying out for the cheerleading squad, he counters with: "You have a sacred birthright, Buffy. You've been chosen to destroy vampires; not wave pompoms at people" (1.3). The question, though, is whether she can do both.

In "Homecoming" (3.5), Buffy's increasing isolation from the high school social scene, combined with Cordelia's incessant ridicule, leads Buffy to compete against Cordelia for Homecoming Queen. The following conversation between Cordelia and Buffy illustrates the duality of Buffy's identity and her ongoing conflict with the self.

BUFFY: Sorry, Cordy, but you have no idea who you're messing with.
CORDELIA: What? The Slayer?
BUFFY: I'm not talking about the Slayer. I'm talking about Buffy. You've awakened the Prom Queen within.

Buffy's quest for Homecoming Queen is a quest to find a part of herself that is not consumed by her calling. The episode provides an opportunity for Buffy and Cordelia to try on each other's life. Buffy, the Slayer, tries to become Homecoming Queen, while Cordelia, the Homecoming Queen, gets mistaken for a Slayer. Buffy keeps trying to be something she is not, when what she really needs is to accept who she is. The essence of Buffy's struggle is the desire to be "normal," to be perceived as one of the group.

Buffy's Moral Code

Buffy's identity struggle reflects many of the same emotions that teenagers deal with as they try to navigate the social maze of their high school years. They must learn to balance their construction of a normal life with the steady encroachment of adult responsibilities. The trunk in Buffy's room, which has personal items on top and Slayer weapons hidden in a secret compartment below, serves as a visual metaphor for the identity-confusion of the teenage years. Joss Whedon comments that in this trunk we "see all the things a normal girl might have and then we see what lies beneath and that's a literal, visual metaphor for the way we feel when we're young."[1] Buffy represents all teenagers who feels their parents just don't remember how difficult high school can be.[2]

So what makes Buffy slay? She never sought to be chosen, never asked for the power. Joss Whedon's answer is that Buffy slays out of "a sense of responsibility."[3] Buffy operates with a strict moral code. The source of this moral code is a deep and abiding sense of the value inherent in human beings. This concept finds expression in various philosophical and religious systems,[4] including the Judeo-Christian tradition where the value of humanity goes back to the idea of creation in the image of God. Although *Buffy*'s use of this concept cannot easily be traced to any single influence, it manifests in Buffy's life in a need to protect and serve others.

Buffy's moral code does not make her flawless. She is not a

paragon of virtue who never acts immorally. Rather what identifies her is an awareness that along with her power comes a responsibility for others, and Buffy relentlessly sacrifices her own interests in the pursuit of that duty. Her moral code compels her to help people, whether that be as simple as stopping a student from defacing museum property or as grandiose as saving the world. The value she places on human life even compels her to turn herself in to the police when she (mistakenly) believes herself to be the cause of a girl's death. Spike, desperate to keep her from this action, tells her that one dead girl means little in comparison with the countless people she has saved (6.13). Yet for Buffy, it means everything. Each human life is precious, and she refuses to compromise the value of human life in order to save herself. Contrast this attitude with the trio of nerds who are the real cause of the girl's death and who describe their getting away with murder as "cool" (6.13).

Unlike the Slayer Kendra who gave up her family, friends, and any semblance of a normal life for an all-consuming pursuit of duty, Buffy works hard to remain both a person and a Slayer. She studies for final exams while attempting to thwart an apocalypse (2.21), two events not mutually exclusive in the minds of students, and prepares for the SAT's in a cemetery, pausing long enough to stake a vampire with her number two pencil (3.6). By season seven, her efforts at juggling the person and the Slayer lead some Sunnydale high students to conclude that Buffy is a "high-functioning schizophrenic" (7.12).

Above all Buffy desires a normal life. Although she never abandons that desire, she continually sacrifices it in the service of others. Buffy sacrifices her social status, her reputation, and her college school of choice so that she can protect people from evil. Even her love life falls on the sacrificial altar. In "Never Kill A Boy On the First Date" (1.5), Buffy begs Giles to let her go on a date with a boy named Owen. "Clark Kent has a job," she tells him. "I just want to go on a date." When she then has to flee in the middle of the date to go track a vampire, Buffy tells Owen that she feels like two different people, one who wants to stay and the other who has to leave. Not taking the hint, Owen follows her to a funeral home where he is knocked unconscious during the battle between Buffy and the vampire. At that moment, Buffy realizes that because she is the Slayer, her personal desire for a normal social life may put the lives of those she cares about in danger; so she later tells Owen that it's over. The moment at which Buffy's duty puts Owen's life in danger occurs at a funeral home, perhaps representing the death of her social life.

"Inca Mummy Girl" (2.4) is another episode that addresses the conflict between Buffy's personal desire for a normal life and the responsibility of her calling. Buffy's dresser drawer serves as another visual metaphor. Containing a hairbrush, two crosses, a stake, and a jar of holy water, it represents the duality of her life and the intermingling, yet seemingly incongruous nature, of the girl and the Slayer. The mummy in question is a type of Buffy, a teenage girl who, centuries ago, was chosen by her Inca tribe to be a human sacrifice. Now awakened, she must literally suck the life out of people in order to remain alive. It is a fitting parallel to Buffy who feels like her "job" of being the Slayer is sucking the life out of her.

The episode is framed at the beginning and end by ruminations on sacrifice. First, Buffy asks Giles if she can leave their training session early. When he reminds her that she has responsibilities, Buffy expresses a blasé attitude towards the sacrifices she must make.

> BUFFY (showing fake excitement): Oh, I know this one! (Doing her best impersonation of Giles) 'Slaying entails certain sacrifices blah blah bitty blah. Give me a scone.'
> GILES: It's as if you know me.

Buffy's attitude becomes more serious later when she has to abandon her plans to attend the school dance so she can investigate some recent murders. Both Buffy and the mummy girl, who is staying at Buffy's house as a foreign exchange student, are bitter about the sacrifices they have had to make. Speaking of herself, the mummy girl says, "Who knows what she had to give up to fulfill her duty to others?" Buffy understands, for when Giles comes to her house the night of the dance and comments on being happy to find her home, she bitterly replies, "Yup. Not at the dance, not with my friends, not with a life." Buffy speaks as though she has no choice in the matter, as though her life is being taken away from her without her consent. Yet, Buffy does not slay because she has to, but because she chooses to. The moral code that Buffy follows is not inherent in the persona of the Slayer; it is inherent in the person of Buffy. She chooses a life of sacrifice. When an Inca bodyguard tells the mummy girl that, as the Chosen One, she must die and has no choice in the matter, she proves him wrong by choosing instead to kill others as an act of self-preservation.

At the end of the episode, Buffy tries to defend the mummy girl's actions. We return to the theme of sacrifice, only here with the idea that Buffy's sacrifices are a choice, not a burden. Recalling the moment when she died at the hands of the Master, Buffy explains her sympathy for the mummy girl.

> BUFFY: She was gypped. She was just a girl and she had her life taken away from her . . . I remember how I felt when I heard the prophecy that I was gonna die. I wasn't exactly obsessed with doing the right thing.
>
> XANDER: Yeah, but you did. You gave up your life.

Both Buffy and the Inca mummy girl were faced with a choice: one chose to fulfill her own desires at the expense of others, while the other chose to sacrifice her life, literally and socially, in service.

Where's the Reward?

Buffy struggles to do good in a world where goodness often goes unrewarded. It is a testimony to her moral character that she does not seek applause or recognition for her actions. If anything, the performance of her duty brings punishment, hardship, and pain. What superhero gets grounded for climbing into her bedroom window in the middle of the night after an evening fighting evil (2.12)? Buffy's attempts to save the world are met with expulsion from school, grounding, and a reputation as a juvenile delinquent. She fights evil on a daily basis, has saved the world numerous times, yet her favorite high school teacher can't even remember her name (3.5). Joss Whedon says the scene in the second episode (1.2) where Buffy is forbidden by the Principal from leaving school grounds is intended to show that Buffy always gets in trouble when she tries to do the right thing.[5] Buffy's morality is not driven by affirmation. She does what is right simply because it is right. She is a model for all who fly under the radar, who daily try to do good for its own sake.

That said, there are rare moments of commendation, most notably at the Senior Prom where Buffy receives the "Class Protector" award, a new category devised just for her because, as presenter Jonathan notes, "Most of the people here have been saved by you, or helped by you at one time or another" (3.20). Nevertheless, the moments of recognition are few and are not the reason Buffy slays. When Buffy mentions that as a young girl she would dress up as "Power Girl" and pretend to save her cousin (2.18), we learn that the Slayer is more definitive of her identity than she herself is perhaps willing to admit.

Reconciliation

Buffy's struggle to maintain a normal life is increasingly balanced by a growing awareness that slaying is not just what she does but who she is. This realization most clearly unfolds over two sets of back-to-back episodes. The first set is the two-part episode titled "What's My Line?" (2.9-10). The setting is Career Week at school, an event that causes Buffy to contemplate her future. When her career assessment identifies for her a future in law enforcement, she is depressed at the thought of never being able to escape her duty. When an assassin dressed as a police officer later attacks Buffy at school, Buffy is in essence being attacked by her own potential future.

The Career Week setting raises the question of whether being the Slayer is a job or a calling. Up until this episode, Buffy has consistently viewed her duties as a job (1.7; 2.3). In "What's My Line, Part One" (2.9), she tells Giles that being a Slayer is a "gig" that she never chose; to which Giles replies that slaying is not a "gig," but a "sacred duty." This is a lesson Buffy has yet to take to heart. In "What's My Line, Part Two" (2.10), Buffy meets Kendra, the other Vampire Slayer, and realizes that the responsibility to fight demons is no longer hers alone. In fact, she contemplates letting Kendra take over all the responsibility so that she can have a normal life. Yet, when danger threatens once again and Buffy rises to meet it, she learns that she cannot separate the Slayer from the girl. This realization is helped along by Kendra who tells her, "You talk about slaying like it's a job. It's not. It's who you are."

By season seven we see how much Buffy has grown in her acceptance of who she is when she tells the vampire Holden that slaying is not a job, but a "calling" (7.7). She has a higher purpose in life, a moral responsibility fulfilled through self-denial and sacrifice. What happens, however, when the sacrifice proves too great? Buffy is aided in her fight by family and friends who support her and give her strength of will. But the true test of one's moral character is how one responds when everything is taken away. The biblical character Job experiences such devastation. Satan strips away his support system of family, friends, wealth, and health, believing that Job's righteousness will then be exposed as a fraud. Job's moral character, however, is proven true when he refuses to allow loss to compromise his integrity.

In the second set of back-to-back episodes, "Becoming, Part Two" (2.22) and "Anne" (3.1), Buffy undergoes her own Job-like trial. She is expelled from school, wanted by the police, and Kendra is dead. Furthermore, her mother, who has just found out that her daughter is a Vampire Slayer, forbids her from leaving the house, laying down the ultimatum that if Buffy leaves, she cannot come back. Again Buffy is called upon to sacrifice that which she holds most dear as she walks out of her mother's house, explaining that "I have to save the world ... again" (2.22).

As Buffy prepares for her final showdown with Angel, she tells Whistler that she is prepared to do whatever it takes to win. Whistler says it is not about what she has to do, but "what are you prepared to give up?" She will be called upon to sacrifice once again, only this time it is a sacrifice greater than the giving of her own life. Any parent can appreciate that the greatest sacrifice in the Bible is not when Jesus gave up his own life, but when God gave up his son. It is far easier to sacrifice oneself than it is to sacrifice one you love. As Buffy is about to defeat the soulless Angelus in battle, Willow's soul restoration spell works, and Angel is back. But by then it is too late. The destruction of the world has begun and the only way Buffy can stop it is to kill the man she loves, to sacrifice his life for the world. She does this while wearing around her neck the cross he gave her, the symbol of sacrifice. Everything has been taken away and the lingering question for her is the same as that for Job: what will she become now that all is gone?

Several months pass by the time the next episode opens and Buffy has run away to Los Angeles where she is trying to hide from her calling and from the memory of what she has lost. The episode is a treatise on the problem of teenage runaways and the title "Anne" points to the importance of names in this episode. Buffy has rejected her name and her calling and now goes by her middle name of Anne. Working as a waitress in a diner, she meets two runaways whose names, Lily and Ricky, are tattooed on their arms. Lily is a runaway from Sunnydale, who at that time was going by the name of Chanterelle. She was saved from vampires by Buffy in an earlier episode (2.7). Like Anne/Buffy, Lily/Chanterelle is trying to hide from her past and to find a new identity. She admits that prior to being Chanterelle, she was in a cult and went by the name Sister Sunshine. When Buffy asks her what her real name is, she falls silent. She has no identity of her own to claim.

A theme of this episode is hope. Many teenage runaways flee a bad situation in the hope of finding a better one. Too often, however, the reality is that the street robs them of their hope and strips them of their identity. Buffy runs into several elderly homeless people who repeat over and over the phrase, "I'm no one." One of these elderly people is Ricky. Local demons have been luring teenage runaways into another dimension where they are subjected to hard labor for decades. When they become too old to work, they are spit back out onto the street. Because time passes differently there, many decades in this dimension equal about one day of the real world's time. The metaphor is clear: the despair and hardship of a life on the street drains the life out of young people.

The leader of the demons, Ken, lures Lily into the demon dimension with the promise of hope under the guise of religion. Later, however, Ken describes this dimension as "hell" because, "What is hell but the total absence of hope?" It is an apt description of the reality for teenage runaways who seek a better life but find only a type of hell carved out of hopelessness.

There is a connection between hope and names in this episode. In the demon dimension, Ken tells Lily that Ricky had remembered her name long after he had forgotten his own. He held onto her name because it represented his hope. Likewise, Lily initially remembers that "Anne's" real name is Buffy because Buffy represents her hope. Buffy herself will mark the restoration of her own hope by reclaiming her name. Buffy finds herself imprisoned in the demon dimension with Lily and others. Buffy can hide from her own problems, but can she turn a blind eye to the suffering of others? Her moral code would suggest no. One of the demons asks all newcomers the question: "Who are you?" Unless they answer "no one," they are beaten. The intent is to strip them of any personal identity and thus any hope. When the demon comes to Buffy, she perks up with a familiar gleam in her eye and informs him, "I'm Buffy . . . the Vampire Slayer. And you are?" She has reclaimed her identity, with respect to both person and calling, and has found her hope in the helping of others. Consequently, after defeating the demons and rescuing the captives, Buffy prepares to return to Sunnydale, but not before handing over her waitress nametag to Lily, who has decided to go by the name of Anne. By giving her Buffy's own name, Buffy has given her hope.

As a moral role model, Buffy represents the belief that o

of power must be governed by a responsibility to use that power selflessly in the service of others. Although Buffy alone has the calling and the power, she is not alone in the fight against evil. Even more remarkable than her own sacrificial actions are those of Xander, Willow, Oz, and others who have not been called, who have not been invested with a sacred duty, and yet willingly fight side by side with Buffy. Without the aid of super strength they risk their lives in battle for the protection of others. It is a rare television show that consistently offers up teenagers who model the virtue of self-sacrifice.

BUFFY AS CHRIST-FIGURE

The Vampire Religion

Season one of *Buffy* consistently associates vampires with religion. This demonic appropriation of religion occurs elsewhere, most notably with The First, but the highest concentration comes in the first season with the Master. These vampires speak in religious language and engage in religious rituals. The Master surrounds himself with a cohort of vampire disciples who worship him in the church where he is entombed and even seek his forgiveness (1.2). The scene in "The Harvest" (1.2) where the vampire Luke (same name as one of Jesus' apostles) drinks the Master's blood and then receives a mark on his forehead plays like "an inversion of the Christian rituals of Communion and Ash Wednesday."[6]

The function of this imagery is to establish the demonic as "antichrist," as wholly evil and opposed to all that is good. That the Master is imprisoned within an underground church (1.2) and is described as ruling "for a thousand years" (1.7) evokes early Christian and Jewish apocalyptic traditions of the binding and 1000 year reign of Satan. In biblical teaching, "antichrist" type of figures are religious figures who distort or oppose Christian practice and teaching through religious claims (2 Thessalonians 2:3-10; 1 John 2:18-19; lation 13). This establishment of the demonic as orientation sets up a contrast with Buffy as Christ figure.

Buffy claims to be "fascinated by the concept of that this fascination plays out is in the identification of Buffy as Christ figure. The predominant symbol of Buffy's Slayerhood is the cross, representing the sacrificial nature of her calling. The cross is featured prominently in the opening credits of every episode. The very first time we see Buffy she is asleep, having a dream about vampires in which there is a glimpse of a cross (1.1). Also in the first episode, Angel shows up and hands Buffy a cross necklace, which she then regularly wears around her neck. The cross no doubt represents protection against vampires, but it also symbolizes what it means to be a Slayer. In "Restless" (4.22), Giles' dream focuses on his responsibility for Buffy. After telling her that she has "a sacred birthright to protect mankind," Giles says of his own role as Watcher: "This is my business. Blood of the lamb and all that." "Blood of the lamb" is the language of sacrifice, particularly applied in Christian tradition to the sacrifice of Christ, suggesting that Giles sees his role as one of teaching Buffy how to be a Christ-like figure.[8] On three occasions, Buffy journeys into the desert and experiences a time of testing (4.22; 5.18; 7.15), not unlike Jesus' forty days of testing in the desert. Wendy Love Anderson notes in reference to common perceptions about *Buffy* that "a truly anti-Christian show could hardly have such an obvious Christ figure as its protagonist."[9] The clearest representations of Buffy as Christ figure occur in two episodes: "Prophecy Girl" and "The Gift."

"Prophecy Girl" (1.12)

The title "Prophecy Girl" refers to Buffy's destiny. Throughout the episode, Buffy prominently wears the cross necklace that Angel gave her, yet she does not fully understand the significance of that symbol and the sacrifice it represents. Early on in the episode, she describes the sacrifices she has to make in rather superficial terms: "I'm putting my life on the line battling the undead. Look, I broke a nail, okay?"

When prophecy reveals that Buffy will die the following night, suddenly the enormity of her calling strikes home. On the night before the Crucifixion, Jesus went to the Garden of Gethsemane and wrestled with his destiny, pouring out in prayer his desire not to die (Mark 14:35-36). When faced with the prospect of her own death, Buffy endures her own Gethsemane-like trial. Having just learned that she is destined to die, Buffy decides to thwart prophecy by resigning from her duties as Slayer. She tells Giles that she quits, ripping off her cross necklace and throwing it on the floor.

That the cross represents her calling, her destiny, is clear. By ripping off the cross and throwing it on the floor, she is rejecting that destiny and that calling. She is rejecting the sacrifice that the cross represents. She is deep within a Gethsemane struggle.

The turning point comes when vampires kill some students on school grounds. The next day Buffy consoles Willow after the tragedy. Recognizing the selfishness of her actions and that she is the only one who can save the world, Buffy informs Willow that she will do what her duty demands. Immediately Buffy returns to the library and picks up the cross from the floor, reclaiming her calling. She places it around her neck and goes off to die. Buffy's insistence on returning for her cross is quite telling. She knows she will die so the reclaiming of the cross is clearly not for simple protection. It represents her destiny and the sacrifice to which she has been called. Like Jesus, she responds to her Gethsemane moment by willingly accepting her fate.

When Buffy arrives at the Master's lair, he informs her that she is "the lamb." The double meaning here is evident. Buffy is the sacrifice that will set the Master free, but she is also the sacrificial lamb whose death will save the world. Like Christ, Buffy dies and is resurrected, and her resurrection represents a victory over evil. Claiming to feel stronger than before, post-resurrection Buffy defeats the Master and saves the world.

"The Gift" (5.22)

Season five of *Buffy* once again involves her coming to terms with the nature of her calling. *Buffy* writer and producer David Fury describes Buffy's growth over seasons four and five as representing a sort of spiritual maturation.

> Buffy comes to a kind of religious epiphany about being The Slayer ... That spiritual journey will continue through next season [five] where she will re-embrace her role as The Slayer. The allegory is you become disillusioned with your faith or church and then you come back again on your own terms.[10]

Buffy embarks on a quest in season five to understand the nature of her power. When Spike tells her that "Death is your art" (5.7), she recognizes the truth of that statement. She deals in death every day. Her confusion over her purpose is enhanced when she goes to the desert for a time of testing. She meets the spirit of the first Slayer who tells her that "Death is your gift" and that love will lead her to it (5.18). Buffy finds this impossible to believe. She says, "Death is not a gift. My mother just died. I know this. If I have to kill demons because it makes the world a better place, then I kill demons, but it's not a gift to anybody" (5.18).

Is death her art or her gift? In Christianity, the concept of death as a gift is a foundational premise. Christ's sacrifice on the cross with its attendant shedding of blood functions as a symbol of selfless love and a gift to the world. In "The Gift" (5.22), Buffy comes to realize the true nature of sacrifice. The episode opens with a "Previously on *Buffy the Vampire Slayer*" montage that begins with the very first episode of season one and rapidly covers the series all the way up to the present, indicating that "The Gift" represents the culmination of her Slayerhood harkening back to the very beginning. Glory is about to shed Dawn's blood, opening the portal that will lead the world into chaos. Blood is closely tied to the notion of sacrifice in this episode. Blood opens the portal and only blood can close it. When Spike says this is so because "it's always got to be blood," he highlights the tenuous connection between life and death. Because blood is life, even the shedding of blood in death can be a symbolic prelude to life.

As Buffy goes off to face Glory, she is still under the impression that death being her gift means that "a Slayer really is just a killer after all." When the defining moment comes, however, Buffy gains an awareness of her true purpose. Her destiny comes clear, and she embraces it willingly. Buffy understands now that the sacrifice of oneself, motivated by love, can be the greatest gift of all. Just as Jesus delivered final instructions and words of comfort to his disciples (John 14-16), Buffy offers final words to her friends and family in which she gives them advice on how to live in the world and assures them that she has figured out that "this is the work that I have to do." Dressed in white (the archetypal color of sacrifice), she then leaps off of the tower towards the portal with her arms outstretched in the shape of a cross.

At the start of the next season, Buffy will experience a resurrection, but for now her death lingers. She came to appreciate the concept of devotion and the meaning of the symbol she wore around her neck. Her death became a gift to the world. "The Gift" concludes with a shot of the headstone adorning Buffy's grave, which reads: "She saved the world. A lot."

FAITH: POWER, CORRUPTION, AND REDEMPTION

The Fall

The Vampire Slayer Faith is everything Buffy is not. Arriving in Sunnydale with no family, no friends, and no Watcher, she lacks the support network that keeps Buffy grounded. Faith is openly jealous of Buffy, longing for the family and the place to belong that Buffy has. Although she tries, Faith never really becomes a part of the group. The irony of her name relates to her inability to connect with others, as writer Douglas Petrie notes: "She's the most faithless character we've got. She doesn't trust herself, or anyone around her."[11] Faith is marginalized not only socially, but also physically. Whereas Buffy lives in a nice home in the middle of town, Faith occupies an eighteen-dollar a day motel room on the outskirts. Faith's downfall begins with the realization of her growing isolation and her unwillingness to trust Buffy. The episode "Revelations" (3.7) concludes with contrasting scenes that highlight Faith's marginalization. The camera cuts from a scene in the school library where the whole gang is present, minus Faith, to Faith alone in her motel room. Buffy then shows up at Faith's room to make amends, but Faith rejects her offer of trust. The episode closes with Faith sitting alone on her bed.

Failing to find purpose in family and friends, Faith seeks solace in the exercise of her power. What ultimately distinguishes Buffy from Faith is not their different social situations, but the fact that Faith lacks the moral compass that guides Buffy. While Buffy is always cognizant of the moral responsibility attending her power, Faith finds such rules constraining. The result is that where Buffy often laments her power, Faith relishes it. Faith's power ultimately corrupts her because she enjoys it too much. *Buffy* writer Jane Espenson notes:

> There's something nice about being able to put the joy in the bad guy and suggesting that evil is more fun. That probably comes from a Puritan ethic that doing good can't be fun. That if you're having fun you're doing evil. It makes Buffy being on the good side all the more heroic. Faith was weak and went for the fun. But Buffy's heroic and strong.[12]

In contrast to Buffy, Faith refuses to sacrifice fun for duty.

The pivotal episode "Bad Girls" (3.14) illustrates the dangers of peer pressure by exploring the intoxicating effect of power.[13] Faith finally convinces Buffy to embrace the fun of slaying. As she does so, Buffy starts to become more like Faith. She isolates herself from her friends and skips her Chemistry test. As is often the case with peer pressure, Faith's influence on Buffy leads to erosion of Buffy's moral structure. While the two of them are out on patrol, Faith breaks into a sporting goods store and gives Buffy a lesson on Slayer power as she steals a weapon from a glass case. She instructs Buffy, "Life for a Slayer is very simple: want . . . take . . . have." The lesson sinks in and Buffy does the same.

The next night provides the real contrast between Buffy and Faith. Filled with remorse over her actions, Buffy is back to her old self. Faith, however, maintains her irresponsible exercise of power, and the decision proves fatal. When a human being surprises them while they are on patrol, the more disciplined Buffy immediately recognizes him as human, but Faith, caught up in the fun, fails to do so and accidentally kills him.

Their immediate reaction is quite telling: Faith turns to run, but Buffy looks back towards the body. This contrast highlights the difference between the acceptance and avoidance of responsibility. Buffy's response to thinking she had accidentally killed a human in "Dead Things" (6.13) was to turn herself over to the police, even though she knew she would never be caught, because her moral code demanded it. Faith, by contrast, disposes of the body and denies any culpability. Buffy tries to get through to Faith by telling her, "Faith, you don't get it. You *killed* a man." Faith's reply is chilling: "No, *you* don't get it. I don't care" (3.14).

Joss Whedon comments that the reason why Buffy could never take the path that Faith does is because Buffy is "moral," meaning that Faith represents "everything that Buffy would never let herself be."[14] The corrupting influence of power for Faith is tied to the belief that power breeds superiority. For Buffy, however, power comes with the price tag of responsibility and a moral obligation to serve. Faith's physical superiority, however, has bred in her a sense of moral superiority.

> BUFFY: We help people! It doesn't mean we can do whatever we want. . . .
> FAITH: You're still not seeing the big picture, B. Something made us different. We're warriors. We're built to kill.

BUFFY: To kill demons! But it does *not* mean that we get to pass judgment on people like we're better than everybody else!
FAITH: We *are* better!
(Buffy is taken aback)
FAITH: That's right, better. People need us to survive. In the balance, nobody's gonna cry over some random bystander who got caught in the crossfire.
BUFFY (sadly): I am.
FAITH: Well, that's your loss. ("Consequences"; 3.15)

Faith's subsequent descent into evil is the result of her failure to accept moral responsibility for her actions. Her journey towards redemption is therefore a journey towards a deeper moral understanding of her identity.

The Turning Point

The turning point in Faith's redemptive arc unfolds over the course of two episodes. Faith's jealousy of Buffy is based in a desire to have what Buffy has in terms of family, friends, and recognition, but does not involve any longing for Buffy's moral code. In season three, Faith makes this clear when she tells Buffy that she has no desire to be like her: "Little Miss Goody-Two-Shoes? It ain't gonna happen, B" (3.15). But in fact it does happen. In "This Year's Girl" (4.15), Faith awakens from her coma and seeks revenge against Buffy. Faith is still highly disdainful of Buffy's moral stance, calling her "self-righteous" and "'better than thou' Buffy." But thanks to a posthumous gift from the Mayor that allows her to swap bodies with Buffy, Faith gets her wish to have Buffy's life.

In the following episode "Who Are You" (4.16), written and directed by Joss Whedon, Faith's moral crisis reaches the breaking point. With Buffy temporarily out of commission, Faith, who now inhabits Buffy's body, tries to *be* Buffy. Deep down, Faith is disgusted with what she has become, and the chance to start over with a new identity, with Buffy's identity, is tempting. One of the first things Faith does in her new body is to take a bath, as though she is trying to wash away the old Faith. Later Faith asks Joyce, now her "mother," if she can borrow some lipstick. When Joyce comments that the lipstick is the same color ("The Harlot") that Faith had previously borrowed, Faith (as Buffy) tosses it back and says, "Burn it." She is trying to kill off her old self.

Faith books a flight out of town for the next morning because she knows she will not be able to pass as Buffy for long. In the meantime, though, she needs people to buy the ruse so Faith stares in the mirror at Buffy's face and practices being Buffy. It is noteworthy that she defines the essence of Buffy in terms of a moral code. Faith practices being Buffy by looking in the mirror and repeating over and over, "You can't do that! Because it's wrong." For the true Faith, though, these words are mere pretense, a veneer of morality designed to deceive.

As Faith experiences Buffy's life over the next several hours, she is forced to recognize certain truths about herself. When Joyce hugs her, she grimaces and pulls away because she experiences true affection and acceptance for the first time. As she hangs out with Willow and the rest of the gang, Faith learns to see herself through the eyes of others, and it's not a pretty sight. When a young woman is attacked by a vampire, Faith kills it in order to keep up the pretense of being Buffy; yet, she is genuinely surprised and uncertain when the woman unexpectedly thanks her.

Inside Buffy's body, however, Faith is still Faith and continues to hold Buffy's moral stance in contempt. She runs into Spike who says, "You know why I really hate you, Summers?" Before he can answer, she does it for him, describing her own feelings about Buffy.

> FAITH: 'Cause I could do anything I want, and instead I choose to pout and whine and feel the burden of Slayerness. I mean, I could be rich. I could be famous. I could have anything. Anyone. Even you, Spike . . . And you know why I don't? Because it's wrong. (She chuckles)

Faith's mockery of Buffy's moral integrity, however, belies a growing appreciation for who Buffy is, coupled with a growing contempt for herself. The more time she spends in Buffy's body, the more like her she becomes. The turning point comes as Faith awaits her flight out of town at the airport. While there, a news report on the television reveals that a group of vampires are holding people hostage in a church. For the first time since her downfall, Faith is morally conflicted. With Buffy out of commission, she is the Slayer, the only one who can save those people. Doing so, however, means having to sacrifice her chance of escape.

Faith shows up at the church and insists on going in, explaining that "I'm Buffy. I have to do this." That Faith's initial step towards redemption occurs in a church is surely significant. It is here that she confesses the truth about herself and begins to experience the weight of moral responsibility. Through her identification with Buffy, Faith has acquired a moral compass. She tells the lead vampire, "You're *not* gonna kill these people." When he asks why not, she repeats the words she had previously mocked, only this time meaning them fully: "Because it's wrong."

The real Buffy, in Faith's body, shows up at that moment and Faith attacks her. The visual impact of this scene is crucial as Faith (in Buffy's body) repeatedly punches her own face in a fit of self-loathing and cries out, "You're nothing! You're disgusting!" Having experienced Buffy's life, Faith fully recognizes the emptiness of her own. The episode concludes with Faith, now back in her own body, fleeing town in despair.

Redemption

Faith's story continues on the *Buffy* spin-off show *Angel*. Faith travels to Los Angeles where she goes on a rampage. Still reeling from self-loathing, she attacks Angel in the hope that he will kill her. Instead, he tries to help her, only to be arrested for harboring the wanted fugitive. Faith's journey has come full circle. Her downward spiral began when she refused to take responsibility for her actions. Now she understands the moral responsibility of power and the value of sacrifice; so, she turns herself into the police, both to save Angel and to bear the penalty for her crimes.

For more than two years, Faith remains in prison until the call of her Slayer duty compels her to break out. The ease with which she breaks out of prison only highlights the fact that she alone kept herself there. When Spike comments that she had the power to break out anytime with nothing to stop her, Faith replies, "I stopped me" (7.18). Faith has learned the difference between the irresponsible display of power and the restraint of power in sacrifice and service.

Faith's storyline represents the pitfalls of any moral evaluation of a serialized television show that simply focuses on selected actions or episodes in the life of a character. For much of her run, the character of Faith glorifies irresponsible sexuality, murderous violence, lying, and self-absorption. She uses power for selfish and immoral means. Taken alone, those elements would justify a negative moral critique. Paying attention to the entire story arc of the character, however, reveals that those actions are by no means a glorification of immorality, but instead serve as an illustration of how the exercise of power outside of moral boundaries is self-destructive. Only by an open exploration of the dark side of Faith does her redemption ring true. The *immoral* portrayal of her character is what ultimately exposes the *moral* perspective of this show.

Through these two Slayers, *Buffy the Vampire Slayer* models two different ways of addressing moral responsibility. Faith represents who Buffy would be without a moral code and without the support of family and friends. Although both serve the moral vision of the show, Buffy does so as a positive example and Faith as a negative one. In Buffy, we see modeled the virtue of self-sacrifice and devotion to moral responsibility. In Faith, we see modeled an open rejection of the same. Yet, Faith's immoral posturing ultimately serves as a means of moral discourse; for with her character, we witness the *process of learning* the value of moral responsibility and self-sacrifice.

Chapter 9

Systems of Power: Technology, Magic, and Institutional Authority

In chapter six I explored human nature's capacity for good or evil, with varying degrees of each, and how the exercise of free will determines the fulfillment of that capacity. Last chapter I examined the moral responsibility of power and how power carries with it an obligation of service. In this chapter, these concepts come together in the examination of systems of power.

The grouping of technology, magic, and institutional authority may seem odd, except that all are systems of power and thus subject to a similar moral evaluation. From *Buffy*'s perspective all systems of power are inherently neutral with respect to moral value. They are merely a source of power. What makes them good or evil, morally speaking, is how that power is structured and used. An institution in and of itself is not corrupt, but that institution may organize power in such a way as to be both corrupt and a corrupter.

The moral responsibility of systems of power mirrors that of a Vampire Slayer. Like Buffy, power may be used as a means for service, or, like Faith, as an end in itself. An institution that uses its power to serve has nobly fulfilled its duty. By contrast, when an institution's power serves only the institution, it becomes demonic in *Buffy*'s world. A closer analysis of how these three systems of power operate in *Buffy the Vampire Slayer* highlights a vital aspect of the show's moral vision.

TECHNOLOGY

The sheer number and sophistication of technological advancements that mark the beginning of the twenty-first century is staggering. Technology is evolving at a pace faster than human society can adapt to. Anya, when asked if she understands computers, embodies this phenomenon.

> ANYA: Well, at first it was confusing. Just the idea of computers was like, 'Whoa, I'm eleven hundred years old. I had trouble adjusting to the idea of Lutherans' (5.15).

Technology barges ahead without concern for a society's ethical and moral boundaries. Twenty-first century lawmakers, moral philosophers, and religious leaders are struggling to catch up, often having to close the barn door after the horse has left. What are the moral and ethical implications of cloning? Where should the ethical lines be drawn? How does one protect society from the proliferation of pornography on the Internet without sacrificing freedom of expression? The Internet alone is such a rapidly changing form of technology that exploration of the moral and legal implications attending its various facets has barely begun. More disturbing, by the time society catches up and fully addresses these questions, the answers may be irrelevant as novel and more progressive technological advancements will have created new dangers and other ambiguous ethical situations to chase after.

Nevertheless, on *Buffy* technology is far from immoral in itself. Willow regularly employs the Internet as a resource in the fight against evil. Even the latest in military hardware can be a welcome ally. Although partial to wooden stakes, Buffy is not averse to using the occasional rocket launcher, should the situation call for it (2.14). In such circumstances, the moral valuation placed on technology depends on the use to which it is put.

During the first three seasons of *Buffy*, the episode providing the most sustained critique of technology is "I, Robot . . . You Jane" (1.8). Sunnydale High's computer teacher, Jenny Calendar, clashes with Giles over the importance of computer technology to the advancement of knowledge. Jenny views computer technology as a boon to humanity, even calling the computer "the good box." For her, the Internet is the great equalizer, making knowledge fully accessible across gender and ethnic lines. Giles, on the other hand, is horrified by the effects that Internet technology has had on the dynamics of human relationships. Fritz, one of Jenny's computer students, snidely informs Giles that, "If you're not jacked in, you're not alive." For Giles, however, that very act is what leads to a kind of social death. When Jenny argues that the Internet is "creating a new society," Giles replies, "A society in which human interaction is all but obsolete? In which people can be completely manipulated by technology?"

Their debate finds concrete expression in a new threat: a demon has inhabited the Internet. This demonization of the Internet is a metaphor for the dangers that unchecked technological advancement can produce. We first meet this demon, named Moloch the Corruptor, in a flashback set in 1418. Moloch corrupts young people by offering false love. He promises a young boy everything he desires in exchange for his love. When the boy professes love for Moloch, Moloch kills him, a stark metaphor for the false promises of the Internet. A society that becomes so enamored of a new technology that it fails to notice the dangers sows the seeds of its own destruction. Giles describes Moloch (and by metaphorical extension the Internet) as "a very deadly and seductive demon. He draws people to him with promises of love, power, knowledge." It is interesting that Moloch is initially trapped by a magic spell and bound within the pages of a book, held captive there as long as the book is never read. When that book is later scanned into a computer, Moloch is set free. The metaphor is instructive: contained within a book, Moloch is restrained; but once placed on the Internet, he is free to corrupt. Information that is wholly unsupervised and unrestrained is a potentially dangerous force. The pornography, gambling, and illegal scams that permeate the web have indeed wielded a corrupting influence on society.

The benefits that the Internet has produced are incalculable and its value immeasurable. It is a tremendous source of power. Yet as with all power, turning a blind eye to its potential for corruption can be deadly. After Jenny insists that the "divine exists in cyber space same as out here," Giles counters with, "What's in cyber space at the moment is less than divine." Giles recognizes the power of information and access used for destructive means. When Moloch changes one student's history paper into a pro-Nazi manifesto and alters another student's medical records so that he is administered medicine to which he is allergic, it serves as a wake-up call to a twenty-first century society facing the prospect of ever-more destructive computer viruses and the threat of cyber terrorism.

Although the metaphor of demonic possession sets up this broad critique of the ethical and moral dangers of the Internet, the episode filters that broad critique through the specific problem of Internet predators. Willow innocently enters a chat room and begins an Internet "relationship" with Moloch who presents himself as an eighteen-year-old kid named Malcolm. Excited at the prospect of someone actually being interested in her, Willow develops a serious crush on Malcolm, despite having never seen him. Although luring Willow with the promise of love, Malcolm actually causes Willow to forsake her flesh and blood relationships with Buffy and Xander, fulfilling Giles' fear that the Internet de-values human interaction. Ultimately Willow triumphs over Malcolm and the corrupting influence of the Internet because she recognizes the emptiness of their promises. She thus offers a model of resistance to technological corruption by refusing to become a slave to technology through blind devotion to its promises of love, power, and knowledge.

MAGIC

Buffy the Vampire Slayer's portrayal of magic has been a source of contention among many Christians because it is taken as a glorification of witchcraft. To suggest, however, that because Willow is a positive role model, she therefore glorifies witchcraft would be like saying that because *Buffy* utilizes "good" vampires like Angel and eventually Spike, the show therefore glorifies vampirism. In fact, magic is treated to the same principle of moral evaluation as technology. Both witches and vampires have access to power. What distinguishes a good vampire from an evil vampire or a good witch from a bad witch is how they use that power. Spike and Angel do not become good simply because they possess a soul. With that soul comes free will and it is their subsequent *choice* to use their power for good that marks their redemption. Likewise, any moral evaluation of the role of magic on *Buffy* needs to pay attention to its usage in context.

First, the portrayal of magic on *Buffy* is not an attempt to represent either positively or negatively the Wiccan religion or any modern form of witchcraft.[1] Willow rejects her college's Wiccan group and claims that her magic is "old-agey" as opposed to "new-agey" (7.11). Willow's magic fits more comfortably within a pre-modern worldview like that of Greek mythology than in a contemporary context.

Second, as with other supernatural elements on the show, magic is metaphorical. In the episode "Witch" (1.3) magic is a metaphor for the relationship between mothers and daughters. *Buffy* executive producer Marti Noxon says that witches on *Buffy* tap into the idea of witch as "a cultural metaphor for women's power."[2] Thus, Willow's growth in magical proficiency mirrors her growth from a shy, insecure girl to a more confident, empowered woman. At other times, magic functions as a sexual metaphor as with the development of Willow and Tara's relationship. Willow's growing reliance on magic in seasons five and six is a clear metaphor for drug addiction. *Buffy* writer Jane Espenson says they also use witches to represent social outcasts. With reference to an episode she co-wrote called "Gingerbread" (3.11), Espenson says that the witches in that show were "a metaphor for kids who get in trouble for the stuff you find in their locker. They're counterculture kids reconceptualized as witches."[3] This brief survey highlights the error of assuming that a positive portrayal of witchcraft on a show necessarily equals a glorification of the occult. On *Buffy*, magic is as much a form of social commentary as anything.

Third, on *Buffy* the moral evaluation of magic depends upon the means and ends of its usage. It is a consistent pattern on *Buffy* that magic used for selfish ends or without respect for its power ultimately results in destruction or pain. Willow learns this lesson early on when Giles scolds her for practicing spells without proper supervision. When asked what she has been conjuring, Willow confesses "fire out of ice, which next time I won't do on the bedspread" (3.3). That magic is dangerous is a constant refrain. "Bad magic" is used for all sorts of nefarious schemes from a basic love spell to world destruction and murder. Giles notes that Willow's destructive and murderous use of magic derived from an unhealthy rage and desire for vengeance (6.22).

The valuation of magic is not consistently negative, however, for magic used wisely and for noble ends is a valuable asset. Both Willow and Giles use magic to save lives, stop demonic enemies, or counter dangerous magic spells. On one occasion, they do a spell designed to "confront and expel all evil" (2.19). Power is a tool for service and the ideal function of magic on *Buffy* is to "help people" (6.8). It is when that ideal is turned inward and magic functions only to help oneself or to further one's own selfish goals that magic becomes demonic. Marti Noxon states the governing principle well:

On *Buffy*, we play with the idea of witchcraft or magic, and it's always about the intention of the person who uses it. Magic per se is not a bad thing. What they do with it is either going to be good or bad.[4]

We see the truth of this statement played out in the visual contrast between the black-eyed, black-haired Willow who uses magic in a selfish desire to destroy the world (6.22) and white-eyed, white-haired Willow who later uses magic to save the world (7.22).

INSTITUTIONAL AUTHORITY

An initial wave of scholarly analysis, much of it coming from a Marxist or feminist slant, consistently pegged *Buffy the Vampire Slayer* as anti-authoritarian and opposed in principle to the institutionalization of power.[5] More recent contributions reject this position by arguing that *Buffy*'s view of institutions is not nearly as liberal or anti-authoritarian as many scholars assume.[6] Buinicki and Enns state:

> Therefore, these apparent subversions of institutional power merely signal a resistance to the excessive use of power, to outdated institutional models rather than to institutional power in general . . . They ultimately reaffirm the role of institutions in maintaining social order.[7]

I argue similarly that *Buffy*'s view of institutional authority follows the same dynamic as its attitude towards magic and technology, affirming their value in both principle and practice, while exposing their corrupt, flawed, or irresponsible uses of power. To illustrate this we will look at Buffy's attitude towards three forms of institutional authority: education, the government, and institutionalized religion.

Education

Most educational authority figures play a peripheral role at best on *Buffy*. When teachers, coaches, or school counselors are featured, they typically behave monstrously (literally) or else end up dead. *Buffy*'s attitude towards educational authority, however, is best represented by its depiction of three principals, each of whom represents an educational model.

On Buffy's first day as a transfer student at Sunnydale High, she meets Principal Flutie. Flutie is a caricature of a liberal approach to educational philosophy. Tolerance-obsessed and non-authoritarian, he cares more about student self-image than about genuine achievement. In line with his de-valuing of his own institutional authority, Principal Flutie requests that students call him "Bob." He informs Buffy: "We want to service your needs, and help you to respect our needs" (1.1). But respect is what Principal Flutie fails to receive. He becomes the embodiment of the idea that "if you try to be the students' friend, they will eat you alive," for that is precisely his fate.

Flutie's successor, Principal Snyder, vows to put an end to Flutie's "touchy-feely, relating nonsense" (1.9). A hard-core disciplinarian, Snyder is all about the enforcement of rules. He makes this clear to Buffy when he catches her in the hallway after school while she's investigating a student's murder: "There are things I will not tolerate. Students loitering on campus after school. Horrible murders with hearts being removed. And also smoking" (1.9). Where Flutie was overly accommodating, Snyder has no faith whatsoever in the students. For him, discipline resolves all problems. He explains his philosophy to Buffy, Xander and Willow as follows:

> SNYDER: Kids today need discipline. It's not a popular word these days. Discipline. I know Principal Flutie would have said 'kids need understanding, kids are human beings.' That's the kind of wooly-headed, liberal thinking that leads to being eaten (1.9).

The irony is that an authority higher than himself, the Mayor as newly made snake demon (3.22), will eventually eat Snyder himself — perhaps a comment on the cannibalistic nature of political bureaucracy.

Both Flutie and Snyder represent a sharp critique of the failings of certain educational models with respect to their use of power. Where Snyder exemplifies the oppressive employment of power, Flutie exemplifies an irresponsible abdication of power by failing to use his authority to provide appropriate structure and discipline. These critiques, however, do not represent an anti-institutional stance towards educational authority in *Buffy*, but rather a comment on the bankrupt nature of certain educational philosophies.

If *Buffy* were truly anti-institutional in its attitude towards educational authority, it would not provide us with a third educational model in the figure of Principal Wood. *Buffy* presents Robin Wood, the new principal of the rebuilt Sunnydale High, as a positive educational authority figure who uses power responsibly. An African-American (diversity in education), Principal Wood cares about his students and seeks their overall welfare; yet, he willingly imparts discipline when called for. As such, he represents a mediating position between the caricatured positions of Principal Flutie and Principal Snyder, embodying the ideals of each philosophy while avoiding their respective abuses of power.

Government

Buffy's overall negative portrayal of the Initiative does not represent an anti-government stance, but only a critique of governmental corruption. At times, the Initiative is a beneficial institution, keeping the peace during times of potential riots (4.10) and reducing the number of dangerous elements (demons) in the population. Willow initially grants the Initiative "good guy" status for its anti-demon stance (4.13). Riley Finn is an institutional man to the core: government soldier, regular churchgoer, and college educator. His desertion of the Initiative is a reaction against its corrupt practices and not a rejection of governmental institution, for his desertion ultimately does not take. When the opportunity arises, Riley joins with another government-connected, demon hunting agency.

The problem with the Initiative is not that it is a governmental system of power, but that it exercises that power without concern for moral boundaries. Both the goal of the Initiative (harnessing demonic power for itself) and the means of achieving that goal ("amoral science"[8]) violate the principle that power mandates service. Professor Walsh insists to Buffy, however, that both the Initiative and Buffy are after the same goal (the destruction of demons) and that the only difference between them is their methodology, or as Walsh puts it, "We use the latest in scientific technology and state-of-the-art weaponry and you, if I understand correctly, poke them with a sharp stick" (4.12). In fact their goal is not the same. Buffy seeks to destroy demonic forces in the service of humanity; the Initiative seeks to harness those forces in the pursuit of more power. Its means of accomplishing this is through science and technology.

Buffy's critique of the Initiative therefore coincides with its critique of technology. Advancements in science and technology that progress beyond the capacity for moral, ethical, and legal safeguards to keep up can create a society's own worst enemy. The Initiative's disregard for proper boundaries in the desire to push technological progress ever further parallels Willow's similar disregard with respect to magic. Both, however, contrast with Buffy's perspective on the exercise of power when she says, "There are limits to what we can do. There should be. Willow doesn't want to believe that. And now she's messing with forces that want to hurt her" (3.20).

Maggie Walsh's creation of the cyborg Adam is a deliberate take on the Frankenstein story, which addresses "fears about industrialization and science and their effects on morality and humanity,"[9] and a commentary on the dangers of unchecked science. When Adam's first act is to kill his creator (4.13), it is a pointed acknowledgment of humanity's tendency towards self-destructive behavior under the guise of progress.

Two scenes in the episode "Goodbye Iowa" (4.14) reiterate this point. Once free, Adam encounters a young boy in the woods, a la Frankenstein. The young boy is shown playing with a cyborg soldier action figure, just before being killed by the real thing. It is no stretch to read this as a commentary on how the turning of guns into children's toys has resulted in the social problem of children dying of accidental gunshot wounds. The second scene creates an interesting parallel between Adam and Wile E. Coyote. Buffy and the gang are hiding in Xander's basement. In the morning, a RoadRunner cartoon is on the TV. In all Road Runner cartoons, Wile E. Coyote attempts to capture his prey by the use of Acme technology, yet only succeeds at repeatedly "killing" himself. Buffy pauses to watch Wile E. be destroyed by another of his technological plots and comments, "That would never happen." The irony, of course, is that it does. The Initiative, by disregarding moral guidance in the pursuit of technological advancement, has sown the seeds of its own destruction. As with Maggie Walsh, the Initiative is ultimately destroyed by the very creature it helped create.

When Riley's friend and fellow soldier, Forrest, is killed and then revived as a cyborg made in Adam's image, Riley exclaims, "Oh, God." Forrest replies, "God has nothing to do with it" (4.21). He is exactly right. Adam, as with his namesake, is a new creation — but not a divine one. The relentless pursuit of power and knowledge without regard for God or humanity gives birth to a monstrous creation that inevitably devours its own creators.

Represented in *Buffy*'s treatment of government is the same standard of moral evaluation used for individuals, that is that the corruption of power results from a failure to wield that power in the service of humanity. So the demonization of institutional authority on *Buffy* no more represents an anti-institutional ethic than its demonization of certain individuals represents anti-individualism. The governing principle is the responsible or irresponsible use of power, a principle that also sheds light on *Buffy*'s portrayal of institutionalized religion.

Institutionalized Religion

Positive religious figures on *Buffy* are not absent, but they are rare. Whether they be ministers presiding at funerals (3.8; 5.16) or an order of monks risking their lives to protect the Key from Glory (5.5), some religious figures are portrayed neither as inept nor corrupt. Christian media critics, however, who lament the relative absence of positive religious role models on *Buffy* mistake that absence for antagonism towards Christianity as a whole, rather than focusing on the reasons why religion is portrayed as it is. *Buffy* is no more opposed to Christianity in principle than it is to education, government, or technology.

The key to understanding *Buffy*'s depiction of religious authority is to recognize that religion, as with any other system of power, is also capable of moral corruption. That *Buffy* regularly employs Christian themes and describes certain characters in Christ-like ways represents a positive attitude towards aspects of Christian teaching and ideals. Nevertheless, *Buffy* deals in social satire and the way religious authority gets portrayed on the show is an attempt to expose the historical failings of Christianity, just as with any other system of power.

The monks who seek to protect the Key (i.e. Dawn) are balanced by the religious order of the Knights of Byzantium whose goal is to destroy the Key (i.e. kill Dawn) under the guise of it being "the will of God" (5.13). An order of religious knights who use God as an excuse for murder is a thinly veiled depiction of the sin of the Crusades. Likewise, the murder of Father Gabriel by a vengeful Native American spirit in an attempt to redress wrongs done against his people may function in "Pangs" (4.8) as a comment on the role played by some missionaries in the process of colonization.[10]

In another episode (4.18), Riley's house becomes possessed by a poltergeist "born out of intense adolescent emotion and sexual energy."

Through investigation, Giles, Anya, and Xander learn that the house had once been a home for runaway children run by Genevieve Holt. A religious woman, Mrs. Holt claims to have "educated them in the way of the Lord" and to have "punished them when they were dirty." That education involved hacking off girls' hair and holding children under water in the bathtub. When Giles and Xander confront Mrs. Holt, she refuses to listen to them, claiming, "I can smell the sin on each and every one of you." Xander replies, "Well let me tell you something, lady. She who smelt it dealt it!"

Christianity, as it has been practiced historically, has its own dark secrets. Physical, sexual, and emotional abuse that for decades has been inflicted on children at church-run orphanages and foster homes only shows that institutionalized religion has indeed dealt its share of sin. Many religious leaders choose to ignore the church's failings, preferring instead to present a hypocritical facade while at the same time preaching confession and repentance to others. Yet when religious leaders use their power to harm rather than help children, they have defied the will of God and their calling to service.

These examples also provide a model for understanding Caleb, the fallen priest who appears in season seven. Caleb raised the ire of several Christian watchdog groups due to his heretical comments and the fact that he did evil while continuing to wear his priestly clothing. The key to understanding Caleb, though, is his attitude towards women. Caleb is a hardcore misogynist who views all women as "dirty." His take on the creation story is: "There once was a woman, and she was foul, like all women, for Adam's rib was dirty" (7.18). Caleb is an over-the-top caricature of the church's historical oppression of women. For centuries the church has gone to Genesis and used the order of creation and Eve's eating of the apple, just as Caleb does, as a justification for all kinds of oppressive acts towards women. Caleb represents the idea that whenever Christianity abuses its power by oppressing rather than honoring and serving women, it's actions become monstrous.

Buffy the Vampire Slayer's portrayal of how institutional authority has abused its power stands in stark contrast to Buffy herself who wields her power sacrificially and responsibly. This leads to the question: how does Buffy herself view institutional authority?

BUFFY AND SUBMISSION TO AUTHORITY

Many Christians use a particular theological principle to delineate Christian responsibility with respect to institutional authority. The principal states that obedience to God trumps obedience to human authorities. Submission and obedience to institutional authorities is a mark of Christian responsibility, except for when the obedience demanded by those authorities contradicts one's calling as a follower of God. Now, no doubt, this principle has at times been abused and misconstrued to justify a variety of anti-authoritarian practices and illegal behavior; yet, in its ideal form, it represents a distinctive mark of the Christian conscience.

Buffy adopts a similar principle in her own perspective on institutional authority, although it is tempered with a pragmatic slant. With rare exception, Buffy submits to authority when that authority does not contradict her calling as the Slayer. Her moral responsibility as the Slayer, however, trumps her responsibility to human authority. At school Buffy obeys her teachers and principal and accepts discipline when meted out by authority figures, even when she believes that discipline to be undeserved. Yet, when Professor Walsh abuses her power by acting insensitively towards an emotionally scarred Willow, Buffy does not hesitate to call her on it (4.7). When Principal Flutie or Snyder hinders her duty as the Slayer, she will defy and disobey.

Buffy quits the Watcher's Council when it fails to help her in the exercise of her duty (3.21), yet she later rejoins the Council under revised terms when doing so aids her purpose (5.12). As long as the Initiative appears to be working towards the same goal as she, Buffy has no qualms about becoming an adjunct member. Even after the Initiative's true agenda is revealed, Buffy continues to work with members to hunt down Adam.

Buffy's view of law enforcement is most instructive for understanding her position on institutional authority. Buffy rejects Faith's argument that Slayers are beyond the law, asserting instead, "We help people! It doesn't mean we can do whatever we want" (3.15). In fact, Buffy regularly submits to legal authority whenever demonic elements are not at play. After Buffy believes she accidentally killed Ted, Buffy confesses to the police despite her mother's attempts to cover for her (2.11). Likewise, Buffy submits to human authority when she believes herself responsible for Katrina's death (6.13). Even though there is no evidence linking her to the crime, and Dawn pleads with her not to do it, Buffy insists on turning herself in to the police. On the way to the police station, Spike tries to stop her, asking, "What do you think you're doing?" Buffy simply replies, "The right thing" (6.13). When Warren kills Tara, it is noteworthy that Buffy refuses to go after Warren and try to kill him. Because Warren is human and he killed Tara by human means (a gun), Buffy understands his punishment to fall under human authority. She tells Xander and Dawn that "the human world has its own rules for dealing with people like him." When Xander counters that those rules don't work very well, Buffy says, "Sometimes they do. Sometimes they don't. We can't control the universe" (6.20). The efficiency of the human legal system is not an issue for Buffy. Human actions are their province and so she readily surrenders her authority to theirs.

When demonic or supernatural elements are at play, however, Buffy's calling and duty overrule all human authority. The same Buffy who tried to surrender to police when Katrina died, beats up a cop who tries to arrest her while the end of the world is threatening, and only she can stop it (2.22). When Buffy believes that Giles has fallen victim to a demon, she breaks into a shop to search for evidence, explaining, "I do not have time to play by the rules tonight" (4.12). Buffy's insistence that a Slayer is not above the law comes under revision when her duty is at stake. After Anya returns to being a vengeance demon and slaughters several people, Buffy announces her intention to handle the situation her way: "Human rules don't apply. There's only me. I am the law" (7.5). For Buffy, submission to institutional authority is a moral obligation; yet, her calling carries with it a higher moral obligation that supersedes human authority.

Chapter 10

Together or Alone? The Dynamics of Community and Family

Slayer tradition holds that "She *alone* will stand against the vampires, the demons, and the forces of darkness" (italics mine). Only the Slayer has the power, only the Slayer bears the ultimate responsibility for holding back the onslaught of demonic powers. It is a recurring refrain, and Buffy is constantly reminded and reminding herself of her aloneness. Whistler tells her early on in what becomes a motif: "In the end, you're always by yourself. You're all you've got" (2.22). By season seven, the idea reaches a fevered pitch. Giles tells Buffy that no one but she has the power to protect the world (7.10). Spike tells Robin Wood, "I know Slayers. No matter how many people they've got around them, they fight alone" (7.17). Buffy tells Faith that the price of being a Slayer is always being alone (7.21).

A companion theme to the solitude of the Slayer is the independence of *Buffy*'s teenage protagonists. Aside from Giles and Joyce Summers, adults play a tangential role in the lives of Buffy, Xander and Willow. Over seven seasons, Xander's parents appear in only one episode, while Willow's mother makes one appearance that illustrates her lack of involvement in Willow's life when she keeps referring to Buffy as "Bunny" (3.11). Joyce Summers, by contrast, is a devoted and loving mother, but hardly an attentive parent. After all, she fails to notice that her daughter sneaks out of her room virtually every night to prowl about in cemeteries. For the most part, these kids make their own life decisions and are left to find their own way.

With respect to these themes, *Buffy* is a mirror held up to contemporary American culture. America is a nation obsessed with independence and individualism. To stand on one's own, to be self-sufficient, to have the money, health, and power to become an island unto oneself is a prized American virtue. We define adulthood in terms of how many people we no longer need. Young people grow up eager to leave home and cut off all dependent ties so they can go off alone and "find themselves," in the belief that one cannot find oneself in a community.

Ironically, an approach to television morality that focuses the issue primarily on sex, violence, and profanity creates a situation in which Christian media critics might decry the presence of violence or profanity in one television show, while praising another that advocates a view of individualism that runs counter to the very foundations of Christianity. From its origin, Christianity was communal, and Christians were mutually dependent on one another. Part of this was due to the quality of ancient Mediterranean culture, part to the status of Christians as a marginalized minority, and part to the philosophy espoused by Jesus and the leaders of the early church. In such a climate, group associations were essential to survival. Early Christianity's focus on community and dependence had a theological underpinning as well. Jesus' admonitions to love and serve one another require a communal context for full expression. The community is a place where Christians are to rely upon one another for strength, forgiveness, comfort, and physical needs, all of which require a willingness to be dependent.

Many American churches, however, are increasingly influenced by the spirit of individualism — at times to the detriment of their own theology. The effects of individualism and independence on religious practice is by no means limited to Christianity, however, as other religious movements have also come to reflect the spirit of American individualism. The state of religion in America is increasingly defined less by communities of reference than by an independent spirituality that seeks some kind of personal and individual relationship with the divine.

On one level, *Buffy* appears to tap into a similar cultural stream through its themes of individualism and independence. However, the show consistently treats these themes with a healthy dose of suspicion, undercutting them with its perspective on the importance of community and family — a perspective that ultimately confirms the falsity of the claim that Buffy must fight *alone*.[1]

COMMUNITY

Community Ethics

Buffy the Vampire Slayer places a high premium on community. Buffy, Xander, Willow and Giles form the core members of an open community that welcomes others as they come into their lives. The foundation of this community is friendship and deep, abiding respect for one another. Their community operates with an ethic that is a model of virtuous behavior. The following are six components of that community ethic.

Acceptance. *Buffy* does not portray the members of this community as saints or flawless individuals. Sometimes they lie, do things that hurt one another, or keep secrets. But what they always do is provide for each other a place of unconditional acceptance and forgiveness. To belong to this community is to belong to a group of people who are accepting of others despite their flaws because they recognize the flaws in themselves. In "The Dark Age" (2.8), Giles' past comes back to haunt him (literally), putting Buffy and other members of the community in danger. At the conclusion of the episode, Giles wallows in guilt; yet Buffy comes to him not with recriminations but with full acceptance. The community is a place where acceptance trumps personal feelings. Despite his hatred of Angel, Xander jumps to Angel's defense when Kendra, an outsider to the community, suggests that Angel must die for being a vampire. Xander says, "Angel's our friend . . . except I don't like him" (2.10). Although Xander holds no fondness whatsoever for Angel, the demands of community require that he accept him fully.

Tough Love. Acceptance of one another in community does not entail condoning or ignoring wrongful behavior. The members of Buffy's community rarely hold back their disapproval when a member behaves inappropriately. Whether it be telling each other the hard truth that they need, but do not want, to hear (5.10) or holding an intervention when one member's behavior becomes potentially destructive (4.2), this community holds each other accountable for their actions. That accountability, however, is always expressed with a spirit of acceptance.

Loyalty. The members of Buffy's community are fiercely loyal to one another because their association is founded upon friendship and common purpose. When one member is hurting, in need, or in danger, the others are there. When Buffy is overwhelmed with the responsibility of preparing refreshments for the Student-Teacher conference while keeping up her Slayer duties, Xander and Willow come to her aid. Xander's offer of help even extends to whittling stakes and whistling a "jaunty tune" (2.3). Having experienced this loyalty herself, Buffy extends it to others. The Mayor is so sure of Buffy's loyalty to her friends that he compares Buffy to a dog whose "friendship is stronger than reason, stronger than it's own sense of self-preservation" (3.19). Even when Faith tries to sever her ties to the community by betraying Buffy, Buffy's loyalty is steadfast:

> FAITH: You don't give up, do you?
> BUFFY: Not on my friends, no. (3.15)

Faith's exclusion from the community is her own doing because she rejects the loyalty that Buffy offers and fails to trust in the community's willingness to accept her.

Trust. Trust is the glue that holds this community together. The members trust each other with their lives. They support and aid one another even when doubtful of the correctness of the choices made. Trust is so foundational to the contours of this community that a rejection or deep violation of it results in exclusion. In fact on *Buffy* this seems to be the only cause for expulsion from the community. Jenny Calendar finds herself on the outside because she betrays their trust in her (2.14). In season seven, the breakdown of trust between Buffy and the rest of the community results in her temporary exclusion (7.19). "Revelations" (3.7) contrasts Xander's trust in the community with Faith's lack of trust. Both are upset when Buffy chooses not to inform them of Angel's return from his hell dimension. Their varying responses to this reveal why one remains a central member of the community and the other does not. Xander expresses his concern that Angel could become dangerous again, yet he leaves the decision about Angel up to Buffy stating simply: "I trust you." The episode then cuts from this scene to Faith in her motel room. Buffy shows up to mend their recent differences, only Faith does not seem interested. Faith instead isolates herself from the community, claiming, "You can't trust people."

Sacrifice. True friendship and community entail sacrifice. *Buffy* is a television show in which its teenage protagonists unhesitatingly risk their lives for each other week after week. In the second episode of the series, an initial member of the community, Jesse, is captured by vampires and taken into the sewers. As Buffy goes in after him, Xander follows on her heels. She tells Xander to leave, but he makes his priorities clear when he says, "Jesse's my bud, okay? If I can help him out, that's what I gotta do . . . Besides, it's this or Chem class" (1.2). The bonds of their community require a commitment to one another so deep that one's personal welfare is sacrificed for the good of others.

Anya's attempts to readjust to human life after 1100 years as a demon often provides a unique perspective on moral issues. In one of her early appearances before she fully joins the community, she tries to convince Xander to flee town with her and thus avoid the coming apocalypse. She assures him that if he stays, he will die — a possibility he willingly accepts.

> ANYA: Come with me.
> XANDER: I can't.
> ANYA: Why not?
> XANDER: I got friends on the line.
> ANYA: So?
> XANDER: That humanity thing's still a work in progress, isn't it?
> (3.21)

Joining humanity on *Buffy* requires an appreciation of the value of community and friendship, and the willingness to sacrifice for it.

Dependence. The lesson that Buffy continually learns and relearns throughout this series is that she is not much good without her friends. Despite her physical power, they are the true source of her strength. They provide physical aid in her battles and emotional support in her life. When she wants to give up, they get her back on track. They have survived by depending upon one another. In the musical episode "Once More, With Feeling" (6.7), an underworld being ("some sort of Lord of the Dance. Oh, but not the scary one. Just a demon.") causes everyone to sing out their deepest feelings. Buffy acknowledges the strength she has drawn from her community when she sings, "What can't we face if we're together? What's in this place that we can't weather?" In the final showdown with the musical demon, however, Giles sends Buffy off to face him alone until he recognizes the wrongness of that choice. Giles, together with the rest of their community, shows up to aid Buffy. As Buffy begins to sing a solo, Giles says, "She needs backup," and sends in Anya and Tara to sing harmony. That's the strength of Buffy's community: backup is always there.

A fitting metaphor for dependence on one another's strength in community comes in the episode where Willow, following her murderous rampage, is terrified that the gang will not accept her back. After sustaining a severe injury, she tries magically to draw power from the earth to heal herself, but confesses that she is too weak. Buffy holds out her hands to Willow, telling Willow that she can draw all the strength she needs from her (7.3). An individualistic life that shuns community also shuns the strength that can only be drawn from others.

Redemptive Community

Redemption on *Buffy* is a communal event. The acceptance, trust, and mutual dependence that one finds in true community foster redemptive action. Spike's first real connection with Buffy's community comes when he goes to them for help after receiving the implant in his head. Tied up to a chair, he is a reluctant and not terribly welcome member. After a fierce battle in Giles' living room that results in Spike's chair, and thus Spike, being knocked over onto the ground, Spike yells out: "What happened? Did *we* win?" (4.8; italics mine). Spike's verbal inclusion of himself within the community forms the first step in his long journey towards redemption.

Spike's gradual incorporation into the community begins to have an effect on him. When Buffy and Riley are trapped inside a house, Xander vows to go in after them and asks who is going to come with him. Spike immediately volunteers. When they all look at him in shock, he explains (sort of):

> SPIKE: I know I'm not the first choice for heroics . . . and Buffy's tried to kill me more than once. And, I don't fancy a single one of you at all. But . . . (pauses) Actually, all that sounds pretty convincing. (walks away) (4.18)

Exposure to community has softened Spike, making him willing to sacrifice and offer help — at least until his rambling monologue reminds him of his former set of values. Spike's gradual acceptance into the community mirrors his gradual movement towards redemption.

Anya also finds redemption in community. After her renewed vengeance gig goes horribly awry, Anya returns to mortal form once again, only this time with a severe identity crisis. Convinced that she has no identity of her own apart from vengeance, Anya cuts herself off from the community in an attempt to be alone and find herself. While insisting to Buffy that she wants to be alone, Anya exposes the lie of independence — the idea that one can truly thrive without help. She says, "Look, I don't need anyone's help. Or, OK, clearly I do, but I don't want to need anyone's help, so stop helping" (7.6). At the root of independence lies a desire to be self-sufficient, when the truth is that no one can survive this world without help. Anya, however, decides to rejoin the community, and she eventually finds herself in the context of community by learning the value of sacrifice and ultimately giving her life to save another.

Faith is another individual who achieves redemption through community. Her initial step down the road to redemption occurs with the body switch and her subsequent inclusion within Buffy's family and circle of friends. Experiencing true community for the first time, she feels remorse for her actions. Then, with the help of another community (Angel's), she takes responsibility for those actions.

The redemptive power of community derives not simply from an association with others but from the community's ethic. When Faith breaks away from Buffy she joins another community, that of the Mayor, but this new community leads her down a path of immorality. Likewise, Andrew belongs to a community, with Warren and Jonathan, that fosters immaturity and self-delusion. Only when Andrew is separated from that community and becomes joined to Buffy's does he set out on the path of redemption, proving that the ultimate issue is not simply membership in a community but what one's community stands for.

"She alone will stand..."

The aloneness of the Slayer and the temptation to give in to that isolation creates a constant tug-of-war with Buffy's desire for community. It is the struggle between individualism and community, independence and dependence. In "When She Was Bad" (2.1), Buffy's sense of detachment as the Slayer is particularly acute, and it causes her to choose the path of independence with disastrous results. Buffy has a dream that sets up the episode, in which the Master, disguised as

Giles, suddenly attacks her while Xander and Willow look on and do nothing to help. She is on her own, feeling isolated, as though she cannot trust her community.

Buffy's plea for independence manifests frequently throughout this episode as first person language, particularly in her constant insistence that "*I* can handle this."[2] When a vampire plot is discovered, Buffy assures Willow and Xander that it is "Nothing *I* can't handle." After Cordelia is kidnapped, Willow asks Buffy, "What do *we* do?" Buffy replies, "*I* go to the Bronze and save the day." When they protest, she says, "*I* can't look after the three of you guys while *I'm* fighting." Willow and Xander warn Buffy that this could be a trap and a deliberate attempt to separate them, but Buffy insists that "*I* can handle this." While on her way, Angel shows up and offers his assistance, but is also firmly rebuffed. He unsuccessfully, however, warns her of the danger in rejecting community.

> ANGEL: You have to trust someone. You can't do this alone.
> BUFFY: I trust me.
> ANGEL: You're not as strong as you think.

Angel's observation is the thematic key to this episode: Buffy is not as strong as she thinks when she goes it alone because her strength is her community. By rejecting them, she has rejected her power. Buffy ignores all of this advice, claims her independence, and goes off alone. The result is that Xander is beaten and Giles and Willow are kidnapped along with Cordelia. One of the ironic features of *Buffy* is that Slayer tradition dictates that the Slayer fight alone, and yet virtually every time Buffy ignores her community and does just that, the results are disastrous.[3] By means of this recurring motif on *Buffy*, "the choice to fight alone, while heroic, is also presented as wrong."[4] As soon as Buffy witnesses the devastation that her insistence on independence has caused, she tells Xander that "we" need to find them. Taking Xander and Angel with her, Buffy saves the day through the strength of community.

The dichotomy between independence and community finds strongest depiction in season four where it manifests as the growing desire for independence that follows a teenager's graduation from high school and the effect that has on community bonds. Now in college, Buffy is trying to find her own way, and her high school friends are becoming less essential to that quest. Buffy is once again alienating herself from her community, and things are falling apart. Riley tells her that "the way people manage is they don't do it alone. They pull each other through. If you weren't so self-involved, you'd see that" (4.11).

This problem finds resolution in the final three episodes of the season. In the aptly titled episode "The Yoko Factor" (4.20), referring to Yoko Ono's role in splitting up The Beatles, Adam instructs Spike to disrupt Buffy's community, thereby disrupting Buffy's strength.[5] Spike sows discord by playing off each member's insecurities. Giles feels he is no longer needed, Willow feels excluded from Buffy's life due to her relationship with Riley, and Xander feels that the college girls have moved on without him. Spike exacerbates all of these feelings and successfully divides the group. As the dissension reaches its height, Buffy tells Xander, Willow, and Giles, "I guess I'm starting to understand why there's no ancient prophecy about a Chosen One . . . and her friends."

The next episode, "Primeval" (4.21), brings resolution. Adam presents a formidable foe, and Buffy is uncertain if she can defeat him. Alone, she does not possess the strength; so they decide she will not go in alone. Willow suggests an enjoining spell in which they combine their essences into one. Willow's essence provides the Spiritus (Spirit), Xander's the Animus (Heart), Giles' the Sophus (Mind), and Buffy's the Manus (Hand). Just before she destroys Adam, this new Combo-Buffy tells him, "You could never hope to grasp the source of our power." That source is her community. Through the sharing of their strength, Buffy and her friends wield a power that the solitary Adam cannot comprehend.

In the final episode of that season, "Restless" (4.22), Buffy dreams that she cannot find her friends. While searching for them, she ends up in the desert for a time of testing. There she encounters Sineya, the very first Slayer. Sineya insists to Buffy that the Slayer always walks alone. The test for Buffy is whether she will accept that, whether she will choose the temptation to isolate herself from her community. Instead Buffy chooses to isolate herself from Slayer tradition when she tells Sineya, "There's trees in the desert since you moved out. And I don't sleep on a bed of bones. Now give me back my friends!" Buffy chooses dependence over independence, community over isolation. She has come to recognize that the true source of her power is not the mystical strength imbued through the Slayer line, but the strength borne out of friendship and community.

"The Wish" (3.9) reveals the reason for Buffy's success as a

Slayer. The beginning of the episode contrasts Buffy's need for community with Faith's isolation. Buffy tells her friends that she survived her struggle with Angel because she had them to rely on. This immediately sets up an opposition to Faith, of whom Buffy comments, "Too much alone time isn't healthy." Faith's isolation from community will eventually be her downfall, which raises the question of what Buffy's life might have been like had she not had family and friends. Enter Cordelia. Cordelia's wish that Buffy had never come to Sunnydale works as a take-off on "It's A Wonderful Life." We get to envision what life in Sunnydale would be like without Buffy.

The real message in this episode, though, is not what Sunnydale is like without Buffy, but what Buffy is like without her community. As the situation in the alternate Sunnydale degenerates rapidly, the alternate Buffy visits Sunnydale at Giles' request. The effects of her isolation are immediately apparent. This friendless Buffy is pessimistic, deadly serious, and emotionally vacant. Dressed in shabby brown clothing with sparse make-up and her hair in a ponytail, this Buffy is as "cold and dispassionate" as Faith.[6] Announcing that she does not "play well with others," she goes off to fight alone and dies. After Cordelia's wish is nullified and things return to normal, the episode concludes with a shot of Buffy sitting outside the school with Xander and Willow. Dressed in a green top and red skirt, she is joyful and laughing. Her friends have made the difference between success and failure, between an emotionless life consumed by duty and a life of fulfillment in the exercise of duty.

By the time *Buffy the Vampire Slayer* ran its course as a series, Buffy had already survived for an unusual length of time for a Slayer and her community of friends is the reason. Kendra, a Slayer without family and friends, dies easily, but Buffy lives on. Her friends have saved her life on numerous occasions and have even proven stronger than death. Both times Buffy died, her friends were there to bring her back (1.12; 6.1). Although Spike has killed two Slayers in the past, he repeatedly fails to take out Buffy. In his first appearance in "School Hard" (2.3), Spike vows to kill the new Slayer but fails when Buffy's mother whacks him in the head with an axe. Spike sulks away lamenting that a "Slayer with family and friends . . . . wasn't in the brochure." Spike's inability to defeat Buffy is a source of puzzlement to him. While tied to a chair in Giles' apartment, Spike watches Xander wave his fingers in front of the temporarily blind Giles who complains that Xander smells like fruit roll-ups. Spike comments, "This is the crack team that foils my every plan? I am deeply shamed" (4.9). What Spike misses is that it is not their skill or intellect or individual ability that constantly defeats him but their friendship. In community they find the strength that eludes each of them as individuals. As the war with The First progresses, Buffy addresses her community and assures them, "There is only one thing on this earth more powerful than evil, and that's us" (7.10). Her message to them serves as a capsule of *Buffy the Vampire Slayer*'s perspective on community — that victory over evil comes through the power of shared lives.

FAMILY VALUE AND (IM)MORAL PARENTING

Joss Whedon's concern that *Buffy* offers an accurate reflection of emotional reality extends to his treatment of the family. Many religious critics do not want the reality of twenty-first century family life portrayed on television but an ideal of what they conceive family life ought to be. In actuality family life today is becoming increasingly dysfunctional and non-traditional. The three main characters on *Buffy* are a reflection of this trend. Xander comes from a verbally abusive family, Willow's parents are seemingly well meaning but ultimately neglectful, and Buffy lives in a single-parent household.

Buffy stands in a long line of shows with teenage protagonists whose parents are on the periphery of their children's lives. The traditional family structure of mother, father, and 2.3 children is virtually non-existent in Buffy's world. But in the interest of distinguishing between portrayal and perspective, *Buffy*'s perspective on family is far more positive and complex than its surface portrayal indicates. First, family dysfunction is never glorified. Xander and Willow are distinctly unsatisfied by their home lives and the deleterious effects that divorce has had on Buffy are never minimized.

Second, what *Buffy* does do is assert the value of non-traditional relationships in an attempt to expand the boundaries of what counts as family. Whedon says, "I really want to get this message out, that it's not about blood."[7] Blood creates relatives, but not necessarily a family. Part of Whedon's interest in this message comes from his feminist reaction to a traditional patriarchal family structure in which the father rules with an iron hand; however, the overriding emphasis appears to be the desire to demonstrate that a created family can potentially be "more lasting and more loving" than a family of blood relations.[8]

Two metaphorical constructions serve as the dominant vehicle for this message. First, Dawn's story arc, in which she suddenly learns that she does not belong to the Summers' family because she is really a mystical key molded into human form, functions as a metaphor for adoption. The episode where Dawn learns this, "Blood Ties" (5.13), touches on several common situations and emotions that adopted children experience. Dawn's confusion over her identity, her desire to know where she came from, her anger, and her resentment towards Buffy and Joyce for not having told her all represent realistic portrayals of the emotional turmoil surrounding an older child's discovery that he or she is adopted. Even when Dawn cuts herself in order to see if she is made of blood, it is a frightening reminder of the self-mutilation that some teenagers (though not necessarily adopted ones) engage in today as a means of dealing with the chaotic and turbulent experiences of adolescence. The message of "Blood Ties," however, is that family is a concept that transcends birth parentage. Therefore, an adopted child can be just as much a part of the family as a birth child. At the conclusion of the episode, Buffy emphasizes this to Dawn.

BUFFY: Are you okay? Did she hurt you?
DAWN: Why do you care?
BUFFY: Because I love you. You're my sister.
DAWN: No I'm not.
BUFFY: Yes you are . . . . It doesn't matter where you came from, or, or how you got here. You are my sister. There's no way you could annoy me so much if you weren't.

This idea of the created family — that one may belong to a family regardless of having been born into it — runs parallel to the concept of community.

Consequently, the second metaphorical construction that governs *Buffy*'s view of family is that community is family. Joss Whedon states that one part of the show's mission is to show how this band of social outcasts (Willow, Buffy, Xander, and Giles) creates their own family.[9] Giles becomes for them the attentive father that they all lack at home. This leads Buffy, while under a spell that makes her think she is engaged to Spike, to ask Giles to give her away at the wedding because "this day is about family — my real family" (4.9).[10] In the episode titled "Family" (5.6), called by Whedon "as much of a didactic message show as I've ever done,"[11] he asserts the community as family theme through a contrast with an abusive patriarch. The episode opens with Tara telling Willow a story about a lost kitten who is adopted by a nice family. It quickly becomes clear that Tara, who has never felt like she really belongs with Willow's group of friends, is this kitten. When Tara's family comes to town, led by the patriarch of the clan, Mr. Maclay, they assert control over Tara and attempt to take her away. The final confrontation occurs at the magic shop where Buffy, Dawn, Giles, Willow, Xander, Anya, and Tara stand on one side with Mr. Maclay and family on the other. When Mr. Maclay demands that Tara be given up to them, Buffy and her community make it clear that he will have to go through them to get her. Mr. Maclay asserts that "*We* are her blood kin!" and questions what claim they have to Tara. Buffy states simply: "We're family." This concept of community as a non-traditional family continues throughout the series, but finds its ultimate representation in season seven where Buffy's entire community of friends plus a couple dozen potential Slayers all live in her house.

This does not suggest that all created families have value. Drusilla refers to herself, Spike, and Angelus as a "family" (2.14) and the Initiative is called a "family" on at least two occasions (4.15; 4.20), indicating that created families can be corrupt and abusive as well. What makes a family of value on *Buffy* is the ethic that binds it together. A family (whether traditional or created) is a community, and the same ethic that guides a successful community (sacrifice, mutual dependence, loyalty, etc.) is the primary determinant of a successful family.

(Im)Moral Parenting

In line with its status as a horror show, *Buffy* addresses the morality of parenting not by presenting positive parental role models, but by presenting horrific ones. Parents bear a tremendous responsibility for the lives of their children and when they fail in that responsibility, either through neglect, immoral action, or well-intentioned mistakes, it can be a frightening thing. This focus on parental failure serves to cast the opposing moral ideal of parenting into greater relief.

"Witch" (1.3) offers a contrast of two mothers. While trying out for the cheerleading team, Buffy meets a fellow contender named Amy. Buffy is immediately jealous of Amy's relationship with her mother when she learns that Amy's mother trains with her three hours a day. Joyce Summers by contrast has been too busy with work to spend time with Buffy. Further straining their relationship is Buffy's sense that she has disappointed her mother as a result of getting into trouble at her old school, thus forcing them to move to Sunnydale.

The paths that these two mothers take with respect to their daughters differ widely. Refusing to accept that her daughter has different interests than she, Amy's mother takes her daughter's life hostage by switching bodies with her. In Amy's body, she tries to reclaim the high school glory she had as a cheerleader, a metaphor for parents who try to re-live their youth through their children, thus robbing them of their childhood. Amy's mother uses her magic to harm some of the cheerleaders, freeing a spot on the team for herself. The obvious influence for this episode is the incident of the Texas mother who attempted murder in order to secure her daughter's cheerleading future. That was an extreme example, but it illustrates the damage that parents can do when they refuse to accept their children as they are. The self-obsession of Amy's mother, however, ultimately highlights the more acceptable approach of Joyce Summers. Both mothers have expectations of their children and both have been disappointed that those expectations were not met, yet Joyce Summers concludes that even though she cannot understand Buffy and does not always agree with her choices, she will always accept and love her regardless.

The episode "Ted" (2.11) illustrates two different kinds of "sins" that parents commit. Buffy's single mother begins to date a seemingly perfect guy, Ted Buchanan, who turns out to be anything but that. Some single parents can be so desperate to remarry in order to meet their own needs that they selfishly ignore moral failings in the prospective spouse, often with tragic results. When Angel says in this episode that "Loneliness is about the scariest thing there is," he is ultimately proven wrong. Being with the wrong person can be far more terrifying.

Ted himself represents a second moral failing of parents. A "family values" type of guy, Ted looks like the perfect father. Generous with compliments and wielding a sunny disposition, Ted charms almost everyone he meets. There is no doubt that Ted is a commentary on the dark side of many religious households. He is a moralistic individual who leads the family in prayer before the evening meal. Beneath this veneer of perfection, however, lies a frightening reality. One of the writers of this episode, David Greenwalt, describes Ted this way:

The soft and sweet side of him is what is so scary; that *other* people don't see that this is a monster. There are a million families in America like that, where Mom and Dad look so good on the outside and go to church on Sunday, but you get inside that house and it's . . . terrifying, because Dad is an abusive totalitarian.[12]

To criticize this kind of presentation as damaging to Christianity's reputation would be unfortunate, for what is in fact most damaging to Christianity's reputation are the very individuals like Ted who mistake an appearance of piety for the real thing. When a church fails to acknowledge and address the moral failings of its members, it succeeds only at propagating them. The fact is that too many Christian husbands fail to adhere to the biblical mandate to love, cherish, respect and mutually submit to their wives. Instead, they distort certain biblical teachings that describe the husband as head of the household by turning them into a justification for the very kind of abusive totalitarianism that Ted represents.

If "Ted" serves as a charge against parental immorality on the right side of the ideological spectrum, then "The Dark Age" (2.8) and "Band Candy" (3.6) offer a charge against the left. Cynthia Bowers argues that these episodes explore "aging Boomers' parenting incompetence and its relationship to drug abuse."[13] In "The Dark Age," Giles' past experimentation with demonic possession by the demon Eyghon, which Bowers reads as a metaphor for LSD, serves as a demonization of "the selfishness, self-absorption, and drugs and sexual experimentation often associated with the 1960's psychedelic youth culture."[14] The participants in this past transgression, which include Ethan Rayne, bear on their bodies the mark of their sins — a tattoo that is connected to Eyghon. When Ethan burns his own tattoo off with acid and then gives Buffy the same tattoo, it represents the attempt "to symbolically transfer the consequences of his own generation's irresponsibilities onto hers."[15] Likewise, in "Band Candy" (a sly reference to cocaine, a.k.a. "nose candy"), the parents of Sunnydale all become addicted to chocolate candy bars that have been magically spiked. These candy bars cause the adults to act in an increasingly immature manner, while the teenagers of Sunnydale are left unaffected. As Bowers notes, in each of these episodes, the teenagers suffer for their parent's irresponsibility: Buffy has to pay for the removal of her tattoo and for damage to her mother's car and they are forced to clean up vandalism at the school (caused by adults).[16] The sins of the parents have been visited upon the children. The source of hope in "Band Candy" comes not from the adult generation, but from the teenagers. The purpose for the spiked candy is to put the adults of Sunnydale out of commission so that a gang of vampires can steal all of the infants from the hospital. That Buffy and her friends race to save the next generation demonstrates that the end to this vicious cycle can only come when the children refuse to pass on the consequences of irresponsibility they inherited from their parents.

Another form of immoral parenting on *Buffy* is the self-absorption that results in a parent's neglect of their child's emotional needs. Some parents equate the providing of physical comforts to their children with successful care. As a society, we have bought into the lie that wealth and privilege are a buffer against self-destructive behavior. Why is it that people were so surprised when the perpetrators of the massacre at Columbine high school turned out to be from a well-to-do family? It is a matter of confusing the satisfaction of physical needs with the satisfaction of emotional needs.

Wrapped up in work or their own personal pursuits, some parents fail to notice the signs of their child in pain. In season six, Buffy, who acts as surrogate mother to Dawn, becomes so engrossed in her own problems that she shirks her responsibility to Dawn, acting as though providing her with food, shelter, and an education is a viable substitute for her own presence. Buffy's recognition of this comes only when Halfrck, a vengeance demon, curses Buffy and her friends for their neglect of Dawn (6.14). Similarly, in "Gingerbread" (3.11), Willow's mother, who once co-authored a paper on "the rise of mysticism among adolescents," completely fails to notice her own daughter's dabbling in the mystic arts which will ultimately become a deadly addiction. The analogy to clueless parents whose children experiment with drugs could not be clearer.

One further example of how *Buffy* addresses parenting problems is the unconventional father-daughter type of relationship between Giles and Buffy and the mother-daughter type of relationship between Buffy and Dawn. Many parents wrestle with the dilemma of how to protect their children from a harsh world, while allowing them to grow and learn independence. Whether out of a selfish desire to hold onto their children longer or a sincere desire to protect them, parents can stifle their children's emotional development.

Rupert Giles embodies this struggle. With Buffy's graduation from high school and foray into college life, Giles recognizes that she requires his guidance as her Watcher (metaphor for parent?) less and less, and he begins to distance himself to give her room to grow. Following the death of her mother, though, Buffy turns to Giles for guidance and begins to rely heavily on him even as she steps more firmly into the adult world. She looks to him to resolve her problems and make life decisions for her. After Giles resolves a financial crisis for her, Buffy tells him how safe it makes her feel to know "you're always gonna be here" (6.5). Yet that is the very difficulty parents face. Knowing that they will not always be there, they have a moral responsibility to make sure their children can stand on their own. So recognizing that he has been standing in the way of her becoming an adult, Giles returns to England leaving Buffy on her own. It is telling that Buffy's fall occurs shortly after Giles leaves.[17] The paradox of letting a child walk on their own is that they may fall down and hurt themselves, but only by letting them fall down do they truly learn to walk.

Buffy, however, has failed to learn this lesson in the context of her own parental role towards Dawn. As a "parent," Buffy is overprotective and smothering, refusing to let Dawn walk alone. Dawn's inability to come out from under Buffy's protective blanket is a source of constant frustration to her. This is a very contemporary problem. By constantly broadcasting reports of child kidnappings, snipers, anthrax outbreaks, pedophilia, and even shark attacks, the media reinforces the message to parents that their children are not safe. The result is that good parenting today is being defined as "protecting children from the experience of life." [18]

Both of Buffy's problems, her own struggle with independence and her smothering of Dawn, find resolution in the sixth season-ender "Grave" (6.22). Earlier in this chapter, I extolled the virtue of mutual dependence in the context of community and family. That is not to minimize the importance of one's personal independence in terms of growth towards adulthood. Yet in a family or community, the independence that comes with adulthood is not separate from dependence upon one another. When Giles returns in this episode, he wonders if maybe he was premature in leaving Buffy.

GILES: I should never have abandoned you.
BUFFY: No. Giles, you were right about everything. It is time I was an adult.
GILES: Sometimes the most adult thing you can do is ask for help

when you need it.
BUFFY: Now you tell me.

Adult independence is not about going it alone, but about knowing when and how to seek help.

Just as Buffy learns that independence from a parental figure does not equal isolation, she also must learn to allow Dawn the freedom to fall. The latter epiphany comes when Buffy and Dawn are trapped and surrounded by monsters. Buffy's first instinct is to protect Dawn, but realizing that there is no way she can win by herself, she asks Dawn for help. When Buffy later tells Dawn, "I got it so wrong. I don't want to protect you from the world. I want to show it to you," she encapsulates a parent's responsibility for the growth of their child. The next season opens with Buffy and Dawn in a cemetery as the same Buffy who formerly shielded Dawn from any sign of danger, now teaches her how to defend herself against vampires. She even lets Dawn get bitten (briefly) because sometimes letting a child get hurt can be the only way to protect them from the things that bite in this world.

The next day Dawn begins her first day at the new Sunnydale high school, and Buffy, like many parents, is terrified of the things Dawn might face without her protection. But Dawn demonstrates how a child's need for independence does not negate the parent-child bond when she briskly walks away from Buffy, who is listing for her all the things to watch out for, and yells back, "I love you. Go away!"

By way of clarification, I must add here one final note. The preceding description of how parental actions can create problems for children should not be taken as an argument against the moral culpability of children for the decisions they make. One message that resonates clearly throughout *Buffy* is that all individuals bear ultimate responsibility for their actions, even though a variety of factors may influence those actions. In this respect, *Buffy* does not reflect the American cultural trend of shifting blame and responsibility to others, whether parents or society. When Faith, who grew up without a father and with an alcoholic mother, takes the path of evil, Willow refuses to let her lay the responsibility for that choice anywhere but on herself. She tells Faith:

> WILLOW: You know, it didn't have to be this way. But you made your choice. I know you had a tough life. I know that some people think you had a lot of bad breaks. Well, boo hoo!

Poor you. You know, you had a lot more in your life than some people (3.19).

Willow's message to Faith clearly enunciates the point that as tragic as a bad childhood may be, it does not excuse one for becoming a bad adult.

Chapter 11

The End as Moral Guidepost

After hearing tales of Buffy's exploits, Riley Finn tells her that he finds himself "needing to know the plural of 'apocalypse'" (4.12). During the run of the series, Buffy faces more apocalypses than birthdays. Even Buffy herself loses count, once asking Giles, "This is how many apocalypses for us now?" (5.22). The terror inherent in apocalyptic threats to end the world is significantly dampened when those threats are more common than political elections. Why then are there so many apocalypses on *Buffy*, and what is their function? Are they simply narrative devices for heightening suspense and providing the show's protagonists a challenging hurdle to overcome? I contend that they are much more than this. They function as a moral guidepost in that they bring clarity to life and thereby inform moral decisions. In order to establish my case, I must first define some terms and set the ideological context out of which my analysis unfolds.

JUDEO-CHRISTIAN ESCHATOLOGY

"Eschatology" is the study of endings. How something ends, whether it be a piece of music, a novel, or a life, is often as significant (if not more) as how it began. An ending may bring closure to an action or idea or effect a transition to a new one. The most common reference point of eschatology, however, is the end of the world.

In this essay, I examine *Buffy the Vampire Slayer* from the perspective of Judeo-Christian apocalyptic thought, but not because I believe that to be the direct source of *Buffy*'s eschatology. Many of the eschatological ideas in *Buffy* are universal, even if they are given specific renderings in different religious and philosophical traditions. However, all modern fantasy from Tolkien on owes a debt to Judeo-Christian apocalyptic, and *Buffy* is no exception. The show's frequent use of the terms "Armageddon" and "apocalypse" acknowledges this debt. So the Judeo-Christian apocalyptic tradition serves as the lens through which I read *Buffy*'s eschatology, both because of the historical connection between the fantasy genre and apocalyptic and because this is the tradition that has most extensively shaped my own eschatological perspective.

Speculation on the end of the world actually functions as a comment on the present state of the world. In contemporary parlance, the term "apocalypse" refers to a threat of imminent world destruction. Originally, though, the term meant something very different. "Apocalypse" has entered our vocabulary by way of the New Testament book of Revelation where it is used only one time. In Revelation 1:1 "apocalypse" simply means "a revelation" or "a revealing." An apocalypse, in this sense, is an unveiling of spiritual truth.

P. D. Hanson draws an important distinction between the terms "apocalypse" and "apocalyptic eschatology."[1] Due to its usage in Revelation, "apocalypse" comes to represent a Judeo-Christian literary genre where the central focus is the unveiling of spiritual truth through divine intermediaries, heavenly journeys, and transcendent revelations. Because Jewish and Christian apocalypses, particularly Revelation, deal so heavily in end-time speculation, the term "apocalypse" later developed in reference to that specific event. By contrast, "apocalyptic eschatology" is a worldview. It is a means of conceptualizing reality. It is a way of talking about life. Under the purview of apocalyptic eschatology, end-of-the-world speculation functions to organize experience. When Hebrew or Christian prophets talk about the future, it is because they are really interested in the present. Looking ahead to the end offers a perspective on the now that cannot be gained any other way.

It would be wrong to assume, however, that apocalyptic eschatology concerns itself only with the end of the world. Other types of cataclysmic endings — of a life, for instance — can be decidedly apocalyptic. After all, what is an apocalypse if not death writ large? Death is a great illuminator of life. That so many significant conversations about life on *Buffy* take place in a cemetery highlights the function of death as a source of enlightenment. In "Conversations With Dead People" (7.7), Buffy encounters Holden Webster, a former high school classmate now turned vampire, in a graveyard. Post-poning their inevitable duel to the death, Buffy and Holden reminisce about old times. Holden, who majored in psychology in college, uses the opportunity to psychoanalyze Buffy, offering her counseling on subjects ranging from her work as the Slayer to her relationships. In a take on the classic psychologist's pose, we see Buffy laying down on a stone sarcophagus as Holden sits on a nearby tombstone and encourages her to open up by assuring her that "I'm here to kill you, not to judge you." Although initially reluctant to receive "emotional therapy from the evil dead," Buffy experiences an epiphany about her life through this encounter. Buffy's receiving of counseling from a dead psychologist in a graveyard is a clear representation of the power of death to give meaning and clarity to life.

LIVING ESCHATOLOGICALLY

Living eschatologically means living one's life with an eye towards its end. This is not the doom-and-gloom mentality that comes from obsession with death and dying. A doom-and-gloom mentality robs life of its joy, whereas eschatological living is a means of embracing the joy of life. Awareness that an end is coming casts the present into clearer focus. Talk with a cancer survivor and he or she will typically articulate a renewed appreciation for life because he or she has tasted the reality of death. In this section, I analyze *Buffy*'s eschatological landscape by focusing on endings that create an appreciation for life, a prioritization of values, and a clarification of moral action. These endings include death, world-ending apocalypses, and metaphorical apocalypses.

Appreciation

A Slayer embodies eschatological living. As a rule, Slayers do not live long and this colors their view of life. Buffy makes sure to impress this point upon potential Slayers by informing them that, "Death is what a Slayer breathes, what a Slayer dreams about when she sleeps. Death is what a Slayer lives" (7.12). This constant awareness of death does not mean that Buffy ignores the value of life. She says, "I realize that every Slayer comes with an expiration mark on the package. But I want mine to be a long time from now. Like a Cheeto" (5.7).

What this acknowledgment of death does bring is a greater appreciation for life and a desire to live it to the fullest. Buffy's dating advice to Willow to "Seize the moment because tomorrow you might be dead" (1.1) represents a philosophical outlook on life whereby the future informs present choices. Despite facing death on an almost daily basis and the ever-present prospect of the end of the world, these kids maintain an active social life. Neither death, nor apocalypse, nor rain of toads keeps them from celebrating birthdays (2.13), going out on dates (7.14), or attending the Prom (3.20). If anything, they make the celebration of life more necessary. In "Never Kill A Boy On the First Date" (1.5), Giles warns Buffy of impending doom just when she is about to go on a first date with Owen. Refusing to let a little thing like the end of the world get in the way of her social life, she holds up her beeper and tells Giles, "If the Apocalypse comes, beep me" (1.5).

The renewed appreciation of life in the face of death affects other characters as well. Spike joins up with Buffy to fight Angel precisely because the very real possibility that the world might end sparks a confession of his fondness for humans ("Happy Meals with legs"), dog racing, and Leicester Square (2.22). No character, however, exemplifies the life evaluation that eschatology can provoke better than Anya. After 1100 years of immortality, the newly mortal Anya's rediscovery of what it means to be human serves as a vehicle for commenting on the universal struggle of humanity. Her experiences with death thus cause her to question the meaning of life.

In the episode "The Body" (5.16), Buffy's mother, Joyce, dies unexpectedly from complications following brain surgery. It is a profound moment on the show as it marks the first time that a person dies of natural causes. The entire episode is a study on death inspired by the death of Joss Whedon's own mother. Whedon's goal was not to offer any existential or religious comment on the meaning of death, but simply to portray realistically the "black ashes in your mouth numbness of death"[2] and how the event of death can reduce a loved one to a body. Questions about the afterlife and the ultimate destination of the dead are left deliberately open. The final scene takes place in the morgue as Dawn looks upon her mother's dead body. Buffy assures her that this body is no longer their mother because their mother is gone. Dawn's reply is: "Where'd she go?" As these words mark the final words of the episode, the question is left to hang unanswered.

Anya is so thoroughly literal-minded and devoid of nuanced thinking that her observations in light of death form an exaggerated portrait of our own insecurities. After sustaining a mild injury to her shoulder, Anya feels the dark hand of death descending upon her. Her response is to embrace life . . . and quickly.

> ANYA: When do we get a car?
> XANDER: A car?
> ANYA: And a boat. No, wait. I-I don't mean a boat. I mean a puppy. Or a child. I have a list somewhere.
> XANDER: What are you talking about?
> ANYA: Just . . . we have to get going. I don't have time just to let these things happen.
> XANDER: There's no hurry.
> ANYA: Yes there is. There's a hurry, Xander. I'm dying . . . I may have as few as fifty years left. (5.3)

Anya's mortal panic represents the fear of a wasted life that many experience when contemplating death. Time, however, forces the panic to give way to a more sustained eschatological outlook as also represented by Anya, who announces after the healing of her shoulder, "I'm feeling better. And I anticipate many years before my death. Excepting disease or airbag failure" (5.3).

Living eschatologically means letting the prospect of death enrich life. An awareness of the end counters the mental sedation that comes from day to day living and creates an appreciation for the joys of life. In the words of Buffy following the averting of an apocalypse: "We saved the world. I say we party" (1.12).

Prioritization

Living eschatologically is not only about gaining a greater appreciation for life, but also about learning what is most important in life. Cordelia's involvement with Buffy teaches her something about priorities. When she enters the library and sees Buffy crying, Cordelia announces: "Is the world ending? I have to research a paper on Bosnia for tomorrow, but if the world's ending, I'm not gonna bother." Of course, ever the pragmatist, Cordelia tacks on an addendum, telling Giles, "But if the world doesn't end, I'm gonna need a note" (3.12). The experience of death and the threat of world-ending destruction relegates most aspects of life (like research papers) to insignificance and causes the more important values, such as relationships with others and service to humanity, to come into focus. The death of Buffy's mother taught her never to put things off and to spend more time with loved ones (4.3; 5.18). It likewise encouraged Xander and Willow to ascribe more value to time spent with family, although in Xander's case he prefers to spend more time with Willow's family (5.17). Xander proposes to Anya in the midst of an apocalypse, not because he fears the world will end, but because he believes it will not. The mere act of facing the possible end causes him to prioritize their relationship (6.3). Personal problems also get minimized in light of the end as Buffy and Angel work together to stop the Mayor's ascension despite a current strain on their relationship (3.21). Willow even effects a kind of reconciliation between the always-bickering Xander and Spike by telling them that if they insist on fighting, "do it after the world ends, okay?" (5.21). Principal Wood sums it up well when he says, "There's nothing like the end of the world to bring people together" (7.15).

In "Help" (7.4), eschatology enlightens Buffy on the importance of service. This episode revolves less around Buffy the Vampire Slayer and more around Buffy the High School Counselor. Buffy took a counseling job at Sunnydale High out of a desire to help students. One of these students, Cassie Newton, wanders into Buffy's office and prophetically announces that she will die on Friday. Cassie's foreknowledge of her own demise merely presents a challenge to Buffy, who is accustomed to fighting and winning against impossible odds. Buffy refuses to accept the inevitable and vows to keep Cassie alive. One of the hardest lessons Buffy has had to learn, though, is that death is an enemy she cannot fight. Twice Buffy saves Cassie's life from external dangers only to have Cassie drop dead from heart failure.

The title of this episode, "Help," contrasts with the helplessness that Buffy feels at her inability to save Cassie. Despite all her power and experience, she could not save this girl. Buffy asks, "What do you do when you know that? When you know that maybe you can't help?" The scene then immediately cuts to the final shot of the episode, which is Buffy back at work the next day sitting at her desk and going through student files. The death of Cassie gave her the answer to her own question. Even when you know that you cannot help everyone, you never stop trying to help those you can.

Clarification

Eschatology clarifies moral decision-making. The renewed appreciation for life and prioritization of values that comes with living eschatologically feeds into the moral choices made. When Buffy is grounded and forbidden to leave the house, she has to make a choice between two right things: obeying her mother or saving the world. This is not easy ethics, but the looming end of the world clarifies her choice (1.2). Willow best illustrates the principle when, following a brush with death, she has an epiphany about her purpose in life.

> WILLOW: The other night, you know, being captured and all, facing off with Faith. Things just, kind of, got clear. I mean, you've been fighting evil here for three years, and I've helped some, and now we're supposed to decide what we want to do with our lives. And I just realized that that's what I want to do. Fight evil, help people. I mean, I-I think it's worth doing. And I don't think you do it because you have to. It's a good fight, Buffy, and I want in (3.19).

Making moral decisions in light of the end is not a guarantee those decisions will be the correct ones. Eschatology does not determine right or wrong, although it can inform moral decisions by revealing what is at stake. What it does is force people to make a deliberate choice, and in that process of choosing they come to grips with what they value most. On *Buffy*, characters sometimes make wrong choices in light of the end. Buffy's friend Ford is terminally ill with a brain tumor. Overwhelmed with the unfairness of his fate, Ford seeks self-preservation at all costs, even to the point of sacrificing the lives of Buffy and others so he can become immortal. When he tries to justify his inequity towards others on the basis that the inequity perpetrated on him has left him without a choice, Buffy corrects him: "You have a choice. You don't have a good choice, but you have a choice. You're opting for mass murder here and nothing you say is gonna make that okay" (2.7). Like Ford, Ben faces his own form of terminal illness — Glory. If she succeeds at activating the Key and returning to her dimension, he will cease to exist. Facing extinction compels him to betray Dawn in an attempt to save himself (5.21).

Ford and Ben illustrate another aspect of the clarifying function of eschatology on *Buffy*. If eschatology forces a choice between good and evil, then on what basis do these characters choose one over the other? If the moral choices made in light of the end are the result of a prioritizing of values, then what is the central value on *Buffy* that marks the dividing line between a right and wrong choice? The moral decision making on *Buffy* is neither the product of adherence to a specific set of religious doctrines nor of a detailed conception of heaven and hell whereby moral choices occur in the context of fear of eternal punishment or hope for eternal reward. Rather, what distinguishes moral choices on *Buffy* is the value placed upon human life. An immoral choice is one that is self-centered with no regard for others. Both Ford and Ben valued their own self-preservation over salvation for others. A moral choice is one that sacrifices self-desire for service to others.

When Buffy first learns of the prophecy that she will die at the hands of the Master, she makes the same choice as Ford and Ben and opts for self-preservation. In her own words, this choice was not "the right thing" (2.4). What changes her "wrong" decision of fleeing to the "right" decision of dying is the realization that others will suffer if she takes the selfish path (1.12). Likewise when facing an apocalypse, Buffy chose to sacrifice Angel, the man whom she loved, in order to save the world (2.22), and she says that she did this because she knew "what was right" (5.22).

Anya, who operates on a moral learning curve, also demonstrates the principle that the extent to which one values human life affects moral decisions. In "Graduation Day, Part One" (3.21), Anya shows contempt for the lives of others when she flees town before the Mayor's ascension. Xander, who has "friends on the line," stays to fight even though he believes he will die. The next time Anya faces an apocalypse, however, she chooses to stay. Acknowledging that "usually when there's an apocalypse, I skedaddle," Anya now stays because of her love for Xander. She has made a tremendous leap in her valuation of human life, although it has only taken her so far. She stays out of worry for Xander's welfare, but confesses to having guilt that "I'm not more worried about everyone else" (5.22). With the final apocalyptic battle of season seven about to break, Anya chooses to stay once again, only this time her decision is based not on romantic love but on a genuine appreciation for human life. She confesses her view of humanity to Andrew.

ANYA: They're incapable of thinking about what they want beyond

the moment. They kill each other, which is clearly insane. And yet, here's the thing. When it's something that really matters, they fight. I mean, they're lame morons for fighting, but they do. They never . . . never quit. So I guess I will keep fighting too.
ANDREW (sighs): That was kind of beautiful. (Anya nods) You . . . you love humans.
ANYA (indignant): I do not.
ANDREW: Yes, you do. You loooove them. (7.21)

The Anya of season three who runs away because she will not be bothered with concern for human life has learned its value, so the Anya of season seven stays and sacrifices her own life to save Andrew's (7.22). Both instances where she confesses her growing appreciation for human life occur in full view of an approaching apocalypse. The end clarifies her values.

The apocalyptic threat of season seven is particularly instructive due to its magnitude. As Anya notes, "Buffy seems to think that this apocalypse is going to actually be, you know, apocalyptic" (7.16). Season seven of *Buffy* sets eschatology in the context of warfare. The book of Revelation offers a helpful perspective on this as it also combines eschatology with warfare imagery. Because the worldview of apocalyptic eschatology is predominantly dualistic, it is attracted to warfare imagery, which divides peoples into enemies and allies. In Revelation, this imagery functions to clarify the options before its audience. The author of Revelation insists to his audience that there is a war going on between God and Satan, and they are part of that war. The options are clear: you can be a part of God's army or Satan's army. While warfare imagery clarifies the options, eschatology forces the choice. The author of Revelation symbolically describes the end for his audience as a means of getting them to make a choice in the present. That choice is based upon foreknowledge of God's plan. By opening up the future to them, the author reveals what will ultimately happen to those who fight on God's side and to those who fight on Satan's. The determination of allegiance resides with the audience, but eschatology has clarified the implications of that choice.

Warfare imagery and language permeate season seven of *Buffy* and clarify the choice set before the citizens of Sunnydale. That choice is set in dualistic terms. Xander goes on a disastrous first date with a girl named Lissa who ties him up and intends to sacrifice him in order to open the hellmouth. She explains her reason to him this way: "The end is coming. The final fight, and everyone is hearing the drumbeat. It's telling us to pick our partners, align ourselves with the good or the evil" (7.14). The factor that determines the choice of partner in this final apocalyptic battle is the value of human life. One side fights for the preservation of human life and the other for its extinction. Buffy has made her choice. She has declared war on evil, the First Evil that is. As Lissa correctly points out, the necessity of making a choice between good or evil becomes clear when "the end is coming." When the end is coming, the luxury of debating shades of gray ceases and the now becomes the moment of moral decision making.

THE AFTERLIFE AND "AFTER LIFE"

In the preceding section I explored the role of eschatology in moral decision making and in the appreciation of life. In this section, I examine eschatology from a different angle; that is, how an eschatological experience of the spiritual affects the interpretation of the physical. Buffy's experience of heaven following her death at the end of season five and her subsequent return to mortal life at the beginning of season six establishes a contrast between spiritual and physical reality.

Buffy's description of the afterlife comes in an episode titled "After Life" (6.3). The depiction or description of heaven in television and film is nothing new, but most such attempts are very superficial. Heaven is a nondescript white light, a celestial family reunion, or a Norman Rockwell-like vision of harps, clouds, and St. Peter at the gate. With few exceptions, these depictions tend to be theologically vacant and sentimental to a fault. By contrast, *Buffy the Vampire Slayer* offers a description of heaven that, while not flawless, reveals a theological depth rarely witnessed in televised conceptions of heaven.

While everyone thinks that Buffy's post-resurrection depression is due to time spent in hell, Buffy confesses the truth to Spike.

> BUFFY: I was happy. Wherever I . . . was . . . I was happy. At peace.
> I knew that everyone I cared about was all right. I knew it.
> Time . . . didn't mean anything . . . nothing had form . . .
> but I was still me, you know? And I was warm . . . and I
> was loved . . . and I was finished. Complete. I don't

> understand about theology or dimensions, or . . . any of it, really . . . but I think I was in heaven.

This short description of "heaven" is not without problems from a theological standpoint. As with the rest of *Buffy*'s cosmology, God's presence in this heaven is ambiguous at best. The attempt to present a heaven that is palatable across denominational and religious lines has relegated God to the background. Whereas the biblical depiction of heaven is God-centered, *Buffy*'s depiction is self-centered, reflecting American cultural values. It is primarily about *her* peace and happiness. Despite these shortcomings, however, this is a quantum leap forward for media descriptions of heaven. It avoids the sappy and superficial stereotypes in favor of emphasis on the completion of one's purpose, the peace of a life fulfilled, and immersion in true love. With specific reference to *Buffy the Vampire Slayer*, this scene transcends the existential secularism that often characterizes the show by asserting a spiritual reward for a life well lived.

The focus of this scene, however, is less on the nature of heaven than on how an experience of heaven affects one's view of earthly life. In the early Judeo-Christian apocalyptic worldview, the unveiling of spiritual reality serves as a means for transforming how one understands the world. Spiritual reality does more than just comment on the physical world; it gets us to see the world through different eyes. Buffy continues her explanation to Spike by describing how her experience of heaven has altered her perception of this world.

> BUFFY: I was in heaven. And now I'm not. I was torn out of there. Pulled out . . . by my friends. Everything here is . . . hard, and bright, and violent. Everything I feel, everything I touch . . . this is hell. Just getting through the next moment, and the one after that . . . knowing what I've lost.

As physical beings, our interpretive matrix for this world is thoroughly colored by our physical experiences. One of the reasons people fear death is because this world is familiar and therefore comfortable, while death is all about uncertainty. An eschatological perspective that includes a conception of heaven, however, suggests that this world cannot begin to compare to the glory to come. That kind of spiritual awakening recasts this world in new terms. Buffy's statement that this world is hell is a metaphorical comment based upon viewing physical reality through new eyes.

Many of the personal difficulties that Buffy encounters in season six are a result of her inability to readjust to life. Loss of interest in the world is a common side effect of eschatological experiences, including existential encounters with death, near-death experiences, and even the "return to life" that forms part of the mythological hero's journey.[3] The eschatological metaphors of death and rebirth that frame the season provide the framework for Buffy's eventual readjustment to life. At the opening of season six, Buffy is literally resurrected out of her grave (6.1-2). Her body is resurrected, but not her spirit. Although physically alive, Buffy shuffles through season six emotionally and spiritually dead. In the final episode of season six titled "Grave" (6.22), Buffy experiences a spiritual and emotional resurrection from her existential grave. While trying to stop Willow's rampage, Buffy and Dawn are in a cemetery and fall into a large hole in the ground. Willow then creates monsters out of rock and earth to attack Buffy. Buffy is in a makeshift grave, surrounded by coffins, and attacked by the earth out of which she came. In the midst of all these symbols of death, Buffy experiences a revelation about life. Having regained her desire to live, she crawls up out of the grave, both literal and metaphorical, that confines her.

METAPHORICAL APOCALYPSES

Another way in which eschatology creates insight into life is through the use of apocalyptic language as a metaphor for the travails of life. Who hasn't felt, for instance, that a break-up with a boyfriend or girlfriend is the end of the world?

> BUFFY: These things happen. People break up and they move on . . .
> for a while it feels like the end of the world, you know, but
> . . . big picture . . .
> GILES: Not so huge.
> BUFFY: Not so huge? I just said it feels like the end of the world,
> don't you listen? (5.11)

Apocalypses on *Buffy* often represent personal crises in life. The real problems teenagers face are blown up to apocalyptic proportions as a way of illustrating their emotional impact. While grounded, Buffy tells her mother how important it is that she be allowed to leave the house.

Joyce replies, "I know. If you don't go out, it'll be the end of the world. Everything is life or death when you're a sixteen year old girl" (1.2). The irony is that in Buffy's case, it may very well be the end of the world if she cannot leave. That emotional dilemma Buffy finds herself in reflects teenage reality where every decision feels like it has ultimate consequences.

In the episode "Doomed" (4.11), the end of the world functions as a metaphor for how people imagine things as worse than they really are. An earthquake convinces Buffy that the end is coming. Although Giles thinks she is overreacting, Buffy becomes so obsessed with the prospect of impending doom that she is unable to enjoy life. Her doom and gloom mentality becomes a self-fulfilling prophecy. Of course, this being *Buffy the Vampire Slayer*, her fear turns out to have substance.

> GILES: It's the end of the world.
> XANDER, WILLOW: Again?
> GILES: It's uh, the earthquake — that symbol — yes.
> BUFFY: I told you. I-I said 'end of the world' and you're like 'poo poo, southern California, poo poo!'
> GILES: I'm so very sorry. My contrition completely dwarfs the impending apocalypse.
> WILLOW: No. It can't be. We've done this already.
> GILES: It's the end of the world, everyone dies. It's rather important really.

Buffy eventually overcomes this apocalyptic crisis, learning in the process that her fear of the end of the world was more powerful than the real thing and that she allowed it to rob her of the joy of living. The human tendency to exaggerate normal crises to apocalyptic proportions is a hindrance to authentic living. When every ache becomes cancer and a huge car repair bill marks the end of financial stability, eschatological thinking gets distorted into a justification for despair. "Doomed" concludes with a scene in which Riley adopts the doom and gloom mentality. When he fails to hide his secret identity as government agent from Buffy's friends, he panics and says, "I'm finished. It's the end of the world." Buffy just smiles, kisses him, and says, "No, it's not." By facing the end of the world, Buffy has learned that eschatology is about allowing the end to put daily crises into proper perspective.

The apocalypses that mark the end of virtually every season of

Buffy metaphorically mark personal endings as well. Buffy's season one battle against the Master represents the end of her childhood illusions of immortality.[4] Buffy is a teenager whose illusion of invincibility is shattered when she truly faces her own mortality for the first time. Her apocalyptic battle with Angel at the end of season two in which she "kills" him to save the world characterizes both the end of their relationship and the culmination of a lesson reiterated throughout the season that moral decisions are not always easy. Season three concludes with an apocalypse on graduation day. The blowing up of the high school is a metaphor for both the end of their high school careers and the end of adolescence. Oz highlights this connection as he and the gang survey the ruins of the high school. He announces: "Guys, take a moment to deal with this. We survived." When they comment on the fierceness of the battle with the Mayor, he corrects them: "Not the battle . . . high school" (3.22).

It is debatable whether the final battle with Adam in season four counts as an apocalypse as such, but it does mark the end of social division between Buffy and her friends. Their illusions of adult independence give way to the realization of how much they need each other. Buffy's climactic battle with Glory in season five brings to fruition her quest to understand her purpose and destiny, culminating in a noble self-sacrifice. Season six's apocalypse signals the end of Buffy and Willow's immaturity and their full advancement into adulthood as they overcome their respective descents into darkness and addiction in favor of accountability and dependence within community. Finally, Buffy's sharing of her power with all potential Slayers during the final apocalypse of the series marks the end of her isolation as the Chosen One.

This chapter demonstrates that the apocalypses on *Buffy the Vampire Slayer* are far more than a device for ratcheting up narrative tension. They are a method for commenting upon life. *Buffy*'s eschatological program exposes life and its emotional struggles to the clarifying effects that come from conceiving of the present in light of the end. By giving greater clarity to life, eschatology thus allows for a more informed method of moral decision making.

Chapter 12

Morals and Consequences

The treatment of moral topics on *Buffy* is complex, reflecting the moral complexity of life. After Anya tricks Willow into helping her with an illicit magic spell, Willow gives Anya a confusing moral lecture: "Look, magic is dangerous, Anya. It's, it's not to be toyed with. Now if you'll excuse me, I have someone else's homework to do" (3.16). Willow's sermonette is counterproductive because of the inconsistency between her moral message to Anya and her own action. Likewise, the incoherence of *Buffy*'s narrative derives from the show's seeming glorification of immorality through its presentation of questionable actions, all the while attempting a moral message through those very same actions. This chapter explores some of the ways in which that happens. The charge of glorifying immorality that has been laid against *Buffy* is partly the result of a misunderstanding of the show's broader moral vision and its methods of moral reasoning. In this chapter I highlight five methods of moral discourse that *Buffy* uses to address moral activity. These methods relate to consequences, context, perspective, metaphor, and theme. Of course, there is much overlap between these in the way that *Buffy* addresses a particular moral issue and some moral topics involve aspects of all five, but what I do here is highlight examples that represent the general approaches.

CONSEQUENCES

Ted Baehr, a leading figure in the media watchdog movement,

writes the following in his book *The Media-Wise Family*: "What boggles the mind is that neither movie nor television characters are ever shown to reap the consequences of their actions."[1] Baehr's comment is a vast overstatement that falters when read in light of *Buffy the Vampire Slayer*, for there have been few if any shows on television as obsessed with portraying consequences as this one. Joyce Summers tells her daughter, "Buffy, you made some bad choices. You just might have to live with some consequences" (3.2). This statement establishes a dominant theme of the show. Mim Udovitch comments that in addition to sexual consequences, the characters on *Buffy* "also have friendship with consequences, school with consequences, popularity with consequences."[2] Todd Hertz, writing for *Christianity Today*, defends *Buffy the Vampire Slayer* to a Christian audience because of its firm commitment to portraying the results of immoral actions. He writes, "*How* a taboo topic is dealt with can be just as important. In *Buffy*, the 'how' is intriguing because of the show's honest portrayal of consequences."[3] As further evidence of this fixation, *Buffy* even has an episode titled "Consequences" that explores the results of Faith's killing of a human being (3.15).

Characters on *Buffy* frequently make bad choices and sometimes engage in immoral or even illegal activity. But to paraphrase Joyce Summers, they always learn that they have to live with the consequences (3.2). As such, the moral message of the show derives not from the actions portrayed but from the consequences reaped. In "Reptile Boy" (2.5), high school student Buffy lies to Giles so that she can attend a college fraternity party. While there she drinks some alcohol and ends up passing out only to awaken chained to a dungeon wall as a potential sacrifice to a serpent demon. Her later *mea culpa* to Giles is instructive:

> BUFFY: I told one lie, I had one drink.
> GILES: Yes, and you were very nearly devoured by a giant demon snake. The words 'let that be a lesson' are a tad redundant at this juncture.

As Giles notes, a didactic lecture ("let that be a lesson") is redundant on *Buffy* because the consequences themselves are the vehicle for the lesson.

Buffy's treatment of magic also illustrates this form of moral discourse. Identifying the very depiction of magic and witchcraft as a glorification of the occult misses the point. On *Buffy*, magic is highly metaphorical, and one of its metaphorical functions is the representation of power. Because magic is a source of power, its use becomes a moral issue. Abuse or misuse of that power is immoral on *Buffy*, represented by the consequences that follow. Anytime a character performs magic out of a selfish motive or with nefarious designs, the results always cause harm to others or to themselves. Even if that power is abused with the best of intentions, consequences still follow. After Giles, Xander, Willow, and Buffy perform the enjoining spell to defeat Adam, the spirit of the first Slayer hunts them. Giles informs the group that their spell must have been an affront to the power of the Slayer.

> BUFFY: You know, you could have brought that up to us *before* we did it.
> GILES: I did. I said there could be dire consequences.
> BUFFY: Yes, but you say that about chewing too fast (4.22).

Giles is the adult voice of warning who attempts to guard Buffy, Willow, and Xander from their own actions. When Willow and Xander conspire to resurrect Buffy at the beginning of season six, they do so only by keeping Giles out of the loop. Despite recognizing that their magical attempt at resurrection is "wrong" (6.1), they proceed anyway. Although the spell succeeds, it does so at a cost: Buffy is tormented, and they are all haunted by a ghostly demon — an obvious metaphor of being haunted by the consequences of one's actions. Spike makes the moral lesson clear: "That's the thing about magic. There's always consequences. Always!" (6.3).

Season six of *Buffy* is all about consequences. More than any other, season six endured harsh criticism for its apparent glorification of immorality, receiving the Parents Television Council's top ranking as the worst show on television. Willow let herself be overtaken by magic with little regard for its effect on others. Buffy engaged in a wreckless sexual relationship with Spike; Dawn took up shoplifting as an after-school hobby; and Warren, Andrew, and Jonathan embarked on a path of increasing immaturity and immorality, culminating in murder.

It would seem that moralist critics have a point. However, no evaluation of the moral worth of *Buffy the Vampire Slayer* would be complete without an acknowledgment that all of those actions bear harsh consequences. Buffy's sexual activity with Spike results in severe emotional torment for her and damage to her relationship with Dawn. Willow's addiction to magic brings great harm to her friends and near destruction of herself. Dawn's thievery also brings repercussions, especially when Anya discovers she stole from the Magic Box. Proving that there is still a little vengeance left in her, Anya says, "And Dawnie, there are two words I want you to get used to. Punitive damages" (6.14). Dawn is forced to return everything that can be returned and pay restitution for the rest. *Buffy* writer, Jane Espenson, comments on how people kept asking her if Dawn and Willow were going to have to pay for their actions. Her standard reply was, "There's always consequences on Buffy. When are there not consequences?"[4] Those consequences extend also to Andrew, Jonathan, and Warren. After Warren is killed, Jonathan and Andrew end up in jail with Willow gunning for them. Andrew refuses to acknowledge their guilt and questions why this is happening to them. He insists they did nothing wrong. Jonathan, however, corrects him: "Yes we did. We signed on, we teamed up, we wanted to see where our plans would take us. Well take a look" (6.21).

Season six of *Buffy* was dark and full of unsavory activity, but that was the point. The purpose of season six, according to Whedon, was to show how people who are making their first forays into adult life and adult relationships often make "really, really bad decisions."[5] Those bad decisions must be set within the context of the entire season in order to be interpreted properly. Turning on any individual episode of season six and witnessing its sometimes graphic portrayal of immorality would provide a negative, but ultimately distorted, view of *Buffy*'s moral message. This is because the consequences of those actions demonstrate that what is ultimately glorified is not immorality but responsible decision making.

CONTEXT (LYING)

Buffy's momentary cheating at miniature golf sparks a tirade from Ted who asserts, "Right is right. Wrong is wrong. Why don't people see that?" When Buffy counters that it is just a game, Ted replies, "I'm not wired that way" (2.11). As a robot, Ted is conditioned to see the world in strict categorical terms. His wiring therefore does not allow him to contextualize moral decisions or distinguish degrees of right and wrong. For human beings, however, the morass of life and the distinctive demands of individual contexts challenge any completely rigid moral perspective.

Recognizing the importance of context in evaluating moral and ethical decisions is not a justification of situational ethics whereby right and wrong is determined solely on the basis of ever-shifting situational factors with no regard for an external moral foundation. It is, however, recognition that contextual factors do play a role in the moral decisions we make and the manner in which we evaluate them. Although most people would agree that killing another human being is morally wrong, the debate becomes more complex and heated when the context shifts to capital punishment, self-defense, war, or abortion. That the same God who delivered the commandment "Do not kill," shortly thereafter orders his people to wipe out entire cities and provides guidelines for capital punishment demonstrates that seemingly absolute rules like the Ten Commandments require contextualization for proper interpretation.

One of the methods of moral reasoning that *Buffy* employs is contextualization. With respect to a particular moral or ethical action, such as lying for instance, the moral evaluation given to that action varies depending on context. The episode "Lie to Me" (2.7) is a study in moral ambiguity, not in the sense of a denial of the categories of right and wrong, but in terms of the difficulty of sometimes distinguishing between the two. Buffy's friend, Ford, tells her, "Everybody lies." That is certainly the case in this episode as every major character lies for one reason or another. The question is whether those lies all weigh equally on the scale. Both Giles and Buffy lie in order to protect her secret identity. Willow lies to Buffy about her inquiries into Ford's background, but feels guilty about it. Angel lies to Buffy about his past with Drusilla, causing Buffy to confront him.

> BUFFY: Who's Drusilla? And don't lie to me. I'm tired of it.
> ANGEL: Some lies are necessary.
> BUFFY: For what?
> ANGEL: Sometimes the truth is worse. You live long enough, you
>   find that out.

Although Angel says the truth can be worse than a lie, it turns out not to be the case in this instance. Angel's lie erodes the trust between him and Buffy, but his telling of the truth brings restoration of that trust. Ford's lies, however, are far more deceptive and deadly because they are grounded in deliberate betrayal. They ultimately lead to a group of innocent people being literally trapped by his lies inside a room that can only be opened from the outside. At the end of the episode, Buffy is confused about who to trust and who not to trust. When she asks Giles if life ever gets easy, he says, "What do you want me to say?" Her answer: "Lie to me." That Buffy tells Angel not to "lie to me" about Drusilla but then asks Giles to "lie to me" about life, is a way of arguing that context allows for distinctions to be made in the lies that are told.

Buffy frequently distinguishes between lies on the basis of intent. Lies that proceed from impure motives reap harsh consequences. Buffy lies to Giles in order to go to a party and almost gets eaten by a giant snake (2.5). She lies to her friends about Angel and has to endure their sorrow and anger over her violation of their trust (3.7). Dawn lies to Buffy about sleeping over at a friend's house so that she can sneak out with some guys and, as a result, gets attacked by a vampire (6.6). On the other hand, some lies are deemed an acceptable means to a desired end. Buffy, Xander, and Willow lie to their parents in order to save the world (2.13); Xander lies in order to spare Cordelia a healthy dose of humiliation (3.20); and Buffy lies to a dying girl in order to spare her emotional pain (5.15).

Good intent, however, does not always absolve one of culpability. Jenny Calendar's lie to Giles and Buffy about her past results in a deep sense of betrayal. Although Jenny explains that she lied out of duty to her people and as such thought that lying was the right thing to do (2.17), her good intent fails to nullify the terrible consequences of her lie. This indicates that on *Buffy* the result of a lie in terms of its effect on others is as much a contextual factor as intent.

If the moral evaluation of lying is contextually bound on *Buffy*, it would not be surprising to find that the same holds true for honesty. Attention to context on *Buffy* suggests that lying, whether right or wrong in and of itself, can serve a noble end. Context, however, also reveals that honesty may not always be a morally pure act. Cordelia is a truth-teller, but one with no regard for how her honesty affects others. She has no interest in massaging the truth, claiming that tact "is just not saying true stuff" (2.18). Yet her words of truth often inflict emotional pain and suffering on the unsuspecting around her. Former vengeance demon Anya, states flatly: "I used to tell the truth all the time when I was evil" (7.8). This raises an interesting question: if the truth can serve the cause of evil, is it possible that a lie can serve the cause of goodness? *Buffy*'s answer is yes. In this way, *Buffy* evokes the traditional debate on the ends versus the means, and suggests that the resolution to this debate is at least partly governed by context. This is a controversial debate and *Buffy the Vampire Slayer* is certainly open to criticism on this point. Regardless of the position one takes in this debate, however, the fact that *Buffy the Vampire Slayer* raises it demonstrates how an awareness of context can be a means of engaging in moral discourse.

PERSPECTIVE (ALCOHOL)

As mentioned in an earlier chapter, the focus of many religious media critics on the portrayal of immoral acts on television often causes them to overlook a show's perspective of those same acts. *Buffy*'s treatment of alcohol represents this distinction. *Buffy*'s position on alcohol use is not one of abstinence. Characters, including Buffy, Xander, and Willow, are shown drinking and at times as drunk. Spike drinks frequently and on one occasion helps Riley drown his sorrows with a bottle (5.10). These portrayals of drinking activity are not always cast in a negative light and are at times used for humor. But close attention paid to *Buffy*'s overall perspective on alcohol demonstrates that this portrayal is certainly not an attempt to glorify alcohol.

Buffy's attitude towards alcohol is not about determining right or wrong, but about offering a realistic perspective on alcohol use. When a number of potential Slayers, most of whom are underage, ask Buffy if she drinks alcohol, she replies, "Sure I do. I mean, no. That would be wrong" (7.12). The dissonance between Buffy's action (she drinks) and her moral claim (drinking is wrong) shows that the goal is not to place a strict moral assessment on the act of drinking, but to acknowledge its role in society without shying away from its dangers.

Buffy undercuts its portrayal of drinking by highlighting the falsity of alcohol's promises and denying its claim to coolness. Buffy compares keg parties unfavorably to the hellmouth (3.8). While preparing for an apocalyptic battle, Giles asks Willow if she needs anything. She says that she could use some courage, prompting Spike to offer her his flask of alcohol. She looks at it contemptuously and says, "The real kind" (5.22). In one scene, Buffy and Spike are in his car on a stakeout and he takes a flask out of the glove compartment and offers some to her.

BUFFY: Ew.
SPIKE: It's not blood, it's bourbon.
BUFFY (slower): Eeeeew. (5.14)

The scene that best represents *Buffy*'s tendency to portray drinking while simultaneously undercutting that portrayal occurs during a birthday party at The Bronze. Riley, Buffy, Xander and Giles all stand around holding plastic cups full of beer. When the underage Dawn complains about having to have her hand stamped, Xander jokingly informs her that it is "to keep you from boozing it up." Dawn's sincere reply is: "Oh please. Only losers drink alcohol" (5.6).

In the episode "Reptile Boy" (2.5), Buffy's refusal to drink beer is presented as the mature choice in contrast to the immaturity of the college boys. It is only under peer pressure that she succumbs and takes a drink, announcing first, "I'm tired of being mature." That she is then nearly eaten by a giant demon snake is a comment on the potentially lethal combination of alcohol and immaturity.

One may also derive *Buffy*'s perspective on alcohol from its use of metaphor. The character of Angel, a bloodsucker who regains his soul and so must forever fight the temptation to drink blood again, functions as a metaphor for alcohol addiction. Joss Whedon describes the creation of the spin-off series *Angel* as an attempt to address "addiction and how you get through that and come out the other side, how you redeem yourself from a terrible life."[6]

Likewise, the episode "Beer Bad" (4.5) serves up a metaphor for the effects of beer. Maggie Walsh's psychology lecture sets the stage by discussing the "pleasure principle" and how the "id" wants what it wants regardless of the consequences. The desire for beer is a manifestation of this "pleasure principle." Xander becomes a bartender in a pub and Buffy is shown drinking a lot of beer, extolling it as "nice," "comforting," and "foamy." That positive portrayal, however, must be grounded by the episode's perspective on beer.

Buffy meets up with four intellectual college boys who pressure her to drink with them. When Buffy says her mother always taught her that beer was evil, one of them counters by saying, "Had the earliest morality developed under the influence of beer there would be no good or evil. There would just be kinda nice and pretty cool." This tacit acknowledgment that beer erodes a person's ability to make moral judgments finds further expression in the idea that beer robs people of their intellect. The owner of the pub spikes the beer with a magical potion that turns those who drink it into Neanderthals. This metaphor ("beer drinkers are Neanderthals") is Whedon's attempt to represent the reality of college life. He says, "Buffy's gonna drink beer, and it's going to turn her into a caveman. Now, I've been to college, and that's what happens."[7] Furthermore, the episode takes other jabs at beer that highlight its negative side. Buffy describes her hangover as "suffering the afterness of a bad night of badness." The clearest comment on this episode's perspective on beer, however, comes when Giles learns that Buffy herself has become a Neanderthal.

> GILES: I can't believe you served Buffy that beer.
> XANDER: I didn't know it was evil.
> GILES: But you knew it was beer.

Clearly the portrayal of individuals drinking on this show does not rise to the level of a glorification of alcohol. Although *Buffy* stops short of identifying the drinking of alcohol itself as morally wrong and does portray contexts in which drinking alcohol receives neither explicit nor implicit disapproval, the overriding perspective of the show towards alcohol is one of suspicion of its value and caution towards its use. What this illustrates is that a show's message about an action is not discernable from its portrayal alone, but only through the interplay of portrayal and perspective.

METAPHOR (DRUG ADDICTION)

It is striking that over seven seasons *Buffy* contains no depiction of illicit drug use whatsoever. There are no occurrences of marijuana, cocaine, heroine, ecstasy, or any other illicit drug. On the surface, drug use appears not to be a problem for any of the denizens of Sunnydale. Subtextually, however, drug abuse is a prevalent topic. The distinguishing feature of *Buffy*'s treatment of drug abuse is that it addresses the topic exclusively through metaphor.

That Buffy is given a drink at a frat party and passes out, only to wake up chained to a wall and menaced by a giant snake, serves as a metaphor for date-rape drugs (2.5). In "Go Fish" (2.20), a win-at-all-costs swimming coach gives his team a performance-enhancing substance that turns them into fish creatures. Steroids, anyone? We have already mentioned how the demon Eyghon in the episode "The Dark Age" (2.8) represents drug use. He is a demon who possesses individuals and grants them a "euphoric feeling of power." Giles describes possession by Eyghon as an "extraordinary high." Because Eyghon, however, is a possessor who cannot be controlled by his host, he wreaks great havoc on those who have "used" him. Even Glory's possession of Ben reads like a drug metaphor. When Ben loses his job because of Glory, he says of her, "This is so unfair. You're taking everything away from me. Everything I worked for, I earned, I care about. These are my choices, this is my life, and you're ruining it!" (5.19). These words sound like an addict speaking to the substance that has taken over his life.

The most extensive treatment of drug abuse is Willow's addiction to magic. As with the Harry Potter books, preachers and Christian media critics have attacked *Buffy* for a perceived glorification of the occult. These misconstrued attacks falter because they fail to pay close enough attention to the function of magic on *Buffy* and the context in which it is portrayed. Magic functions primarily in Willow's story as a metaphor for drug use. Marti Noxon notes that Willow's addiction storyline was about "adult crossroads" and the need for taking responsibility for one's life.[8] Willow's growing obsession with magic in seasons four and five has her reveling in a power she cannot control. In season five, we see Willow stealing in order to do magic, rationalizing it, and then trying to blame Anya when the results prove disastrous (5.11). She has a growing problem but will not take responsibility for it.

Willow's addiction to magic reaches the crisis point in season six. She is using magic too much and for selfish reasons. She craves the power that it gives her and becomes oblivious to its deleterious effects on her relationships (6.6). Throughout, Tara has been Willow's anchor, holding her back from the path of self-destruction. When Willow finally recognizes the strain that her magic habit has put on their relationship, she promises to go a week without magic. She doesn't even last a day and does a spell that causes great harm. As a result, Tara leaves her (6.8).

Tara's absence marks Willow's downfall. Without Tara as her conscience, Willow must learn to take responsibility for herself, a decision she strongly resists. When Willow says that Tara left her "for no good reason" (6.9), she demonstrates an addict's denial of personal accountability.

In "Wrecked" (6.10), Willow hits rock bottom. Frustrated by her inability to do as much magic as she would like, Willow visits a warlock named Rack who, according to Spike, "deals in magic. Black stuff, dangerous." Once inside, Rack's place resembles something like an opium den, but the outside is invisible to the naked eye. It is a testimony to the omnipresence of the drug trade in a society that refuses to acknowledge or recognize it. At Rack's place, Willow takes in more magic, literally floating to the ceiling in a visual representation of being "high." It is only when Willow, still high off the magic, crashes a car into a concrete pillar and injures her passenger (Dawn) that she begs Buffy for help. Willow finally takes responsibility for her actions and the episode concludes with her lying in bed and experiencing magic withdrawal symptoms. Making the "magic as drug addiction" metaphor unmistakable, Willow later joins Spellcasters Anonymous (6.14) and removes all magic paraphernalia from her room, including the candles because, as Buffy explains to Dawn, "to you and me they're just candles, but to witches they're like bongs" (6.11). In season seven, Willow's magic undergoes a slight metaphorical shift. According to Giles, the magic has now become internalized within Willow in a manner that transcends what it was before (7.1). The result is that Willow cannot completely remove magic from her life, but must learn to deal with its constant presence. The focus of the metaphor thus shifts from drug addiction to the struggle to respect and control the power within.

The treatment of magic on *Buffy* illustrates again the problem of assuming without an adequate awareness of a show's methodology of moral discourse that the mere portrayal of an act is a tacit approval of that act. Watching any individual episode in which magic occurs paints a distorted picture of magic's role on *Buffy*. Only by viewing magical activity within the entire context of the series and by paying attention to the means of moral discourse (in this case metaphor) can one engage in a responsible critique of that activity.

THEME (SOCIAL JUSTICE)

Another method of moral discourse employed on *Buffy* is the exploration of a theme. *Buffy* offers comment on some moral issues, such as social justice, by the way it ties that issue into a larger prevailing theme. *Buffy the Vampire Slayer* is all about power. It is a dominant structuring theme on the show. We have looked at Buffy's sense of moral responsibility for her power and Faith's contrasting lack of respect for that power. We have examined the corruption of power with respect to technology, magic and institutional authority. We have discussed the power of shared lives in community. The pervasive issue running throughout these topics is the morally responsible versus morally irresponsible use of power.

Social justice is about the relationship between the powerful and the powerless. It is grounded in the principle that the possession of power carries with it the price tag of responsibility, in this case responsibility for the weak, the outcasts, the marginalized ones of the earth. *Buffy* places a high premium on the underdog and the empowerment of society's powerless. The choice of a frivolous, tiny, blond teenager as the show's warrior hero is a representation of the human desire to prove oneself more powerful and "more significant than the world believed."[9]

When Joyce Summers announces at a Sunnydale rally that "silence is this town's disease" (3.11), she is acknowledging a society's tendency to ignore its social problems.[10] *Buffy*, however, refuses to be silent on social issues and explores them by repeatedly connecting them to the issue of power. The frat boys who sold their souls for prosperity by sacrificing girls to a demon illustrate how privilege and wealth is often built off the backs of the less fortunate (2.5). When an on-campus gang of vampires focuses their killing specifically on isolated freshmen, it becomes a metaphor for a type of class warfare in which the college campus, as a microcosm of society, becomes a place where the powerful prey on the weak (4.1). This same theme was dealt with more extensively in the first season episode "The Pack" (1.6). The oppressive power of high school cliques comes into view when Xander and four others become possessed by the animal spirits of hyenas. This plays out as a metaphor of the teenage tendency to prey on the weak. Xander, however, breaks the cycle when Willow comes under attack, risking his own life to protect her. Through Xander's actions, he reveals the message of the episode, which is that power should be used for protection, not oppression, of the weak.

The character of Cordelia frequently serves as a medium for addressing issues of social justice. Cordelia embodies the power of popularity. Although popularity by itself is not a moral issue, it is a form of power. When that power is used to demean or oppress others, it becomes a form of social injustice. Cordelia's division of the world into winners and losers is essentially a division between the popular and the unpopular. When Xander expresses "moral outrage at swim team perks," Cordelia educates him on her philosophy.

> CORDELIA: But the truth is certain people are entitled to special privileges. They're called 'winners.' That's the way the world works.
> XANDER: And what about that nutty 'All Men Are Created Equal' thing?
> CORDELIA: Propaganda spouted out by the ugly and less-deserving. (2.20)

In "Out of Mind, Out of Sight" (1.11), Cordelia becomes the vehicle for addressing the anger of the social outcast towards society. Cordelia represents the privileged individual who is oblivious towards the less fortunate around her. Marcie Ross is one of Cordelia's victims, a member of the high school band whose attempts to socialize with Cordelia have been firmly ignored. Marcie's social invisibility becomes a literal invisibility, illustrating that in a high school context unpopularity is a form of invisibility. Invisible and angry, Marcie embarks on a path of murder, trying to kill those who most ignored her, which, of course, puts Cordelia at the top of the list.

Marcie is not simply a victim of society and she is never absolved of responsibility for her actions, but the focus of the episode is on how a society can contribute to the anger of the outcast. Buffy and Cordelia represent two different responses to Marcie's plight. When Buffy learns of Marcie's condition, she confesses that this is something "we" did to her by failing to recognize her presence among them. When Cordelia, however, is shown a picture of Marcie, the girl she so mercilessly tormented, she replies, "I've never seen this girl before in my life." Cordelia's obsession with popularity blinds her to the less fortunate around her. The Cordelia who claims earlier in this episode that popularity is "not just my right but my responsibility" has failed in that responsibility by using her popularity to oppress and ignore. Marcie left a one-word message at the sight of her three attacks. When put together they read: Look . . . Listen . . . Learn. Through attention paid to the marginalized and disenfranchised, a society can learn the value of power well used.

When Cordelia begins to date Xander, she refuses to tell her friends out of shame. In violation of her own code, she is associating with a known "loser." Once the secret is out, Cordelia finds herself ostracized by her former friends and on the receiving end of the same ridicule she so mercilessly doled out to others. Cracking under the pressure, Cordelia breaks up with Xander on Valentine's Day because she cannot stand being unpopular. Back in the good graces of her friends, Cordelia resumes her former ways — that is until her friends start to ridicule Xander. Having experienced the plight of the outsider, however briefly, Cordelia has learned that privilege does not excuse verbal oppression of others. She rebukes her friends and informs them, "I'll date whoever I wanna date. No matter how lame he is" (2.16). Cordelia's learning curve, however, bends only so far. Despite her newfound appreciation for those who stand outside her winners' circle, Cordelia measures it as a sign of her growth when she is able to tell Xander that he doesn't have to try out for the championship swim team next year because she will be just as happy if he is on the football team (2.20).

Cordelia's story arc constantly taps into this ongoing theme of social justice as a responsibility of those who wield power. In some ways, she is a caricature of our nation's obsession with fame and worship of the "beautiful." As such, Cordelia's character functions as a mirror reflecting the emptiness and shallowness of popularity and privilege as an end in itself.

One other example of how *Buffy* illustrates a moral principle through the reiteration of a theme is the show's focus on female empowerment. Historically, women have often been among those marginalized and deemed weak by western society so the empowerment of women on *Buffy* is a comment on social justice. Joss Whedon asserts that the primary mission of his show is to explore "adolescent rites of passage" and "the getting of strength."[11] This mission came to fulfillment at the conclusion of the series. Commenting on the power Buffy possesses and how she is never respected for that power, Whedon mentions that the final episode "deals very specifically with how she decides to use that power and what she thinks of it and what it's really for, and that to me is very important."[12] What Buffy chooses to do is to share her power with other girls. Suddenly we see a young Japanese woman standing up at a family meal, filled with strength; we see a nervous little girl at the plate in a softball game all of a sudden choking up with newfound confidence; we see a young abused woman grabbing the wrist of the man trying to slap her and rising up to defend herself (7.22). Buffy has learned the value of power: it is not to be hoarded and protected as a means of self-preservation. Rather it is to be shared in the service of humanity. This final episode of *Buffy* encapsulates Whedon's mission and his desire to alter cultural attitudes towards women. He says:

> Honestly, I hope the legacy of the show would be that there's a generation of girls who have the kind of hero a lot of them didn't get to have in their mythos and a lot of guys who are a lot more comfortable with the idea of a girl who has that much power.[13]

This brief survey illustrates that the methods of moral discourse on a television show like *Buffy the Vampire Slayer* can be multi-faceted. Moral issues get explored from a variety of angles and communicated by a variety of means. In light of this, an evaluation of a show's moral worth that is based upon the sheer occurrence of sexual references, acts of violence, or profanity seems inordinately simplistic. Any such evaluation that fails to explore a show's portrayal of consequences, its underlying perspective on moral issues, its narrative context, and its use of narrative features like theme and metaphor runs the risk of misrepresentation. In continuation of this discussion, the following two chapters relate these issues to the controversial topics of sexuality and violence.

Chapter 13

Sexuality

With the possible exception of violence, nothing has logged more time at the center of the controversy over media and morality than sex. It is the linchpin of the sex, violence, and profanity trifecta that form the basis of most moralistic attacks on film and television. Medved's comments are representative when he says that what characterizes Hollywood is "the glorification of sexual adventurism and the focus on physical pleasure as an end in itself" and that sex on television is represented as "a glorious form of recreation that has nothing to do with responsibility or commitment."[1] Donald Wildmon adds, "When 88% of all sexual activity portrayed on TV occurs between people not married to each other, television makes lust more attractive than love."[2]

A casual viewing of *Buffy the Vampire Slayer* would seem to support these conclusions. Characters engage in sexual activity outside the boundaries of marriage with the attitude that such is a viable choice. *Buffy* also fits well within current Hollywood trends with its liberal portrayal of homosexuality. But the issue, again, is not *Buffy*'s portrayal of sexuality, but its perspective on sexuality. In his book, *Hollywood Worldviews*, Brian Godawa includes a section that examines the use of sex, violence, and profanity in the Bible. The evidence demonstrates that the portrayal of these features in the Bible is not at all inconsistent with moral exhortation. According to Godawa, "context" is the factor that distinguishes "between moral *exhortation* and immoral *exploitation* of sin."[3]

With respect to *Buffy*, this means that *how* sexuality is presented is of more significance than *that* it is presented. *Buffy the Vampire Slayer* is a show about real life viewed through a fantasy lens. The goal is to create an emotional resonance that rings true to real life. Joss Whedon says:

> The show works only if it resonates. That's the most important thing in the show. People forget this. People like to talk about the monsters and the makeup and the fangs and the horns and the whatnot. But the fact of the matter is the only thing that separates this show from any other, if in fact it is separate, is the kind of emotional resonance that we can get to by playing the entire thing as true life, just a little bit wonkier.[4]

Consequently, *Buffy*'s treatment of sexuality is less about the rightness or wrongness of sexual activity than it is about the emotional impact and emotional consequences of engaging in it.

Buffy the Vampire Slayer is not a show for children. Designed for late teens and up, the show addresses the sexual issues encountered within those age groups. This is neither done lightly nor without regard for a storyteller's responsibility. Writer Douglas Petrie says, "I don't see that we've ever done anything gratuitously."[5] What he means is that story, rather than a desire to tantalize and boost ratings, drives all presentations of sexuality on the show. So my discussion of *Buffy*'s sexuality unfolds with an eye towards story. In the sections that follow, I survey this show's use of sexuality in a chronological fashion, noting how the changing life stages of the characters evoke differing sexual issues, and then conclude with a summary of *Buffy*'s perspective on sexuality.

THE HIGH SCHOOL YEARS

Given the current standards of most teen-oriented shows on television, the most striking feature about the first three seasons of *Buffy* is just how little sex there actually is. This is a show in which the three main characters (Buffy, Willow, Xander) are all virgins and remain so well into the second (Buffy) and third seasons (Xander, Willow). Even then, the number of times these characters have sex during their high school years is a combined total of three (once each). Even when presented with temptation, these teens behave nobly. Xander's love spell aimed at Cordelia goes awry and causes Buffy to fall for him. Yet when Buffy throws herself at him, Xander, who has long had a crush on Buffy, resists her advances (2.16).

Despite the paucity of sexual activity in the first three seasons, sexuality is a pervasive theme. The message that reverberates throughout the first three seasons is that sex can be dangerous and laden with harsh consequences. Angel's statement to Buffy that things which seem good and powerful can be painful was spoken with reference to the ability to hear people's thoughts (3.18), but in principle applies equally well to the subject of sexuality. The first episode to really tackle the issue of sex is "Teacher's Pet" (1.4). A gorgeous substitute teacher comes to Sunnydale High and quickly captures the attention of the male student population. Underneath her human disguise, she is a giant praying mantis known as "The Virgin Thief." After luring virgin male students to her home, she mates with them and then devours them. It is a potent reminder in the age of AIDS that sex can kill. It also suggests that young people who move too quickly into adult sexual relationships for which they are unprepared can be easily devoured. Towards the end of the episode, Xander is embarrassed when everyone learns he is a virgin, but finds himself consoled by Willow who assures him that being a virgin at this stage in their life is "the right thing, the smart thing."

The episode "Bad Eggs" (2.12) addresses teenage sex and responsibility. In Sex Education class, the teacher lectures about the overwhelming flood of teenage hormones that constantly urge teenagers to act upon their desires; yet, the teacher argues that, in the midst of these hormonal surges, "it's often difficult to remember that there are negative consequences to having sex." The class members are then assigned to care for an egg as a way of impressing upon them the consequence of teenage pregnancy. Of course, this being *Buffy*, the metaphor of egg as a baby gets exaggerated. Inside the eggs, are little monsters that latch onto their host, taking over their lives and turning them into mindless automatons — a not too subtle depiction of how children can impact the lives of teenage mothers. It is interesting that this episode about teenage sexual *responsibility* occurs immediately before the two episodes in which Buffy learns the consequences of sexual *irresponsibility* by sleeping with Angel.

The character of Oz represents the adolescent struggle between hormonal urges and moral values. As a werewolf, he embodies the conflict between the human and the animal within. *Buffy* writer Marti Noxon says, "A young man turning into a werewolf is a very strong metaphor for a sort of teenage sexuality and the kinds of things that are going on in puberty."[6] At issue is whether Oz will allow those animal urges to define his behavior. On two occasions, Willow makes advances towards Oz, initially wanting him to make out with her for the first time (2.14) and then later wanting him to sleep with her for the first time (3.10). On both occasions Oz's human nature triumphs over the animal, and he gently refuses because he knows that her motives were not pure (in the first instance, it was to make Xander jealous and in the second, it was out of guilt).

The most sustained comment on sexual activity during the first two seasons is the relationship between Buffy and Angel. Buffy and Angel are wrong for each other on so many levels. She's in her mid-teens; he's celebrated a bicentennial. She kills vampires; he is one. It's a classic case of a young girl romanticizing the bad guy.

The back-to-back episodes "Surprise" (2.13) and "Innocence" (2.14) explore Buffy and Angel's first sexual encounter. It's Buffy's birthday, a fact not incidental to the message of these episodes. She is about to get older, both physically and emotionally. Early on in "Surprise" Buffy shares with Willow her concerns over whether she should have sex with Angel.

> BUFFY: Willow, what am I gonna do?
> WILLOW: What do you wanna do?
> BUFFY: I don't know. I mean "want" isn't always the right thing to do. To act on "want" can be wrong.
> WILLOW: True.
> BUFFY: But to not act on "want" . . . what if I never feel this way again?

At the end of the episode, Buffy acts on her passions with Angel.

The following episode "Innocence" (2.14) examines the "rather appalling consequences of that act."[7] As a result of sex with Buffy, Angel loses his soul — a dire consequence of the gypsy curse that restored his soul to him in the first place. Angel has now become Angelus once again.[8] Angel's loss of his soul and turn towards evil after having sex with Buffy is a clear metaphor for the horror of the man seeming to become a different person afterwards. Whedon notes that "Innocence" works on two levels: the mythic level in which it represents the hero's moment of loss and challenge and the personal level in which it is basically "a show about 'I slept with somebody and now he doesn't call me anymore.'"[9] Christine Jarvis argues that Angel's transformation fulfills three fears of young women: "that sex is violence, that the boy will cease to value the girl after sex and that the act itself will be much less important to him than to her."[10]

Rarely has a sexual act on television generated such extensive and drawn out consequences as Buffy and Angel's tryst. Buffy experiences severe emotional anguish over the event and frequently expresses regret. Warning Buffy that she should stay away from Angelus on Valentine's Day because he is prone to displays of brutality, Giles says to Buffy, "Better safe than sorry." She replies, "It's a little late for both" (2.16). The immaturity of Buffy's choice is also emphasized, as represented by her mother's response.

> JOYCE: You don't get to get out of this. You had sex with a boy you didn't even see fit to tell me you were dating!
> BUFFY: I made a mistake.
> JOYCE: Well don't just say that to shut me up because I think you really did (2.17).

When Angel begins to stalk Buffy, Giles points out that once a vampire has been invited into a home, he can always enter thereafter of his own accord. Xander makes the metaphor obvious when he says, "You know I think there may be a valuable lesson for you gals here about inviting strange men into your bedrooms" (2.17). The consequences of Buffy's action play out horrifically as Angel murders several people, including Jenny Calendar, tortures Giles, and eventually must be killed by Buffy herself.

Joss Whedon says that "Innocence" was his attempt to deal with the issue of sex in a serious way.[11] Although *Buffy* never takes the position that sexual activity outside of marriage is wrong, it does go to great lengths to emphasize the emotional horror that can arise out of sexual relationships. This grows out of a view that sex is a powerful force ruled by powerful passions and therefore can be potentially dangerous and damaging. Writing for *National Review*, Chandler Rosenberger defends the show's portrayal of Angel and Buffy's sexual activity because he sees in it the message that sex is risky "not only because it has physical consequences, but — more importantly — because it unleashes such powerful passions. Where is the sex-ed class that teaches *that*?"[12] The title of this episode points to the loss of childhood innocence that comes with growth towards adulthood and one's initial foray into adult sexual experiences. The episode is not a comment on Buffy's moral character per se (i.e. loss of her moral innocence), but an exploration of the real-life emotional horror that can stem from a young person's premature involvement in adult sexual relationships.

Buffy's first sexual experience came about after much reflection and deliberation and resulted in great emotional pain. The other Slayer, Faith, models a different attitude towards sexual behavior. Faith's sexual adventurism and libertarianism is embodied in her "use 'em and lose 'em" policy towards men (3.7). When she says, "All men are beasts" (3.4), Faith reveals herself to have just as distorted a view of men as the seventh season's Caleb has of women. Faith's sexual irresponsibility is symptomatic of the moral laxity that eventually leads to her downfall.

If this is true, then we should expect to find that her journey towards redemption includes learning to value men and acquiring an appreciation of the responsibility attached to sexual activity. In the body-swapping episode, "Who Are You" (4.16), Faith (in Buffy's body) decides to have fun by going to visit Riley. As she gradually learns the value of morality by having adopted Buffy's persona, here she also learns to see sex from a new angle. For Faith, sex has always been about fun, power and control. Convinced that all men are beasts, Faith attempts to assert control by coming on to Riley (who thinks she is Buffy), tempting him with, "Am I a bad girl? Do you wanna hurt me?" Riley, however, replies by kissing her tenderly. Then, while in the middle of sex, Riley softly says to her, "I love you." Faith is immediately disgusted and desperately pushes him off, shouting "No." For her, tenderness, not violence, is a form of rape. Distraught, Faith insists to Riley that what they have been doing is "meaningless"; but then when he notes that she is shaking and tries to touch her, she flinches back. Despite her protest that sex is meaningless, Faith has, for the first time, experienced sex as meaningful — and it has shaken her to the core.

Faith next returns to Sunnydale in the seventh season, having gained a moral compass but still holding to her negative perception of men. After another of her characteristic one-night-stands, this time with Robin Wood, Faith blows him off in her typically isolationist manner. This time, however, her conquest confronts her. Robin Wood gets her to acknowledge the possibility that her emotional solitude and defensiveness may be causing her to miss out on a lot of decent guys.

When Wood is injured in the final climactic battle of the season, Faith's genuine concern for him shows that she has taken his message to heart and for the first time is learning commitment to one man. Her journey of redemption balances her moral growth with a growing appreciation for the power of sexuality and the value of men.

THE EARLY COLLEGE YEARS

Seasons four and five of *Buffy* bring with them an increase in sexual activity that coincides with the characters taking on greater adult roles as they make their initial journeys into post-high school life. This increase in sexual activity did not go unnoticed by media watchdogs. The Parents Television Council ranked season four of *Buffy* as the fourth worst show on television, with sexual activity and innuendo as the primary cause. They state: "All sex among these young college freshmen is portrayed almost exclusively as romantic or fun, with no reference made to the consequences of such behavior."[13] This comment is baffling when examined in light of the actual evidence from season four.

One of the initial episodes of the season, "The Harsh Light of Day" (4.3), is about little besides sexual consequences. Three couples engage in sex in this episode: Spike and Harmony, Anya and Xander, and Buffy and Parker Abrams. Each of the females has sex for different reasons, but the results are similar. The vampires Harmony and Spike engage in sex simply for pleasure; yet once Harmony realizes that she means little else to Spike, she is deeply hurt. Anya proposes having sex to Xander as a way for them to get over their feelings for each other and move on. Her view of sex is strictly utilitarian. Xander, however, is wary.

> XANDER: It's just we hardly know each other. I mean I like you. And you have a certain directness that I admire. But sexual interc — what you're talking about, well — and I'm actually turning into a woman as I say this — but it's about expressing something. And accepting consequences.

Anya responds by reiterating her utilitarian point of view when she says, "I like you. You're funny, and you're nicely shaped. And frankly, it's ludicrous to have these interlocking bodies and not . . . interlock."

For Anya sex is simply about achieving the goal of getting over each other. When she and Xander do have sex, however, she finds herself feeling more committed to him and angry that he does not seem to acknowledge the depth of meaning that they shared. What she learned from her sexual experience was that it was indeed about consequences and things being expressed. Buffy's rendezvous with Parker Abrams also leads to pain. After their sexual encounter, Parker moves quickly on to his next conquest and has little interest in furthering their relationship, much to Buffy's shock and despair. She had been looking for acceptance, but found only rejection. The episode concludes with individual shots of Buffy, Anya, and Harmony walking all alone and looking sorrowful. This is anything but a depiction of sex as exclusively romantic, fun, and devoid of consequences.

The consequences of sexual activity continue throughout the season, particularly with reference to the effects of infidelity on others. Infidelity on *Buffy* always brings pain. The foundation for this theme occurs in season three when Cordelia discovers her boyfriend Xander kissing Willow in an abandoned factory. When she turns to run away, Cordelia falls through a hole in the floor and is impaled on a metal spike (3.8). Cordelia's impalement is a visual metaphor for the emotional impalement of being cheated on in a relationship. It is no wonder that Cordelia will later want to discuss with Willow "the ethics of boyfriend stealing" (3.16). The emotional impalement from infidelity continues as a theme in season four. That Riley was having sex with Buffy's body in the episode where Faith inhabits her body does little to dampen the hurt that Buffy experiences because she knows that sex is about an emotional connection and not just a physical act (4.16). Likewise, when Willow discovers her boyfriend Oz with Veruca, her pain is nearly unbearable. Buffy comments, "I've never seen her like this. It's like it hurts too much to form words" (4.6). These consequences of bad sexual choices put the lie to the statement that sex in season four is all about fun.

The most sexually charged episode of season four, "Where the Wild Things Are" (4.18), represents the fine line between sexual freedom and sexual responsibility that *Buffy* consistently attempts to navigate. *Buffy* adopts the position that sexual activity for these college-age individuals is a viable choice. Nevertheless, it also asserts that sex is an act of great emotional power and can therefore be damaging and dangerous, requiring maturity and responsibility for proper expression. In this episode, sexual repression forced upon children in a religiously oriented orphanage manifests as a poltergeist. Triggering this manifestation is the unrestrained sexual activity between Buffy and Riley.[14] Although the theme of the episode is the danger of sexual repression, "Where the Wild Things Are" does not go so far as to suggest that repressing sexual desires is bad and indulging them good. Rather, *Buffy* adopts a mediating position between sexual freedom and sexual restraint. The denial of natural sexual expression is perceived as unhealthy repression, while sexual expression without the restraint of personal responsibility is deemed equally problematic. The attempt to juxtapose sexual freedom and sexual responsibility plays out in the final scene after Riley and Buffy have been made aware of the destructive consequences of their lack of sexual restraint.

> BUFFY: If Riley and I hadn't . . . gotten so wrapped up in each other, none of this would've happened.
> ANYA: True. Feel shame.

The look that Buffy and Riley then share reveals that they do indeed feel shame for the harm their sexual activity caused, though not necessarily for the activity itself.

Being a horror show, when *Buffy* self-consciously takes on sex as an issue, it typically focuses on the negative consequences of bad sexual choices. Balancing that, however, are occasional portraits of sexuality rendered more positively. In "I Was Made to Love You" (5.15), Warren creates a female robot as a consort for himself, ultimately demonstrating the point that sex without love is empty. Similarly, the same Anya whose earlier view of sex led her to treat it as a utilitarian formula, later gains a more exalted perspective on the whole business.

> ANYA: It's not just about two bodies smooshing together. It's about life. It's about *making* life . . . It all makes me feel like I'm part of something bigger (5.17).

This brief survey of the early college years on *Buffy* demonstrates that, while not rising to the level of a traditional Judeo-Christian view of sexuality, these two seasons in no way reduce sexuality to fun, romance, and avoidance of consequence. A more accurate description would be that they present sexuality as being about love, responsibility, and the acceptance of consequences.

ADULTHOOD

Season six of *Buffy* contains the most extensive and graphic portrayal of sexual behavior on the series, primarily the perverted relationship between Buffy and Spike. Some attributed season six's increase in sexual activity to the shift to a new network (from the WB to UPN) with more lax standards, while others saw it as a blatant attempt to garner attention and ratings. Joss Whedon ascribes it to good storytelling. He argues that storytelling requires an exploration of the dark side of humanity if it is to ring true.[15] Now appealing to one's narrative responsibility does not absolve the storyteller of his or her moral responsibility to the audience. Personally, I believe that the portrayal of Buffy and Spike's sexual activity during this season was carried on too long and at times crossed the line of good taste. The same message could have been communicated without needing to resort to some of the more graphic scenes that were presented. Whether or not the writers always succeeded, however, their goal was to use sexuality to serve the larger story.

By season six, the main characters are all now in their early twenties and entering full force into the adult world. The intention for this season was to explore the adult problems and bad choices that come when the persistent immaturity of adolescence meets the freedom of early adulthood. For Buffy, the cycle of bad decisions begins after her resurrection from the dead. Her inability to readjust to life mirrors a young adults' challenge of adapting to the adult world. Buffy's experience with death has left her disillusioned with life and emotionally bankrupt. Consequently, she desires anything that will make her feel again. Her quest leads her to Spike. They embark upon a degrading sexual relationship characterized by the intermingling of violence and sex.

It is important to recognize that Buffy never attempts to legitimize her relationship with Spike. In fact, as with Willow's magical activity, it is played as a metaphor for addiction, with Buffy consistently reiterating the wrongness of their activity while at the same time seeming incapable of breaking it off. *Buffy* writer and executive producer Marti Noxon says that Buffy and Spike's relationship is primarily "about the wrongness of it" and about the consequences that come from choosing to be with the wrong person.[16] Elsewhere she explains the rationale behind their relationship and the reason for the darker tone of season six.

She's made a choice right now that is very adult, because she's in a relationship that is a lot more sexual and less romanticized. But there's also going to be a price to pay for that, because it's obviously not the healthiest situation. So she's dealing with something that I think only happens when you get out of that sort of dreamy, romantic teen-age period.[17]

The back-to-back episodes "Smashed" (6.9) and "Wrecked" (6.10) set the stage for her and Spike's relationship. In "Smashed," Buffy and Spike have sex for the first time. Despite her protestations that he is an "evil, disgusting thing," she finds herself continually drawn to him, culminating in a violent encounter in an abandoned house. They begin beating each other and throwing each other into walls, causing more damage to the house. The damage done to the house signifies the damage they do to each other. Their physical battle becomes intermingled with kissing and eventually sex. The violence of their actions causes the house to fall apart around them and the floor to give way. The image of Buffy and Spike falling through the floor into the basement while in the midst of passion represents how her life has hit rock bottom. Whedon says, "When the house came down around Buffy as she slept with Spike that first time, it was a metaphor for her life. Her life was crashing down around her."[18] That she is oblivious to the collapse of the house, as represented by her post-sex comment to Spike ("when did the building fall down?"), demonstrates how one is usually unaware of the effects of bad decisions until it is too late (6.10).

The self-loathing and shame that Buffy experiences following her night with Spike, coupled with her continued desire for him, is a realistic and effective representation of temptation. She tells Spike, "Last night was the end of this freak show"; yet, barely seconds later, she is kissing him again (6.10). Though she refers to their encounter in the abandoned house as "the most perverse . . . degrading experience of my life," she is still drawn to him (6.10). "Wrecked" concludes with Buffy in her room, garlic on her window and bedframe, sitting on her bed and looking around nervously as she twirls a cross in her hands. She is an embodiment of one who struggles with a sin, vows never to do it again, yet fears that she cannot trust herself to resist the temptation when it shows its face.

Buffy writer Douglas Petrie describes a general storytelling principle used on the show when he says, "Every good story will, I think go to places where the viewer doesn't want to go because you love these characters and you don't want to see certain things. But you've got to take them through the dark to get to the light."[19] This perverted relationship between Buffy and Spike forms one of those dark times that both Buffy and Spike will have to work through. Towards the end of season six, Buffy conquers her temptation and announces to Spike that she will no longer have sex with him because she does not love him (6.18). The aborting of their relationship ultimately leads to Spike's rape attempt, a devastating consequence of their inability to separate sex and violence (6.19).

The sexual activity of season six cannot be treated in isolation but is only properly understood when juxtaposed with season seven. Both Buffy and Spike, courtesy of his newly restored soul, find a kind of redemption from their sordid past together. When Spike first returns to Sunnydale after regaining his soul, Buffy initially misconstrues the situation, thinking he has returned in an attempt to renew their relationship. She says to him, "You thought you would just come back here and . . . *be* with me?" Spike replies, "First time for everything" (7.2). With a new soul, he now sees sex differently. Despite all that they did together, Spike acknowledges that he has never really been with her. His path of redemption includes a more responsible view of sexuality. Whereas the pre-souled Spike had no objection to having sex with Anya earlier (6.18), he now nobly refuses her advances (7.8).

The episode "Touched" (7.20) provides the strongest counterpoint to Buffy and Spike's relationship in season six. The apocalyptic battle with The First is brewing, and Buffy's friends are all anxious and afraid. In an attempt to feel something, they turn to sex. While the song "Only Love" plays, we witness a montage of scenes in which Faith and Robin Wood, Willow and Kennedy, and Anya and Xander engage in sexual activity. The final scene is of Spike and Buffy together in bed, fully clothed, with Buffy sleeping gently in Spike's arms. Despite the genuine feelings of affection Spike and Buffy develop for each other over the course of season seven (in contrast to the perverted lust of season six), they never engage in sexual activity. The other three couples are all seeking to be touched as a way of escaping the fear and pain — just as Buffy did in season six. Through sex, they are trying to fill an emotional void that cannot be filled that way. Buffy and Spike, who previously used sex as a means of feeling alive, now eschew that in favor of something deeper and truer. Their perverted relationship of season six is turned on its head in season seven, a testimony to the importance of keeping a particular story arc within the context of the larger narrative. Buffy and Spike's relationship represents a type of incoherence in the narrative of *Buffy* in that the sexual irresponsibility portrayed in season six was in actuality a means of promoting sexual responsibility.[20]

BUFFY'S PERSPECTIVE ON SEXUALITY

Buffy the Vampire Slayer is certainly open to legitimate criticism for its presentation of sexuality, but that criticism only has value if it flows out of a broader understanding of the show's perspective on sexuality. The place that sexuality occupies within *Buffy*'s moral vision is neither a hedonistic one nor a moralistic one. *Buffy* fits comfortably within a western secular morality that says sex outside of marriage is viable in principle as long as it is governed by love. This covers the treatment of homosexuality on *Buffy* as well. Willow's turn towards homosexuality in season four and following generated criticism from many religious viewers. In its perspective on homosexuality, *Buffy* certainly does stand at odds with traditional Judeo-Christian teaching, but it rarely attempts to exploit Willow's homosexuality. It is treated the same as other sexual relations on the show, that is as a means of commenting on the emotion of life. In fact, none of the sexuality on *Buffy* is glorified or cast in the dreamy tones of fantasy romance. If anything the opposite is true. In tune with *Buffy*'s genre, much of the sexuality on *Buffy* is about finding the horror in it, and this comes through an honest and sometimes exaggerated portrayal of the negative consequences that can arise.

On the other hand, *Buffy*'s sexual ethic is strongly grounded in commitment. The protagonists on this show do not sleep around. When they do embark on a sexual relationship it is almost always with the presumption of faithfulness and commitment to one person. This is why *Buffy* treats the occasional act of infidelity as horrific and fraught with emotional pain; why *Buffy* presents the libidinous character of Parker Abrams as such a vile human being; and why, when Xander gets divided into two personas and Anya wants to sleep with both, she is told it would be "wrong" (5.3). Even though both are technically Xander, as long as they occupy separate bodies, it is viewed as infidelity.

As with just about everything on *Buffy*, the show's perspective on sexuality comes down to emotional resonance. Whedon says:

> I don't want to make a reactionary statement. I don't want to say, 'Never have sex.' I don't want to say, 'Quick, go have it now.' I want to say, 'Some people have it. Everybody thinks about it. Here's how we deal with it.' The thing with Angel wasn't, 'Don't sleep with your boyfriend' . . . It was about what happens when you sleep with a guy and he stops calling you . . . It was about the emotion of it.[21]

Media watchdog groups and many religious viewers typically evaluate a show like *Buffy* on how well or how poorly it moralizes on an issue, that is the extent to which it clearly and unambiguously identifies a behavior as right or wrong. *Buffy*'s method of moral discourse, however, characteristically attempts to avoid overt moralizing. *Buffy* is less about the rightness and wrongness of sexual activity per se as how to navigate the emotional minefield of sexuality. This show typically engages moral issues indirectly through narrative constructions of emotional reality. Consequently, any critique of *Buffy*'s morality that does not engage it at the level of story and emotion remains woefully incomplete.

Chapter 14

Violence and Vengeance

The cultural debates over media violence are so prolific and well documented that I need not repeat them here other than to offer a few general comments. The charge is that the media's portrayal of excessive and gratuitous violence desensitizes people to its adverse effects and breeds aggression and imitation.[1] Although personal and parental responsibility is always primary, the media certainly should not be allowed to hide from the critical eye. Although no one can claim that the media bear no responsibility for the proliferation of violence in American society, the extent to which that responsibility extends is unclear. Studies on the direct effects of media violence are contradictory and unable to establish an unambiguous link.[2] William Romanowski is correct that the real issue is not the inclusion of violence in media but "the value and perspective" that the media ascribes to it; in other words, the overall context of violent representations.[3]

The Bible offers a parallel example of the importance of context for the evaluation of violence because the Bible is replete with acts of violence and violent images. Violence is common in the parables of Jesus and central to their message. The history of the ancient nation of Israel cannot be told without profuse amounts of violence. If rendered faithfully on film, the book of Judges would certainly receive an "R" rating (or worse). On the one hand, the portrayal of violence in scripture highlights the reality and depravity of sin. On the other hand, violence in often serves the cause of holiness. The violence that God employs and commands on behalf of Israel serves his redemptive purpose. In the Old Testament prophets, violence can be a refining fire that purifies a people and sparks repentance. It is a form of redemption through violence. The book of *Revelation* attempts to provide hope and comfort to its audience by means of "violent images of imagination and metaphor."[4] The proliferation of violence in the Bible in service to the message of hope, justice, love, and peace is a powerful witness to the need for keeping moral evaluations of violence in context.

THE INCOHERENCE OF VIOLENCE

Buffy the Vampire Slayer represents a kind of incoherent text with respect to violence, and this incoherence has a lot to do with the confusion over its moral agenda. This is a show in which violence is integral to the very premise. Buffy is a Slayer: by definition a person of violence. Her calling and the fulfillment of her mission require violence. Consequently, when Xander feels that the group is slighting his contribution to the cause, he protests, "I've done some quality violence for those people" (3.13). Buffy's first instinct for solving problems is to resort to violence. So when Xander tells her that she does not know how to defeat a particular monster, she replies, "I thought I might try violence" (2.18). On a field trip, Buffy prepares to stop a student from defacing museum property. When Willow suggests a non-violent approach, Buffy counters with the hesitant assertion, "I wasn't gonna use violence. I don't *always* use violence . . . Do I?" Xander's reply to Buffy is informative: "The important thing is, you believe that" (2.4).

The show's protagonists threaten violence as a form of revenge. Even gentle Willow, after giving Riley dating advice on how to talk to Buffy, adds a final caveat: "And remember, if you hurt her, I will beat you to death with a shovel" (4.7). Likewise, when Dawn reunites with Spike for the first time after his attempted rape of Buffy, she makes her intentions clear: "I can't take you in a fight or anything, even with a chip in your head. But you do sleep. If you hurt my sister at all . . . touch her . . . you're gonna wake up on fire" (7.2). At times violence is treated flippantly and with humor as when Dawn and Anya take turns hitting their hostage Andrew (7.10). This sometimes casual attitude towards violence surfaces in the following exchange between Dawn and Andrew:

DAWN: Buffy said if you talked enough, I'm allowed to kill you.
ANDREW (timidly): Not even.
DAWN (cocks her head to the side): Even.
ANDREW: License to kill, huh? (nods) Pretty cool. (7.11)

From these examples and others, it appears that *Buffy* glorifies violence through its casual, pervasive, and often humorous treatment of it.

Yet the incoherence arises from the fact that the underlying message of *Buffy* is actually one of restraint and of the seriousness of human violence. Violence is not a violation of Buffy's moral code, but integral to it.[5] Violence is an expression of power and, as with all power on *Buffy*, is subject to moral evaluation based on usage. When Buffy and her friends use violence, it is typically for protection of the innocent, for battle against evil, and "as an instrument of social change."[6] *Buffy* is a show that relishes the exercise of violence while simultaneously arguing for its responsible use. This incoherence finds expression in Buffy herself who "is a demon-killer obsessed with the morality of killing."[7] Consequently, a moral evaluation of *Buffy* that focuses strictly on its narrative presentation of violence without attention to its underlying perspective on violence misreads the narrative.

THE RESPONSIBILITY OF NARRATIVE

Joss Whedon suggests that the portrayal of violence is inherent to the act of storytelling. Consequently, if one is to tell stories responsibly as a means of dealing emotionally with the reality of violence in the world, then the storyteller must engage violence honestly. Yet at the same time that the storyteller bears the responsibility to allow violence to grow out of the story, he or she also bears the responsibility to address violence in a way that neither glorifies nor promotes it. He says about his responsibility as a storyteller:

> I've thought about this a lot . . . I think we have a grave responsibility. I think it would be belittling our audience to say that if we poke a stick in somebody's eye on the show they're all going to do it, because they're a little more intelligent than that. But you absolutely have to think about what it will mean. At the same time, I feel strongly . . . that we have a responsibility to be irresponsible. As

storytellers, I've always been very offended by the whole, 'let's rewrite all the fairytales' where the three little pigs settle their differences with the wolf by talking about their feelings.[8]

Buffy engages reality through fantasy. These fairytale-like stories of monsters and demons are a funhouse mirror reflection of real life, distorting the surface picture while still capturing the substance. Most of the violence on *Buffy* is fantasy violence — largely bloodless, sterile, and at times comical. Whedon says it was essential that the vampires look like demons when Buffy fights them and that they explode into dust when killed so that it would be clear that this is fantasy violence.[9] By contrast, "The Body" (5.16) is an attempt to deal with the death of Buffy's mother in a realistic fashion. Throughout the episode, there is neither violence nor any distinct fantasy element — until the last scene. While Buffy and Dawn are in the morgue at the hospital, one of the corpses on a nearby table arises as a vampire and attacks them, only to be dispatched by Buffy and explode into dust. This abrupt break in the realistic tone of the episode serves as a comment on the difference between a fantasy death (the vampire) and a "real" death (Joyce).

At times the line between fantasy and real violence can become blurred, leading to heightened questioning about media responsibility. In the episode "Earshot" (3.18), Buffy temporarily gains the ability to hear people's thoughts and overhears someone at school planning a killing spree. When Xander expresses surprise that a student might want to kill other students, Cordelia chimes in with "Yeah, because *that* never happens in American High Schools." The problem with the episode is that it was filmed shortly *before* the student massacre at Columbine High School on April 20, 1999 and scheduled to air shortly *after*. Because the episode resonated too closely with the reality of high school violence, the network postponed its airing indefinitely, a move Whedon supported.[10] Kathleen McConnell argues that one of the reasons for the postponement of this episode was a recognition that *Buffy* "re-entrenches the myth of high school as hell: Columbine both happened because, and proves that, *Buffy's* central tenet is not fiction." It thus forced the culture to face and ultimately choose to repress the fear that *Buffy* too accurately reflects the reality of American high schools.[11] Regardless of whether that is true, the timing of the episode was so close to the Columbine event that postponement was a valid choice.

When the network later overreacted, however, and postponed the season ending episode "Graduation Day, Part Two" (3.22) out of fear that it might spark violence at graduation ceremonies, Whedon was less understanding because the violence in that episode more clearly resided in the realm of fantasy. It involved students at the Sunnydale graduation packing crossbows and swords in order to combat a sixty-foot tall demon snake. Nevertheless, although Whedon protests that the decision represented a misreading of the nature of violence in *Buffy*, he also recognized the social responsibility he has a storyteller, noting that had they aired the show as scheduled and outbreaks of violence at graduations occurred, "there would have been a very bad taste in everyone's mouth."[12]

In the following sections, I examine *Buffy*'s perspective on violence from several angles. Although I will look at a variety of narrative features and themes, what continually surfaces through this examination is the dialectic between violence as horrific and violence as redemptive.

MONSTER VIOLENCE AND HUMAN VIOLENCE

Most of the violence on *Buffy* resides firmly in the realm of the fantastical. Monsters and demons kill humans, and humans kill monsters and demons. Due to its fantasy nature, much of this violence serves a metaphorical end as it represents battle against the personal and social demons of life. Buffy's constant and firm insistence that there is a vital distinction between being a Slayer and being a killer is a tacit acknowledgment that violence against demons and violence against humans is qualitatively different. It is a testimony to the fantasy nature of the show and its attitude towards real world violence that, with the exception of the Initiative, guns rarely make an appearance on the show. Buffy herself declines guns in favor of the more traditional weaponry of stakes, swords, and crossbows. In "As You Were" (6.15), she tosses aside a gun commenting, "These things? Never useful."

On *Buffy* human death is treated with the utmost gravity, and it is when humans act inhumanely towards other humans that *Buffy* finds its true grounding in horror. Whedon has commented that people are what terrify him the most.[13] There is no act of violence perpetrated by a demon or monster on *Buffy* that can outdo the real world capacity of humans for evil. Thus, on *Buffy*, the disgust and horror expressed at the thought of a human who kills far outweighs that of a demon (1.9; 3.11). The dream monster that hunts comatose Billy Palmer in "Nightmares" is just a pale imitation of the little league coach who put him in the coma to begin with (1.10). When nerdy Warren, initially played for comic relief, kills his ex-girlfriend Katrina and then later kills Tara with a gun, he becomes one of the series' scariest villains because his acts of violence cut so closely to the reality of our nightly newscasts.

The line between fantasy monster and human monster becomes blurry in "Some Assembly Required" (2.2). A student, Chris, chops up the bodies of three girls who died in a car accident in order to create a Frankenstein-like female. Willow tells Buffy not to be too hard on Chris because, after all, "he's not a vampire." Buffy reveals the show's attitude towards humans who do inhuman things when she replies, "No, he's just a ghoul." Willow's extremely violent murder of Warren taps into the horror and unpredictability of the human monster, for she had been the most gentle and compassionate person on the show. Likewise, Faith's transformation into a human monster comes with an act of violence against another human: the murder of Deputy Mayor Allan Finch. Angel says of Faith, "She killed a man. That changes everything for her" (3.15). With an act of violence against another human being, Faith crossed the line from Slayer to "killer" and cemented her status as one of the most horrific kinds of monsters on *Buffy*: the human kind.

REDEMPTIVE VIOLENCE

The two main redemptive events in the biblical story, the exodus of the Israelites from Egypt and the cross of Christ, both combine redemption and violence. Whether used actively or received passively, violence often goes hand in hand with redemption. Violence may be the spark that unites the fiery passion for redemption or an active agent in it. Joss Whedon has recognized this and expressed a personal interest in stories that revolve around the theme of "redemption-through-violence."[14] Significant redemptive moments for several characters on *Buffy* occur in a context of violence. Willow's redemption comes while trying to kill Xander and destroy the world (6.22). Andrew's recognition and acceptance of his guilt occurs only because of the threat of violence (7.16).

Both Faith and Spike represent similar attitudes towards violence in their redemptive journeys. Prior to redemption, both relish violence, finding it fun and freeing. Spike, who claims to "love a good slaughter as much as the next blokc" (2.17) and often seeks out a "spot of violence before bedtime" (5.4), lives to cause harm. Violence is his reason to exist. When each reaches moments of crisis that set them off on the path of redemption, they are moments marked by violence. Faith's acknowledgment of her own moral failings occurs with an act of violence in a church (4.16). Spike's attempted rape of Buffy is the catalyst for his quest to reclaim his soul (6.19). Interestingly, whereas Faith and Spike both lived lives of violence and were set on the path of redemption in contexts of violence, their post-redemption status brings with it a different attitude towards violence. Their pre-redemption attitude of violence as freeing and fun becomes a post-redemption recognition of the seriousness of violence. So when Buffy punches the reformed Faith, the Faith who always retaliated in the past, now does not (7.19). Spike returns to Sunnydale claiming that his soul has provided him with a newfound understanding of violence. When Buffy accuses him of having gone soft, he says, "I haven't quite been relishing the kill the way I used to" (7.15). It is a paradoxical assertion on *Buffy* that just as violence can serve the cause of redemption, redemption creates a more cautious and responsible attitude towards violence.

VIOLENCE AS METAPHOR

Violence can function as a metaphor for emotional expression. It can be an externalization of the internal battles we fight against personal and social demons. After Buffy's death at the hands of the Master and subsequent resuscitation, she engages in a fierce pummeling of the Master's minions. When Xander comments that this battle is Buffy "working out her issues," he points us to the fact that the battle is a visualization of her internal fight against the fear of her own mortality (2.1). In "Dead Man's Party" (3.2), Buffy's defeat of an army of zombies risen from the grave is really a representation of her overcoming the buried issues and emotions that have separated her from her friends. It is no coincidence that as soon as the last zombie is dispatched, Buffy and her friends reunite in a big group hug. The M'Fashnik demon that Buffy encounters in "Flooded" (6.4) is a metaphor for the financial problems threatening to do her in. She first meets this demon in a bank of all places while seeking a loan to pay for the full copper re-pipe she needs to fix her flooded basement. Towards the end of the episode, the demon attacks her in her home (the source of her financial woes). As they battle, Buffy laments and attempts to minimize the financial damage he is causing.

> M'FASHNIK: You have cost me, Slayer.
> BUFFY: I cost *you*? That's a designer lamp, ya mook!

Their battle eventually leads to the basement where Buffy beats him to death with the very pipe that needs fixing. Her killing of the demon is clearly a metaphor for the conquering of her financial problems as she accompanies the beating of the demon with the refrain, "Full . . . copper . . . re-pipe! No . . . more . . . full . . . copper . . . re-pipe!"

Another metaphorical use of violence on *Buffy* is violence as conversation. Lakoff and Johnson contend that one of the root metaphors used to structure communication is "argument is war."[15] On *Buffy*, the metaphor of argument as war becomes embodied in visual form with the portrayal of verbal confrontation as physical confrontation. Buffy and Spike's volatile conversations are typically punctuated with violence as their verbal sparring manifests as physical sparring. Their traded blows accentuate the points they are making. A clear visualization of the metaphor of argument as war occurs when Spike returns to Buffy's house only to discover that her friends have exiled her. Spike confronts Faith over the issue and their subsequent argument is an alternation of counterpoints and counterpunches. Every verbal jab is followed by a physical one (7.20).

The violence inherent in Buffy's identity as Slayer also serves a metaphorical purpose. Her fight against vampires is a representation of society's fight against its own demons. Mimi Marinucci suggests that Buffy's "mission is symbolic of the fight against sexual violence . . . It is her duty to battle the strangers lurking in shadows and dark alleys, eager to prey on the enticing bodies of innocent and unwilling human beings."[16] Warfare imagery becomes pervasive in season seven with Buffy setting herself up as a general who trains and leads an army of potential Slayers in battle against The First and its army of vampires. Buffy acknowledges that as leader of this army, she will have to make decisions resulting in the deaths of good people (7.16-17). She has to look at the big picture and make tough choices. On one level, this theme taps into the ethics of warfare. *Buffy*'s perspective seems to be that although war is ugly, messy, and the cause of too much death, it is at times necessary. Buffy is willing to risk the lives of the potential Slayers and of her friends because she believes in her moral responsibility to protect the world against destructive and demonic forces. As such, the warfare imagery of this season is also metaphorical. The metaphysical (even spiritual) battle of good versus evil is here embodied as a physical war between Buffy and The First Evil.

Any moral evaluation of violent acts on television requires an awareness of that show's method of moral reasoning and its narrative devices. The violence on *Buffy* functions not to promote violence or aggression, but to comment on the reality of life. The violence on *Buffy* at least partly functions as a metaphorical structuring device that organizes our conceptions of violence and of the issues and emotional demons we symbolically fight against.

THE CYCLE OF VENGEANCE

Jenny Calendar's uncle tells her, "Vengeance is a living thing" (2.14). It is not a mere weapon to be wielded, but a force all its own that consumes and is never satisfied. Vengeance knows no reason, no boundaries. When vengeance demon Halfrek says that half the time she's not even sure if she's maiming the right guy, it is a testimony to how vengeance can become blind to its victims (6.12). One of the most dangerous aspects of vengeance is its tendency to cloak itself as justice. Halfrek notes that a vengeance demon prefers to be called a "justice demon" (6.14). But vengeance and justice are not interchangeable. Justice is about equity, about a balancing of the scales in fairness. Vengeance is about payback, about a never-ending cycle of violence that escalates until it consumes everything in its path. At least Jenny Calendar's uncle is honest when he says, "It is not justice we serve. It is vengeance" (2.14).

The vengeance demon Anyanka, a.k.a. the human Anya, is at the center of *Buffy*'s most extensive rumination on vengeance. Her career as a vengeance demon began in 880 AD when she was a human girl married to Olaf. This Anya was generous to a fault, wanting to donate her excess rabbits "to the townspeople, exchanging them not for goods or services, but for goodwill and the sense of accomplishment that stems from selflessly giving of yourself to others" (7.5). When Olaf cheats on her with a bar matron, Anya seeks vengeance against him. The ferocity of her retaliation catches the attention of the demon D'Hoffryn who offers Anya an official gig as a vengeance demon (7.5).

Anya embodies the idea that vengeance is a selfish act. It is a self-centered pursuit of retribution with little concern for its effects on others. It is noteworthy that the specialty of vengeance demons is connected to their own personal pain. Halfrek, who has "daddy issues," exacts vengeance against bad parents (6.14). Having been scorned herself, Anya focuses her vengeance on men who wrong women. Hailed as "the single most hard-core vengeance demon on the roster" (7.1), Anya cuts a wide swath of destruction across the next millennium, with her punishments against men ranging from evisceration to making them "double-check spreadsheets for all eternity" (6.1).

When Anya loses her vengeance powers and becomes human again, she retains the self-centeredness that she had cultivated over a millennium given to the pursuit of payback. When Willow pleads with Anya for help, Anya sighs and asks, "Is it difficult or time-consuming?" (7.3). This selfishness manifests particularly as materialism. When Anya begins working for Giles at the Magic Shop, her customer relations leave much to be desired. After taking money from customers, she tells them to "Please go" instead of "Have a nice day" because "I have their money. Who cares what kind of day they have?" (5.5).

Humanity eventually takes its toll on Anya, and she gradually acquires a sense of the value of others. Nevertheless, she reaches a crisis point on the day of her wedding to Xander. A man whom Anya had cursed during her days as a vengeance demon returns and sabotages her wedding by encouraging Xander to break it off (6.16). Vengeance has come full circle. Vengeance never ends, is never sated. It hungers like a living thing. Scorned once again as Xander breaks off the wedding, Anya returns to the fold of vengeance. That Anya goes from human to vengeance demon to human and back to vengeance demon again is a visual representation of this endless cycle of vengeance.

The message is that the only person who can stop the cycle of vengeance is the one who seeks it. Since vengeance is a selfish act, the repudiation of vengeance can only come through selflessness. Anya initially seeks vengeance against Xander, but when the moment for retaliation comes, she relents (6.18). Her genuine concern and affection for him overrides her desire for revenge. After this, Anya continues as a vengeance demon, but an ineffectual one. When Willow sets out to avenge the death of Tara, Anya tries to stop her because she knows the pursuit of vengeance will destroy Willow (6.21). Later Anya reverses one of her own vengeance spells when she witnesses the damage caused (7.2). Afterwards, Anya confesses to Willow that vengeance is not fulfilling for her any more:

> WILLOW: Really? 'Cause I got the impression that you enjoyed, you know, inflicting.
> ANYA: Well, causing pain sounds really cool, I know, but turns out it's really upsetting. Didn't used to be, but now it is. (7.3)

The cycle of vengeance reaches a climax in the aptly titled episode, "Selfless" (7.5). Desperate to prove that she still has the chops as a vengeance demon, Anya performs an act of vengeance that results in the mass slaughter of young men at a college frat house. Her subsequent guilt is palpable as she, smeared with blood, sits in the frat house and says, "What have I done?" In an act of selflessness, Anya seeks to make things right. She offers D'Hoffryn her own life if he will restore the lives of the dead. She has finally broken the cycle of vengeance by returning to the generosity and selflessness of her original nature. D'Hoffryn agrees to the bargain, but takes the life of Anya's friend Halfrek instead as a form of his own vengeance against Anya. When the final battle against The First comes around, Anya brings her character's story to a close by giving her own life in order to save the life of Andrew (7.22). The most selfish of them all has become selfless, and in that act provides a model of the antithesis of vengeance.

SUMMARY

I suggested that *Buffy the Vampire Slayer* was a type of incoherent text with respect to violence in that the show regularly portrays acts of violence, often in very attractive and engaging ways, yet ultimately preaches about the dangers of violence. Too many critics miss the point when they fixate on *Buffy*'s portrayal of violence because they overlook the show's perspective on violence. *Buffy* draws a clear and distinct line between violence against demons and violence against humans. It suggests that violence can be an agent of redemption, and redemption demands a new view of violence.

This topic illustrates that understanding a show's perspective on violence requires attention to its method of moral discourse. A responsible viewer must evaluate metaphorical acts of violence by a different standard than acts of violence portrayed merely to shock and amuse. A responsible viewer must pay attention to context and narrative arcs, or else risk missing the forest for the trees. One could focus on any number of isolated moments involving Anya and come to the conclusion that *Buffy* takes vengeance lightly and uses it simply as a source of amusement. By failing to view those isolated episodes as part of a character's life cycle, these viewers miss the real message, which is that vengeance is a deadly cycle to be stopped only by selfless love. What a similar tragedy it would be to take only isolated moments in a person's life and assume they represent the totality of their moral character. *Buffy* represents the view that life is a process of growth and maturation that involves learning to come out of the darkness and into the light.

Chapter 15

Guilt and Forgiveness

In previous chapters, I discuss a variety of immoral actions and the perspective that *Buffy the Vampire Slayer* gives to them. Whereas those chapters focus on the performance of immoral and harmful acts, this chapter focuses on the *response* to such acts. The themes of guilt and forgiveness relate to other recurring themes on *Buffy*: consequences, power, and community. Guilt is a consequence of bad choices and immoral behavior. It arises from a variety of actions on *Buffy*: causing harm to others, lying, cheating on a boyfriend, and keeping secrets to name a few. This guilt creates a need for forgiveness, which is tied to both power and community. A wronged person possesses power of a sort. If a guilty party seeks forgiveness, the wronged person has the power to alleviate their guilt through forgiveness or to twist it like a vise.

Being in a position of moral superiority, that is being the one providing rather than needing forgiveness, is a position of power. As with all power on *Buffy*, the issue is how that power is used. A refusal to forgive or, even worse, holding out the promise of forgiveness while simultaneously ratcheting up the other person's guilt, is an abuse of that power. To forgive selflessly and unconditionally, however, is an expression of power in service to others. On *Buffy*, the act of forgiveness has close ties to community. In a community where acceptance and mutual dependence are prized virtues, forgiveness is a must.

Buffy the Vampire Slayer takes guilt very seriously, both in terms of its ability to paralyze and in terms of its ability to motivate redemption. Yet, *Buffy* takes the perspective that guilt is ultimately destructive unless coupled with forgiveness.

A USELESS EMOTION?

As the time approaches for the goddess Glory to attempt a return to her own dimension, the veil separating her from her host body (Ben) begins to fade and Glory becomes contaminated by Ben's emotions. One of those emotions is guilt. This perplexes Glory, for a goddess is not supposed to experience human feelings. She declares that human emotions like guilt are "useless" because they overpower rational thought (5.21). Is guilt a useless emotion? Many would suggest so. For some guilt is nothing more than the unwanted remnants of a puritanical age that impede us from doing what we want to do. Guilt is a barrier to true freedom.

The feeling of guilt is akin to the physical experience of pain. Pain is a warning mechanism that alerts us to a problem with our bodies. If we pay due attention to pain and respond to it properly, it can be an extremely useful, though decidedly unpleasant, experience. Likewise, guilt is a warning mechanism that alerts us when something has gone wrong with our souls. Vampires experience no remorse over their actions because they lack souls. On *Buffy* the soul is a necessary prerequisite for guilt. A soul does not guarantee redemptive behavior, but it does create the possibility for remorse. Xander confuses the two while sharing an apartment with the re-ensouled Spike.

> XANDER: I'm just saying . . . once you get back the soul, doesn't that mean you start, like, picking up your own wet towels off the floor?
> WILLOW: No, but maybe you start to feel really bad about leaving them there (7.6).

The feeling of guilt is a warning that something is amiss with one's moral compass and, if strong enough, motivates steps to alleviate that guilt.

One common attempt to alleviate guilt is the self-infliction of physical or emotional punishment. Willow is a paragon for this type of ascetic guilt. She says her response to feeling attracted to guys other than her boyfriend is, "I feel guilty, and I flog and punish" (4.6). When

Willow is caught kissing Xander, she describes her guilt as overwhelming: "I never knew there was anything inside me that could feel this bad" (3.8). Her response is a desire to be punished. She says of Cordelia, who was Xander's girlfriend at the time, "Cordelia belongs to the justified camp. She *should* make us pay. And pay and pay and pay" (3.9). For Willow, punishment is a means of lessening the pain of guilt, yet she finds it to be ultimately ineffectual. The resolution of her pain comes only from Oz's forgiveness.

In Willow's case, she acted immorally, and guilt was the appropriate reaction. Her desire to suffer for her guilt was the problem. An ascetic form of guilt is unhealthy and damaging to a person because, unlike in Willow's case, it is often tied to actions that one *feels* responsible for but is not. So, for instance, Buffy feels guilty over her parents' divorce (1.10) and for not doing enough to try and save her mother after she found her dead (5.17). In these instances, guilt itself is the problem. It becomes a damaging emotion that imprisons the bearer in a self-made cell. Several episodes on *Buffy* explore this form of guilt and offer a resolution for it.

"The Killer In Me"

Given Willow's penchant for self-inflicted guilt and her desire to be punished, it comes as no surprise that she blames herself when Warren kills Tara. "The Killer In Me" (7.13) explores Willow's guilt over Tara's death and Willow's attempt to move on with her life. Unbeknownst to Willow, rival witch Amy casts on her a "standard penance malediction," in which a person's subconscious selects his or her own punishment. Thus, when Willow starts to move on with her life romantically, her appearance suddenly morphs into that of Warren. Gradually Willow is turning into Warren as a physical manifestation of her guilt. She begins to replay in her mind the day that Warren killed Tara, although in Willow's mind, she is the one responsible. She says, "I let her be dead. She's really dead. And I killed her." Adopting the appearance of the man who physically killed Tara is Willow's way of punishing herself for having to figuratively "kill off" Tara in order to move on with her life. Because Willow's punishment was self-motivated in response to an event for which she was not truly responsible, the solution requires that she forgive herself. Thus, the use of the magical curse on this episode functions as a comment on the human tendency to burden ourselves with unnecessary guilt.

"Passion," "Killed By Death," and "I Only Have Eyes For You"

These three episodes, airing in succession, form a trio that addresses Buffy's guilt over Angel's loss of his soul due to their night of passion. Although Buffy accepts responsibility for what she did, she refuses to seek absolution, opting instead to punish herself with guilt. In "Passion" (2.17), Buffy faces the tragic consequences of her tryst with Angel when the soulless Angelus murders Jenny Calendar. In the next episode, "Killed By Death" (2.18), Buffy is hospitalized with the flu. Joyce's comment that Buffy never gets sick, but that she has been down ever since Jenny's death, suggests that Buffy's flu is a physical manifestation of her guilt over the death of Jenny. Compounding that is the fact that Buffy has a fear of hospitals stemming from her eight-year old cousin's death in a hospital while Buffy was present. Buffy's guilt, manifesting as the flu, is consuming her for failing to stop those deaths. While in the hospital, Buffy claims to see an invisible demon that brings death to children, the same demon that killed her cousin. By defeating the demon and by learning that she was in fact not responsible for her cousin's death, Buffy is able to forgive herself for her cousin's death. She is not yet, however, able to forgive herself for Angel.

In "I Only Have Eyes For You" (2.19), Buffy continues to punish herself for causing the loss of Angel's soul and for Jenny's subsequent death. The setting of this episode is the Sadie Hawkins Dance. As the days lead up to the dance, the spirit of a former student named James who had an affair with a teacher named Grace Newman haunts Sunnydale High. When Ms. Newman broke off their relationship, James accidentally killed her with a gun and then, in remorse, killed himself. The spirit of James is continually re-creating the tragedy in the halls of Sunnydale High in the hope of attaining forgiveness.

James' spirit is attracted to Buffy in this episode because it senses in her the same pain and guilt it experiences. Buffy herself subconsciously recognizes the similarity between James' murder of the woman he loved and her "murder" of the Angel she loved. When Buffy describes the punishment that she thinks James deserves, Xander replies, "Yikes. The quality of mercy is not Buffy." Because Buffy sees herself reflected in James, she desires harsh punishment for him as a way of expressing the punishment she feels she deserves. This becomes clear in the following exchange after Giles explains to Buffy that James is caught in a purgatory where he is forced to kill Ms. Newman repeatedly and, therefore, "forgiveness is impossible."

> BUFFY: Good. He doesn't deserve it.
> GILES: To forgive is an act of compassion, Buffy. It's, it's, it's not done because people deserve it, it's done because they need it.
> BUFFY: No. James destroyed the one person he loved the most in a moment of blind passion. That's not something you forgive. No matter why he did what he did. And no matter if he knows now that it was wrong and selfish and stupid. It is just something he's gonna have to live with.
> XANDER: He can't live with it, Buff. He's dead.
> (Buffy turns and storms out)
> CORDELIA: Ok. Overidentify much?

Buffy refuses to allow forgiveness for James because to do so means she would have to forgive herself.

Eventually the spirits of James and Ms. Newman possess both Buffy and Angel respectively. Now Buffy (as James) and Angel (as Ms. Newman) replay the night of the tragic murder. This time, however, when James (in Buffy's body) shoots Ms. Newman (in Angel's body), she doesn't die — the benefit of a vampire's body. Instead she forgives James for what he did. Whedon comments that this episode is really about Buffy learning to forgive herself and coming to the realization that there is "redemption out there for her."[1] Later Buffy comments, "A part of me just doesn't understand why she would forgive him." When Giles asks her if it really matters, she says, "No. I guess not." By re-creating the drama between James and Ms. Newman, Buffy has received a kind of forgiveness from Angel and in that finds the strength to forgive herself.

"The Weight of the World"

Towards the end of season five, Buffy is desperately trying to hide Dawn from Glory. She promises Dawn that she will not let anything happen to her, but then Buffy makes a mistake that results in Dawn's kidnapping (5.20). In doing so, Buffy represents parents who inadvertently bring harm to their child or who blame themselves for a child's abduction, constantly replaying in their mind all the things they could have done differently.

The subsequent episode, "The Weight of the World" (5.21), deals with Buffy's guilt and the heavy emotional burden of destructive thinking. Emotionally paralyzed by the weight of guilt over Dawn's abduction, Buffy shuts down and enters a catatonic state. In this state, she replays in her mind three scenes. In one she is a young girl of about six years old who holds the newborn Dawn in her arms and asks her parents if she can sometimes take care of her sister. This scene clearly taps into her guilt over her failure to do just that. In another scene, a grown up Buffy stands at her mother's grave. Then she walks into her sister's room where Dawn is asleep and begins to smother her with a pillow. She feels responsible for the death of her mother and believes she has now killed Dawn as well. The final scene shows Buffy walking up to a bookshelf and placing a book in it. These three scenes constantly replay in Buffy's mind. She is stuck in a loop of guilt, the never-ending cycle of destructive thoughts that can only be broken by forgiveness.

The scene at the bookshelf provides the key for unlocking Buffy's catatonic state. This scene shows Buffy reliving a moment when she thought that she could not defeat Glory and for a brief second actually longed for defeat. By imagining what a relief it would be for Glory to kill Dawn and then leave this dimension, Buffy believes she has caused Dawn's death. She says, "My thinking it made it happen." That is the destructive power of guilt. How many children have thought in a brief moment of anger that they hate their parents, and then suffer a lifetime of unnecessary guilt when one of them later dies? How many children burden themselves with guilt over a divorce because they blame themselves for it? How many people daily bear the weight of the world on their shoulders because they fail to relinquish guilt for things that they were never responsible for?

Willow helps Buffy break the endless loop of guilt when she magically enters her mind and tells her, "All this . . . it has a name. It's called guilt. It's a feeling, and it's important. But it's not more than that, Buffy." By forgiving herself, Buffy unburdens herself of unnecessary guilt and is able to stop the downward spiral of destructive thinking.

Buffy the Vampire Slayer suggests that guilt can be a useless and even harmful emotion when it results from self-destructive thinking designed to punish oneself for actions or thoughts that are neither immoral nor intentional. In this sense, guilt becomes self-inflicted torture that can be alleviated only through self-directed forgiveness. But what about when guilt results from actions that are immoral, intentional, and harmful?

A USEFUL EMOTION

Anger is an emotion that can be wielded for great destruction and harm. Anger is also an emotion that can lead to the correction of injustice, the defense of the innocent, and activism for righteous causes. Guilt is like anger in that it can serve both destructive and redemptive ends. If guilt is a form of emotional pain designed to signal that something is spiritually wrong with a person, the value of guilt, as with pain, lies in the response to that signal. *Buffy the Vampire Slayer* explores this side of guilt through character arcs.

Faith: Accountability Denied

One of the methods *Buffy the Vampire Slayer* uses to comment on moral issues is the negative example. After Faith kills Deputy Mayor Allan Finch, she is wracked with guilt. The question is what will she do with that guilt? At first, Faith returns to her motel room and furiously scrubs her bloody shirt in the sink trying to remove the guilt by removing the blood. What she fails to recognize is that a cleansing from guilt comes only through confession and accountability. When removing the blood fails to work, Faith removes the body. She is now trying to remove her guilt by burying it. Buffy tells her, "Getting rid of the evidence doesn't make the problem go away." Faith replies, "It does for me" (3.14).

In the next episode, "Consequences" (3.15), Faith breaks into the Mayor's office and sees a picture of Allan Finch. She holds the picture gently and seems to experience a moment of remorse (for Faith a sign of weakness). She puts the picture down and quickly recovers, noting, "Whatever. I'm not lookin' to hug and cry and learn and grow." Faith's problem is precisely that. She refuses to use her guilt as a motivation for growth. Giles comments on this when he says, "She's utterly unable to accept responsibility . . . There is no help for her until she admits what happened." Guilt that leads to confession and accountability is a valuable emotion. It is Faith's denial of her guilt that becomes the destructive force in her life. By accepting her guilt, her life could have taken a different path. Thus we see once again that, with Faith, *Buffy* portrays the immoral actions of a character as a means of offering positive moral comment. This is done less through strict denunciation of the character's immoral actions than it is by showing how characters respond to those actions. Faith's denial of her guilt and of her accountability highlights the necessity of both because we witness where Faith's denial takes her: down the path of evil and self-destruction.

Buffy: Absolution Rejected

Willow's characteristic response to guilt is to seek absolution. At times she attempts this through self-inflicted emotional torment. At other times her attempt at absolution involves acts of penance. When her selfishly motivated magic spell puts her friends in danger, Willow bakes chocolate chip cookies in order to make amends. Anya asks how long she intends to do this and Willow replies, "Oh, until I don't feel so horribly guilty. I figure about a million chips from now. Also, I have to detail Giles' car" (4.9). What lies behind Willow's eager desire for forgiveness is a need to be accepted by her community and to be loved for who she is.

In contrast, Buffy's attitude towards forgiveness in season six is a denial of who she is. Buffy's degenerate relationship with Spike creates a deep level of guilt and shame within her to the extent that when Spike compliments her hair, she cuts it off, asking to be made "different" (6.11). Buffy deals with the guilt by convincing herself that it is not the real her doing these things. She believes that when she came back from the dead, she came back wrong. During a particularly horrid sexual encounter with Spike, Spike taunts her by saying, "What would they think of you . . . if they found out all the things you've done? If they knew . . . who you really are?" (6.13).

That question of identity is at the heart of the matter. Buffy rationalizes her behavior by assuring herself that she came back different. In order to prove this to herself, Buffy asks Tara to investigate her resurrection and find out how she was changed. The news is not good. Tara informs Buffy that, other than receiving the equivalent of a molecular sunburn, there is nothing wrong with her. Buffy is devastated. "There has to be!" she says. "This just can't be me, it isn't me." Buffy confesses her relationship with Spike to Tara and then, in a highly dramatic moment, Buffy tearfully begs Tara, "Please don't forgive me." Buffy falls to her knees, sobbing, and again pleads, "Please *don't* forgive me" (6.13).

What underlies Buffy's rejection of forgiveness is a denial of the truth. If she accepts forgiveness, then she must also accept that it is really her doing these things. She will no longer be able to hide behind the excuse that she came back wrong. As with Faith, Buffy also offers moral exhortation through a negative example. Her insistence on not being forgiven emphasizes the need for accepting forgiveness if true absolution is to occur. Many people have a difficult time accepting forgiveness because they believe, like Willow, that guilt requires punishment. Later Buffy will explain her behavior by stating, "I wanted to be punished. I wanted to hurt like I thought I deserved" (7.7). The biblical doctrine of grace, which is about receiving favor and forgiveness when it is neither deserved nor merited, is one of the most challenging for people to accept ironically because they do not feel worthy of it.

In Buffy's case, the forgiveness at hand is not about wiping the cosmic slate clean or seeking divine absolution. For her, it is about learning to trust in the grace of community. On *Buffy*, forgiveness is a communal virtue. The acceptance that community demands extends itself in unconditional forgiveness. Buffy, Xander, Willow and Giles regularly and consistently forgive one another in a model of grace. The foundation for this community ethic comes in "When She Was Bad" (2.1), the episode where Buffy learns unconditional acceptance. Distraught over how she has treated Xander and Willow, Buffy believes she doesn't deserve forgiveness.

> BUFFY: What am I supposed to say? 'Sorry I almost got your throat slit. What's the homework?'
> GILES: Punishing yourself like this is pointless.
> BUFFY: It's entirely pointy. I was a moron. I put my best friends in mortal danger on the second day of school.

Yet when Buffy reluctantly drags herself into class, she sees that Xander and Willow have saved her a seat. They act towards her as though nothing has happened, and the episode ends with a smile on Buffy's face that shows the realization of forgiveness and how it has freed her from guilt.

This foundation of grace in community makes Buffy's refusal of forgiveness stand out. It seems that the shame Buffy feels over her relationship with Spike is so great that she fears it will test the limits of her community's forgiveness. She realizes otherwise when her later attempt to kill her friends, while in a state of altered consciousness, fails to turn them against her (6.17). Following this event, Buffy tells Spike that she is no longer concerned about her friends finding out about them because "I tried to kill my friends, my sister, last week . . . and guess how much they hate me. Zero. Zero much. So I'm thinking, sleeping with you? They'll deal" (6.18). Through this action, Buffy has learned the power of grace and so she extends it to others. When Willow returns to Sunnydale following her attempt to destroy the world, she is fearful that her friends are no longer her friends. Buffy, however, is the first to accept her back unconditionally, prompting Willow to say, "It's nice to be forgiven. Too bad I need so much of it" (7.3).

Although most acts of forgiveness on *Buffy* are those defined by community acceptance and are essentially about the restoration of damaged relationships, there is also a more spiritual aspect represented. *Buffy* particularly draws on Christian ideas and themes when connecting forgiveness to the idea of redemption and atonement. Spike and Angel provide two examples of this phenomenon.

Spike: Repentance

In the episode titled "Restless" (4.22), written and directed by Joss Whedon, Buffy, Giles, Xander, and Willow have dreams that foreshadow events that are to unfold over the next few seasons. During Giles' dream, he visits Spike's crypt and discovers him posing for photographers. After striking a series of voguish and vampiric poses, Spike adopts a final pose: that of the Crucifixion. Feet together, arms outstretched in the shape of a cross, head bowed to the side, Spike resembles a Christ figure in black leather. It is a provocative scene, this vampire in messianic form. But what does it mean? Whedon has described "Restless" as "a forty-minute poem."[2] Just as poetry is figurative language, this visual poem contains images that are symbolic and fluid in meaning. As such, there is more than one way to interpret Spike's Crucifixion pose and two of those are explored in this chapter and the next.

The cross of Christ is a symbol of grace and forgiveness effected through sacrifice. The shedding of Christ's blood allows for cleansing and absolution. Spike himself comments of sacrifice that "it's always got to be blood" because blood is life (5.22). But the cross is also a symbol of the peace that can only be found in forgiveness and grace. In Matthew 11:28-29, Jesus hints at this when he says, "Come to me all you who are weary and are heavily burdened and I will give you *rest*. Take my yoke upon you and learn from me, because I am gentle and humble in heart, and you shall find *rest* for your souls."[3]

In "Restless," the dreams that each character has represent their various fears, insecurities, and anxieties; in other words, the restlessness of their souls. Spike, however, does not share that affliction because he has no soul. Along with the absence of a soul comes the absence of a conscience. When Spike finally regains his soul at the end of season six, the restlessness of a guilty conscience comes with it. Spike says, "I can't cry the soul out of me. It won't come. I killed, and I can feel 'em. I can feel every one of them" (7.8). All of the people Spike has killed weigh heavily on his soul. With that guilt comes shame. A visual representation of Spike's shame occurs when he and Buffy visit a student's home. An angel decorates the doorjamb of the front door and Spike studiously avoids its glare. Then, inside the house, he sees a cabinet full of numerous angel figurines. One by one, Spike turns them all around so they face away from him (7.6). His inability to bear an angel's glare testifies to the depth of his self-loathing and the restlessness of his soul.

Guilt proves its value when it leads to repentance. Guilt can be rejected and buried, as with Faith, or it can become the motivation for a changed life. Spike opts for the latter. Buffy summarizes the essence of repentance when she tells Spike, "You faced the monster inside of you and you fought back" (7.9). Even Faith recognizes that Spike has become "all repenty" (7.18).

The foundational moment for Spike's repentance comes towards the end of "Beneath You" (7.2). Spike's restored soul is still fresh within him, the red marks on his chest still visible from when he tried to remove the guilt by clawing the soul out of himself. In this episode, Buffy, unaware of the restoration of Spike's soul and still bearing the emotional scars from his attempt to rape her, nonetheless agrees to let him fight beside her for sheer utilitarian reasons. When Spike unintentionally harms a human being, suddenly all of the guilt that he has been trying to suppress comes flooding forth. He yells out, "God, please help me" and runs away.

Buffy finds Spike holed up in a church. As she enters the church, moonlight illuminates a painting on the wall that appears to be Mary holding the baby Jesus. At the front of the church stands a six-foot tall, freestanding cross. Spike's facade of normality is gone. Clearly weary and suffering, Spike confesses to Buffy that he retrieved his soul, what he calls "the spark." He tells her that "it's here, in me, all the time . . . They put the spark in me and now all it does is burn." Looking up to the ceiling as if to God, Spike yells, "It's what you wanted, right?" But Spike is not so sure it is what *he* wants. He says that the voices of all the people he killed are in his head telling him to go "to hell." Although Spike recognizes that hell is where he belongs, in that moment he becomes cognizant of the prospect of grace. Turning towards the front of the church, Spike slowly walks towards the giant cross. His words dripping with both hope and regret, he says while eyeing the cross, "She shall look on him with forgiveness, and everybody will forgive and love. He will be loved." Spike then embraces the cross, laying his arms over the sidebars and gently resting his head upon it. His vampire body begins to sizzle from contact with this cross and smoke rises from it, but Spike pays no notice. He willingly pays this physical penance. He continues to hug the cross, his body hanging off it in a manner not unlike that of Jesus, and says, "Can — can we rest now? Buffy . . . can we rest?"

Spike's plea for rest, spoken while hanging onto a cross, clearly links this event back to his Crucifixion pose in "Restless" and offers insight into one meaning of that enigmatic scene. He is indeed hanging on a cross, but not as a sacrifice. He hangs onto the cross *because of* the sacrifice. It is the symbol for the forgiveness he seeks, for the grace that has heretofore alluded him. It is the source for the hope that he might not end up in the "hell" he deserves. In this act, Spike models repentance as an embracing of the cross and what it stands for. He clings to the cross even while his sins burn him, while the smoke from an unholy life rises off him like incense. Spike seeks a rest from the burden of his guilt by clinging to the cross of the one who promised that "you shall find rest for your souls."

Angel: Amends

Like Spike, Angel bears the guilt from a century of sin.[4] One may wonder why the gypsies who cursed Angel chose to restore his soul as their act of vengeance. Their reasoning was that only with a soul could Angel possibly know "true suffering" (2.21). True suffering, in their definition, comes from a conscience and from recognition of the pain caused by one's sins. They were correct. Angel notes that living without a soul was a form of freedom. "No conscience, no remorse," he says. "It's an easy way to live" (1.7). But a soul brings a constant reminder of one's moral failings. So the Angel with a soul says, "You have no idea what it's like to have done the things I've done . . . and to care" (1.7).

Angel's story is a story of guilt. While describing his attraction to the character of Angel, Whedon says:

> I'm not sure why it is that redemption is so fascinating to me. I think the mistakes I've made in my own life have plagued me, but they're pretty boring mistakes: I committed a series of grisly murders in the eighties and I think I once owned a Wilson-Phillips Album. Apart from that I'm pretty much an average guy, yet I have an enormous burden of guilt . . . Ultimately, the concept of somebody who needed to be redeemed is more interesting to me.[5]

Angel has borne his guilt for over a century, wallowing at times in self-pity and despair. The loss of his soul in the middle of season two, along with the accompanying freedom it brings, only adds to the death toll. Although Angel regains his soul once more at the end of that season, the emotional wounds from his recent acts of evil fester well into season three.

The climactic moment in Angel's battle with guilt occurs in an episode written and directed by Joss Whedon titled "Amends" (3.10). Forgiveness is a big theme for this episode. Oz forgives Willow for her brief indiscretion with Xander, Faith and Buffy temporarily mend the rift between them, and Giles wrestles with forgiving Angel for the murder of his girlfriend Jenny. This theme of forgiveness is not incidental to the setting of the episode: Christmas. This Christmas-themed show is all the more noteworthy considering it is the only episode of *Buffy*'s seven seasons to make Christmas a central feature. It is interesting that most of the episodes on *Buffy* that consistently incorporate Christian themes and ideas in a positive manner are those written by Joss Whedon, a self-proclaimed atheist.

"Amends" begins with a different Christmas setting. It is the year 1838 and Angel is on the hunt. He kills a man named Daniel as Daniel recites the 23rd Psalm. In this act, Angel symbolically repudiates the hope and grace that God offers. Throughout "Amends," the viewer witnesses several flashbacks of horrible murders committed by Angel. This device serves as a potent reminder of the evil within Angel and the very real challenges to his redemption.

Angel has been wondering why he was suddenly and inexplicably returned from the hell to which Buffy sent him at the end of season two. He wants to know what his purpose is. Making matters worse, his deceased victims refuse to stay dead. Angel begins to see many of his former victims all around him, Jenny Calendar included. His past is haunting him, reminding him of the pleasure he once took in evil. When the guilt becomes almost unbearable, temptation strikes. Angel realizes that if he sleeps with Buffy again and loses his soul, then all the pain, all the remorse, all the guilt will vanish away. Not trusting himself to resist this temptation, he chooses suicide and so journeys out onto a hill to await the morning sunrise and the death it will bring.

When Buffy finds him there, Angel tells her that he has figured out his purpose. He is a creature of evil and can be nothing else. Sooner or later, he believes he will give in to the temptation to be free of the burden of a soul and become a killer again. He may be a vampire, but the real danger is his human weakness or, as Angel puts it, "It's not the demon in me that needs killing, Buffy. It's the man." Angel's self-loathing guilt has produced in him a desire for punishment. He tells Buffy, "Am I a thing worth saving, huh? Am I a righteous man?" Angel falls prey to the paradox of grace, rejecting it out of a sense of unworthiness when the very nature of grace is that it is undeserved.

Buffy, however, offers the prospect of grace and forgiveness to Angel. Although Angel believes that Buffy can never understand the evil he has done, she tells him, "I know everything that you did, because you did it to me." Despite her firsthand knowledge of his crimes, Buffy offers her forgiveness. She pleads with him to get inside before the sun rises, telling him that "you have the power to do real good, to make amends. But if you die now, then all that you ever were was a monster."

Then, just as the sun is about to rise in Sunnydale, California, it unexpectedly begins to snow. Considering that the previous day's temperature was seventy degrees and that the snow and clouds block out much of the sun, thwarting Angel's suicide attempt, this "Christmas miracle" becomes a source of hope to Angel. He finds purpose for his life in making amends for the sins of his past.

Through the narrative presentation of these character-based stories, *Buffy the Vampire Slayer* reveals guilt as a potentially useful emotion. By depicting a variety of responses to immoral behavior, *Buffy* suggests that the value of guilt is to be found in the actions it motivates. Guilt can become unhealthy when it is suppressed or when it produces a non-redemptive desire to suffer and a lingering sense of unworthiness. Yet guilt proves its value when it generates confession, repentance, and the moral accountability represented by the desire to make amends.

THE "PANGS" OF CULTURAL GUILT

This discussion of guilt and forgiveness on *Buffy* provides illumination for one of the show's more controversial and, I believe, most misunderstood episodes: the Thanksgiving episode titled "Pangs" (4.8). The story is very simple: a spirit of the Chumash Indians of southern California, named Hus, awakens to seek vengeance for the wrongs done against his people by early colonial settlers. Buffy and her friends rise up to stop it. This story line, however, is really just a backdrop for addressing the heated cultural debate over how a society redresses the wrongs of its past.

This episode raises several intriguing questions about race, colonialism, cultural stereotypes, and cultural guilt. Is it acceptable to force guilt upon a generation for wrongs committed several hundred years prior by their ancestors? Is it acceptable to ignore those wrongs simply because one may not be personally responsible? Should one cease to celebrate Thanksgiving as a modern holiday simply because its origins are less than pure? What does one do with cultural guilt? If *Buffy*'s model is any guide, then one must acknowledge those wrongs and make amends. But this is the real crux of the matter, for the question is how does one make amends for cultural guilt?

This episode has received harsh criticism for its perceived racial stereotyping, cultural bigotry, and demonizing of the Chumash.[6] Although these criticisms have come from a variety of sources, the most sustained academic critique comes from Dominic Alessio who finds *Buffy*'s ambiguous treatment of race in this episode to be highly problematic. He laments the imperialistic mindset of some of the characters and the stereotyping and misrepresentation of the Chumash, such as having them speak English.[7] Most offensive is the ending of the episode where Buffy and her friends defeat the Native American spirits. The offense comes from a reduction of their conflict to a dualism of good and evil. Alessio refers to this ending as both "tragic" and a "cop-out."[8]

Every interpreter brings preconceptions and personal agendas to a text. Although these agendas necessarily play a role in how the text is interpreted, they should not be allowed to overshadow the text. The misunderstood morality of "Pangs" derives in part from the tendency of some interpreters to evaluate the episode on the basis of its relationship to their personal agenda without *first* locating it within its larger narrative context.

I suggest that an analysis of this episode in light of *Buffy*'s overall perspective on guilt and forgiveness yields an assessment more in tune with the show's moral vision. The setting of this episode at Thanksgiving clearly is an attempt to evoke the debate over the historical origins of this country and over the celebration of Thanksgiving as a valid holiday. Several of the major characters in this episode represent varying positions in this debate, with the exception of Anya who simply regards Thanksgiving as "a ritual sacrifice, with pie."

The British characters Giles and Spike represent an imperialistic mindset.

> SPIKE: You won. All right? You came in and you killed them and you took their land. That's what conquering nations do. It's what Caesar did, and he's not going around saying, 'I came, I conquered, I felt really bad about it.' The history of the world isn't people making friends. You had better weapons, and you massacred them. End of story.
>
> GILES: . . . . I made these points earlier, but fine, no one listens to me.

Giles and Spike largely reject the validity of cultural guilt in this instance because they see the colonials as simply engaging in survival of the fittest.

Willow, by contrast, represents an approach that promotes inclusiveness and reparations by using guilt as a club. Willow's viewpoint is made clear toward the beginning of the episode when she and Buffy attend the groundbreaking ceremony at UC Sunnydale's new Cultural Partnership Center. Anthropology professor, Dr. Gerhardt, comments on the appropriateness of this groundbreaking occurring at Thanksgiving because Thanksgiving is about the mutually beneficial interaction of different cultures. Willow does not see it that way.

> WILLOW: What a load of horse hooey.

BUFFY: We have a counterpoint?
WILLOW: Yeah. Thanksgiving isn't about blending of two cultures. It's about one culture wiping out another. And then they make animated specials about the part where, with the maize and the big, big belt buckles. They don't show you the next scene where all the bison die and Squanto takes a musket ball in the stomach.

Much of the episode centers on the conflicting viewpoints of Giles and Willow. Willow wants to understand and empathize with the plight of the Chumash spirit and help him to redress the wrongs done to his people. Giles wants to stop him from harming anyone else. Willow thinks Giles is being "unfeeling guy" and Giles thinks Willow is being naive. When Willow suggests giving land back to Hus, Giles makes his opinion known:

GILES: I'm sure that'll clear everything right up.
BUFFY: Sarcasm accomplishes nothing, Giles.
GILES: It's sort of an end in itself.

As representatives of opposing ends of the ideological spectrum, Willow and Giles are unable to effect a resolution. They model the extent to which this cultural debate often stalls due to the ideological divide when Giles suggests that they keep a level head about all of this, and Willow retorts, "And I happen to think mine is the level head, and yours is the one things would roll off of."

In contrast to both Giles and Willow, Buffy is the figure who ultimately provides a solution. "Pangs" opens with Buffy patrolling in the cemetery. She hunts a vampire who appears startled to see her. This opening is crucial for the setup of the episode because this vampire is a metaphorical representation of oppressed, indigenous peoples. When the vampire sees Buffy, he says, "Why don't you just go back where you came from? Things were great before you came." His comment identifies Buffy as a metaphorical representative of invading colonial forces. When Buffy fights him and stakes him, she symbolically fulfills her role as oppressor. Yet, after Buffy stakes him, she says, "And they say one person can't make a difference." Buffy's comment hangs over the whole episode and provides the central theme. How can one person make a difference? How should individuals respond to atrocities committed by their cultural forebears?

Throughout the episode, Buffy represents a mediating position between Willow and Giles. With her mother out of town, Buffy desperately wants to cook Thanksgiving dinner for her friends. The recent upheavals in her life have made her long for the stability and tradition of the holiday. On the other hand, she also recognizes the wrongs that have been perpetrated on the Chumash, and it causes her to be conflicted. During an early fight with Hus, Buffy freezes out of guilt, later explaining that she prefers her evil to be "'straight up, black hat, tied to the train tracks, soon my electro-ray will destroy Metropolis' bad. Not all mixed up with guilt and the destruction of an indigenous culture."

On one level, it seems as though Buffy is trying to ignore the whole issue in favor of a nice, quiet Thanksgiving dinner. There is an effective juxtaposition throughout the episode: whenever the conversation turns towards the wrongs done to the Chumash, Buffy redirects the conversation towards Thanksgiving dinner or runs off to cook something. Buffy's attempts at redirection are a manifestation of her conflicted conscience. She wants to resolve the conflict with the Chumash spirit *and* celebrate Thanksgiving. She lays down the law with her friends by saying, "We will find a solution. And we will have a nice dinner, ok? Both. End of story." However, that proves to be easier said than done, prompting Buffy to later ask Willow if there is a "non-judgmental way" to kill Hus.

Buffy's sensitivity *both* to the plight of oppressed peoples and to the plight of contemporary individuals made to feel guilty for crimes they never committed is the key to this episode. "Pangs" exposes the flaws in several proposed solutions for the guilt pangs of historical and cultural misdeeds. The Chumash spirit Hus represents one approach. He claims that "I am vengeance" and then proceeds to re-create the very same wrongs done to his people. He kills representatives of those who oppressed his people (a priest, an authority figure) and, because the Chumash were infected with a variety of European diseases, he infects Xander with all of them simultaneously. Hus' solution of vengeance is a failed one because, as Giles says, "Vengeance is never sated, Buffy. Hatred is a cycle. All he will do is kill." The oppressed has become the oppressor in an endless cycle of retribution. By directing his vengeance against an innocent generation, Hus has become as insensitive and violent as his historical oppressors.

Spike best represents the failure of the imperialistic solution, which is its failure to appreciate the plight of its victims. Once Spike finds himself on the receiving end of a violent attack, he finds oppression quite unappealing. Because he is tied to a chair, when the final battle with Hus and his fellow avenging spirits commences, Spike finds himself turning into a human pin cushion full of enemy arrows. His imperialistic bravado quickly comes crashing down. With arrows flying around him, he yells out, "Remember that conquering nation thing? Forget it. Apologize." Spike, as helpless victim, has changed his tune.

Just as vengeful retribution and imperialistic bravado are shown to be bankrupt, so also is Willow's guilt-ridden empathy. Once the Chumash warriors attack them all at Giles' apartment, Willow does not hesitate to pick up a shovel and begin beating the very indigenous people she has championed, calling out with each blow, "Why . . . don't . . . you . . . die!" Afterwards she laments that "two seconds of conflict with an indigenous person, and I turned into General Custer." The flaw in Willow's solution to the problem is that it sounds good in theory, but fails in practice because it casts judgment on an entire group of people (the colonial settlers) without ever being in their proverbial shoes.

With Buffy, however, I believe we witness *Buffy the Vampire Slayer*'s proposed solution to the problem of cultural guilt. The juxtaposition of two statements by Buffy with two scenes featuring Spike lays the foundation for this solution. In the first instance, Buffy invites a reluctant Willow to her Thanksgiving meal. After relenting, Willow asks if they can *not* invite her nemesis Anya. Buffy shoots that idea down saying, "Look, pilgrims aside, isn't that the whole point of Thanksgiving — Everybody has a place to go?" The scene then cuts to a shot of Spike, newly escaped from the Initiative, wandering around the forest with no place to go. In the second instance, Buffy invites Riley over for Thanksgiving, but he declines, explaining that he will be traveling home to Iowa to be with family. He says, "What's the line? Home's the place that, when you have to go there . . . " Buffy finishes it for him: "They have to take you in." The scene then cuts to another shot of Spike, this time returning to his former lair, only to be kicked out by an angry Harmony. Spike is now homeless and looking for a place to be taken in.

"Pangs" suggests that Thanksgiving be evaluated on the basis of what this day now means and not what it may have once meant. Buffy's two comments about having a place to belong and about home being where they have to take you in, identifies the meaning of

Thanksgiving as being about home, family, and community. Just as with the vampire at the beginning of the episode, Spike here represents the Other, racially and socially. He is the homeless, the outcast, and the oppressed. Alessio argues that "the issue of 'race' in [*Buffy the Vampire Slayer*] remains one demon that Buffy can't deal with, one frontier that Buffy is incapable of crossing."[9] I suggest that Spike functions in this episode as a demonstration that Buffy has indeed attempted to cross that frontier. Homeless and with no place to belong, Spike knocks on the door of Giles' apartment and Buffy lets him in. Spike has gone to his enemy for help. If the problem has been that the early colonials killed and oppressed their perceived "enemies" (the Chumash), here that past sin is reversed. Their enemy is not killed, but is made a part of the family in a sense. On Thanksgiving Day, Buffy gives Spike a "home" — he even sits at the table with them during their Thanksgiving meal. When Giles says, "Good work, Buffy. On both counts," he acknowledges that she has created a successful Thanksgiving meal and resolved the Chumash crisis.

But more than that, Buffy has also succeeded at resolving the issue of cultural guilt. In line with the themes that run throughout the series, cultural guilt that is used as a form of emotional punishment for historical wrongs is unhealthy and damaging to a society, but guilt that provokes one to repentance and the making of amends is valuable indeed. In this instance, the way that one makes amends, the way that one person can make a difference, is by not repeating the wrongs of the past. Any society or generation is not responsible for the crimes of its ancestors *unless* it repeats them. The value of cultural guilt comes from its ability to motivate a society to learn from the sins of its past. According to *Buffy the Vampire Slayer*, the celebration of Thanksgiving should not be a celebration of historical wrongs, but an attempt to rectify them through an emphasis on community and acceptance of those different from us (Spike).

Chapter 16

The Vampire, The Witch, and the Warlock: Patterns of Redemption

Redemption is a major theme in *Buffy the Vampire Slayer*. According to Whedon, it is second only to the theme of adolescent (especially female) empowerment.[1] Most major characters have undertaken a redemptive journey to one degree or another. But what is redemption on *Buffy*?

Godawa argues that many Hollywood portrayals of redemption are really just a humanistic form of self-actualization in which people motivate themselves to live better lives.[2] Krzywinska makes a similar claim for *Buffy*, suggesting that its treatment of redemption is more about morality than spirituality.[3] It is no doubt true that *Buffy* avoids traditional Christian conceptions that reduce redemption primarily to the attainment of eternal salvation. On *Buffy* redemption is more about the conquering of internal demons and the moral transformation of a life. Any suggestion, however, that this redemption is strictly about a secular morality devoid of spiritual emphasis presents a false dichotomy. The identification of the secular and the spiritual as mutually exclusive entities is largely a modern invention. For most of the world's history, the sacred and the secular have intermingled. In many ancient cultures, such as ancient Near Eastern, Egyptian and Greco-Roman, the distinction between the sacred and the secular can be difficult to identify. Within early Christianity, for instance, redemption had as much to do with how one lives one's life morally in this world as it does gaining spiritual access to another world.

There is a growing trend in western culture to separate morality from spirituality, but ultimately it is an exercise in self-deception because the two share such a strong symbiotic relationship: to talk of one is to evoke the other, whether consciously or unconsciously. Whedon seems to recognize this based on the extent to which he imbues his moral discourse with spiritual themes and emphases. Redemption is a case in point. Whedon has acknowledged Christian influence on his conception of redemption. Consequently, specific instances of redemption on *Buffy* either employ deliberate Christian themes and imagery or are at least resonant with them. I have already explored some redemptive arcs (Angel, Anya, Faith) in earlier chapters. Here I examine the redemptive journeys of three others that connect the conquering of internal demons with spiritual themes: a vampire (Spike), a witch (Willow), and a warlock (Andrew).

THE WITCH[4]

The premise of *Buffy the Vampire Slayer* centers on the slaying of demons. As a narrative that is grounded in metaphorical comment upon life, *Buffy* teaches that our social and personal demons can be overcome by the power of love, community, and forgiveness. It comes as no surprise then that the act of redemption on *Buffy* involves the slaying of one's internal demons. Anya overcomes her selfish pursuit of vengeance only by learning to act selflessly. Angel's guilt over his past sins against humanity finds a salve in his determination to make amends through service to humanity. Faith's moral bankruptcy is a driving force in her descent into evil, while her ascent begins with recognition of what it means for actions to be "wrong." This pattern of redemption continues with the characters examined in this chapter.

What makes *Buffy*'s treatment of redemption so effective is that viewers live with the characters for a while. In Willow's case, five years pass while viewers watch her grow and mature before she turns evil. It is like the experience of having a sibling or a close friend suddenly and inexplicably descend into darkness. But the truth is that such self-destructive turns are rarely sudden or inexplicable. The seeds are always sown earlier, growing slowly beneath the surface until sprouting forth. With Willow, the signs were there all along.

Signs

Willow's later troubles all grow out of her deep-seated insecurity and lack of emotional control.[5] One of the defining features of Willow's personality is her intense stage fright. She freezes and then flees the stage during the high school talent show (1:9), and her personal fear that manifests in the episode "Nightmares" is having to sing on stage before an audience (1.10). This fear of performance is the fear of exposure. Willow fears the disapproval and rejection that comes from the glare of scrutiny, preferring instead to hide herself away from the public eye. Willow's selection of a ghost for her Halloween costume is telling (2.6). She desires social invisibility. In this early Halloween episode, Buffy offers a prescient comment that hints at what Willow is really hiding. Buffy tries to talk Willow out of her ghost theme by encouraging her to get wild. Willow says, "Oh, I don't get wild. Wild on me? It goes spaz." Buffy replies, "Don't underestimate yourself. You've got it in you." When Buffy then dresses Willow up in a red top and black leather miniskirt, it hints at what is truly inside Willow, for both Vamp Willow and the Dark Willow who will try to destroy the world show a preference for black leather.

Willow's insecurity manifests itself in a desire for acceptance, yet her poor self-image is the constant voice in the back of her head whispering to her that she will never measure up. Consequently, she is her own worst critic. After attaining a very good, but not perfect, score of 740 on the verbal portion of the SAT, Willow freaks out: "I'm, I'm . . . pathetic! Illiterate! I'm Cletus, the slack-jawed yokel!" (3.8). Insecurity also plagues her relationship with Oz. After he admits not mentioning one of his band's gigs to her because he figures she would not want to miss school for it, Willow draws what, for her, seems like the obvious conclusion.

WILLOW: You think I'm boring.
OZ: I'd call that a radical interpretation of the text (3.16).

When Buffy gains the ability to hear people's thoughts in "Earshot," Willow's first thought is that Buffy does not need her anymore (3.18). With her cheerful personality and sweet disposition, Willow puts up a deceptive front. Behind that front, however, is a person deeply unhappy. On two occasions, she confesses that she doesn't like this world very much (3.16; 6.21).

This explains Willow's attraction to magic and the ferocity with which she pursues it. Magic gives her power, makes her special. This power ultimately corrupts her because it is selfishly focused. Although Willow often expresses a desire to use magic to help people, she primarily craves it as a means of helping herself. She begins using magic to resolve personal problems or for personal benefit, such as cheating at poker (4.13). As her addiction to magic takes stronger hold, the selfishness of her actions increases. It becomes a substitute for work and a means for correcting whatever is wrong in her life. When she and Tara have a fight, Willow performs a forget spell — problem solved (6.6). When Tara discovers what Willow did, however, Willow explains that she was only trying to help. Tara replies, "Maybe that's how it started, but you're helping yourself now, fixing things to your liking. Including me" (6.8).

Whereas Willow had always fought to keep her dark side hidden, the magic brings all of her character flaws into the open. In addition to the selfishness, magic exposes Willow's impatience. Willow's desperation to break away from her insecurity and weakness, prompts her to push herself harder than is appropriate. She ignores warnings and forges ahead, trying newer and more dangerous spells that are often beyond her current capability. Even from the beginning, her desire to be more than she is manifests in impatience. Willow tries to get her mother's attention by convincing her that she is a bonafide witch. She says, "I-I can make pencils float. And I can summon the four elements. Okay, two, but four soon" (3.11). When she gains a higher degree of proficiency in magic, Willow selfishly uses her magic to ward off boredom, even using it on her laptop because the Internet is too slow (6.9; 6.11).

Magic exposes a third flaw in Willow's character: lack of emotional control. This is the most dangerous of all because it creates an inability to control her magic power. The first hint of this occurs in "Dopplegangland" when Willow floats a pencil while lecturing Buffy on how magic requires emotional control. Once Willow becomes upset during the conversation, the pencil suddenly spins out of control and buries itself in a tree (3.16). This is the first hint that Willow's combination of magic and passion may prove lethal.

In "Something Blue" (4.9), Willow's impatience and lack of emotional control combine with tragic results. Distraught over her recent break-up with Oz, Willow wants the pain to go away immediately. She says, "Isn't there some way I can just make it go away? Just 'cause I say so? Can't I just make it go 'poof'?" Later she tries just that, weaving a magic spell that allows her will to be done. The opening line of the spell is, "Out of my passions, a web be spun." Thereafter, whenever Willow speaks words out of anger, they become reality. Willow, however, remains oblivious to the damage her words cause. When her emotions overtake her, she becomes blind to the consequences of her actions.

Forever a Sidekick

Magic is such an addictive lure to Willow because it transforms her from shy, unremarkable Willow into the person she wishes she was: confident, capable, and someone to be reckoned with. But like any drug, the effect is temporary. Despite her newfound power, Willow is unable to suppress her insecurity. Although her power has progressed beyond that of Tara, Willow confesses that she still feels like "the junior partner" (5.19). When Buffy calls upon Willow to help them in battle and refers to her as their "big gun," Willow responds that she is more suited to being a cudgel or pointy stick. Buffy then tells Willow, "You're the strongest person here. You know that right?" Willow frowns, unsure, and says, "Well . . . no" (5.22). In the episode "Fear Itself" (4.4), Willow's fear is a manifestation of her insecurity, as represented by the following exchange after she offers to perform a guiding spell to help Buffy.

> BUFFY: Will, let's be realistic here. Okay, your basic spells are usually only fifty-fifty.
> WILLOW (Angry): Oh yeah? Well . . . so is your face!
> BUFFY: What? What does that mean?
> WILLOW: I'm not your sidekick!

The essence of Willow's fear is that what she protests is in fact true. She fears that despite all her progress, she remains only a sidekick.

This theme finds further development in the dream episode "Restless" (4.22). This episode is vital for understanding Willow's arc because it both summarizes earlier themes and foreshadows new ones. In her dream, Willow is waiting to go on a stage as Giles mentions that "everyone that Willow's ever met" is in the audience. This is Willow's deepest fear. On stage, she may be exposed for who she really is. Buffy tells her, "Your costume is perfect. Nobody's gonna know the truth.

You know, about you." Although Willow keeps protesting that she is only wearing her normal outfit, her real "costume" is the veneer that she has constructed in order to mask her insecurity. When Buffy tries to take Willow's costume off, Willow says, "I need it." Buffy then rips off Willow's clothes, commenting that the result is "much more realistic."

At that moment, the dream shifts to Willow standing at the front of a classroom full of students. Her friends are in the classroom mocking her. She stands there wearing the same type of nerdy outfit she wore in the very first episode of the series. This reveals the core of her insecurity. She fears that no matter what she does, she will always remain the same nerd that she was in high school. All the rest is just a costume and acting.

The reason why Willow stands at the front of the class is to deliver a book report. The book she has chosen is "The Lion, the Witch, and the Wardrobe" (a story about redemption). Written by Christian author C. S. Lewis, "The Lion, the Witch, and the Wardrobe" is a children's story that relates aspects of the Christian narrative in symbolic form. Willow's choice of this book is highly significant. The book is about a witch who rules as a despot over the land of Narnia. She uses magic to control others and to deceive them into doing her will. Four children come to Narnia as a group. One of the four children is beguiled by the witch and enticed by addiction. This one betrays his other companions, but ultimately finds redemption.[6] It is difficult not to see in this story a clear parallel to Willow's arc. Beguiled by witchcraft, Willow likewise becomes embroiled in addiction and betrayal. Since "Restless" foreshadows Willow's future descent into the madness of addiction and the deceptive power of witchcraft over her life, one assumes that the value of "The Lion, the Witch, and the Wardrobe" for Whedon is that it hints *both* at Willow's self-destructive future and at her ultimate redemption.

Shortly following this episode, Willow enrolls in a drama course at college (5.2). Does this mean that she has chosen to embrace the actress within her and to hide herself behind the "costume" she wears, continuing the "subterfuge" that Giles claims is the essence of acting (4.22)? It would seem so, for over the next two seasons she relies more and more on magic to overcome her personal weaknesses and to develop the self-perception that she is no longer nerdy Willow. For instance, after Willow performs an illumination spell, she tells Tara, "Isn't this better than using a flashlight like some kind of doofus" (5.4).

The problem for Willow is that along with her growing self-confidence and power comes a degradation of her moral code. When Dawn wants to perform a resurrection spell to bring her mother back from the dead, Willow, unlike Tara, has difficulty recognizing the selfishness involved in the act (5.17). This is a precursor to her later selfish attempt to resurrect Buffy, an act Tara also identifies as "wrong" (6.1). Willow's growing addiction to magic is a desire to become in her own eyes more than she thinks she is. She describes it as the difference between being "plain old Willow or super Willow" (6.10).

Unconditional Acceptance

One of the reasons for the portrayal of immorality on *Buffy* is to set up the need for redemption. It is, in a sense, immorality in the service of morality. The redemption of these characters only rings true if their need for it rings true. Willow's addiction and the other immoral acts portrayed during season six emphasize the depths to which Willow and others have fallen so that their subsequent redemption bears the stamp of authenticity. Joss Whedon says,

> I think as you make your way through life it's hard to maintain a moral structure, and that difficulty and the process of coming out the other side of a dark, even psychological time is to me the most important part of adulthood. I think to an extent every human being needs to be redeemed somewhat or at least needs to look at themselves and say, 'I've made mistakes, I'm off course, I need to change.' Which is probably the hardest thing for a human being to do and maybe that's why it interests me so.[7]

Willow's narrative arc is very much about coming out of a dark and psychological time.

The catalyst for Willow's rampage is the murder of Tara by Warren. The grief and pain it causes Willow results in a complete loss of emotional control and, consequently, a loss of control over her magic. The angrier she becomes, the more her power grows.

Willow had turned to magic in the first place in order to hide from her real self. The raw power of the magic represents the antithesis of everything weak about her. Now, with the magic raging out of control, Willow not only hides from herself but also loses herself. Xander asks

Buffy, "This is still Willow we're dealing with, right?" His question hangs in the air until Willow herself later provides an answer when she tells Giles, "Willow doesn't live here anymore" (6.22). This empowered Willow represents a complete rejection of her weaker self. She says, "Let me tell you something about Willow. She's a loser. And she always has been. People picked on Willow in junior high school, high school, up until college. With her stupid mousy ways. And now? Willow's a junkie" (6.21). Willow's insistence on referring to herself in the third person shows the extent to which she has disowned the real Willow. In one sense, the costume has become the reality.

Willow has fulfilled her lust for power, for importance. She has come out from the wings and now stands at center stage. While attacking Buffy, Willow comments, "Come on, this is a huge deal for me! Six years as a sideman, and now I get to be the Slayer" (6.21). Willow tells Buffy that she has finally figured out that being a Slayer is all about power. She declares, "And there is no one in the world with the power to stop me now" (6.21). That, however, is where she is wrong.

Willow has become more powerful than Buffy, Giles, and Anya combined. Anya notes that not only can't Buffy stop her, but neither can any magic or supernatural force (6.22). Yet Willow was wrong when she said no power in the world could stop her because she overlooked the most powerful force of all: unconditional love.

Willow's redemption derives from a display of unconditional love and acceptance strongly resonant with the sacrifice of Christ. As Willow commences the destruction of the world, Xander shows up specifically referring to himself as a "carpenter." He wins Willow back by demonstrating his acceptance of her no matter what she does or who she tries to become. He tells her that he has come here to be with her because, "You're Willow."

> WILLOW: Don't call me that.
> XANDER: First day of kindergarten. You cried because you broke the yellow crayon, and you were too afraid to tell anyone. You've come pretty far, ending the world. Not a terrific notion. But the thing is? Yeah. I love you. I loved crayon-breaky Willow and I love scary veiny Willow. So if I'm going out, it's here. If you wanna kill the world? Well, then start with me. I've earned that.
> WILLOW: You think I won't?

XANDER: It doesn't matter. I'll still love you (6.22).

Xander's willingness to give his life and his repeated declarations of love, ultimately tap into the real Willow inside. This display of unconditional love is a statement to Willow that she does not have to hide herself behind a facade of strength in order to be accepted and loved. Xander's crayon story points out that he accepts her just as she is — insecurities and flaws intact. Xander's Christ-like display of unconditional love to Willow ends with her collapsing into his arms and weeping as a musical version of the "Prayer of St. Francis" plays. Over this scene of redemption and reconciliation, we hear the first words of the prayer:

> Lord, make me an instrument of your peace;
> where there is hatred, let me sow love;
> where there is injury, pardon;
> where there is doubt, faith;
> where there is despair, hope;
> where there is darkness, light;
> and where there is sadness, joy.

Xander has become that instrument, sowing love, pardon, and hope to overcome Willow's hatred, injury, and despair.

Willow's descent into darkness resulted from a desire to be someone other than the mousy, nerdy Willow. Insecure about her own self worth and weakness, she sought validation in magic. As her fall was tied to a lack of self-esteem, so her redemption is about her learning to accept that she is loved for who she is. In the next episode, Willow is in England with Giles. She expresses surprise that he is mentoring her rather than punishing her. Giles asks her if she wants to be punished. Willow's reply shows that she has slain the demon of poor self-esteem when she replies, "I wanna be Willow" (7.1).

THE WARLOCK

Originally, the term "warlock" meant "teller of lies."[8] Andrew, a summoner of demons, is a warlock in the truest sense. A storyteller, he uses stories to deflect reality. He casts the world around him into the shape of a story, bending it to fit his will. In season six, Andrew is one of three nerds who pester Buffy like hungry mosquitoes. In Andrew's version of events, however, he is a super-villain and Buffy's archnemesis.

This falsely constructed life weakens Andrew's moral structure. Moral decisions become simply another plot point in the story. After Warren kills Katrina and the trio of nerds successfully insulate themselves from blame, Andrew describes their getting away with murder as "kinda cool" (6.13). After all, isn't that what super-villains in stories do? Even after surviving the showdown with dark Willow, Andrew persists in using stories to alter the truth. He simply recasts himself and Jonathan as "outlaws with hearts of gold" (7.7).

In Andrew's narrative world, the nature of reality constantly shifts to meet the demands of his current situation, and Andrew is a character actor who adopts the persona required by the moment. This reliance on stories as the foundation of his world makes him particularly susceptible to deception through story. The First convinces Andrew to kill Jonathan by telling stories. Through story, The First deceives Andrew into believing that his murder of Jonathan will be a noble act and richly rewarded. Later Andrew explains that Jonathan is now "in a place of joy and peace. He told me." Xander corrects him, "No, nobody told you. You got tricked by a fake ghost" (7.10). The teller of lies has himself been deceived.

Andrew's quest for redemption begins when he involuntarily falls in with Buffy and her crowd. Admitting that he "went over to the dark side, but just to pick up a few things," he now claims to fight for the forces of good (7.10). Although Andrew has ostensibly abandoned evil for good, this move is really little more than a twist in the story, for Andrew has not abandoned his self-deceptive ways. Andrew's quest for redemption is, for him, merely another story line. He says, "I'm like Vader in the last five minutes of *Jedi* with redemptive powers minus a redemptive struggle of epic redemption" (7.10). But Andrew will learn that redemption does not come with the ease and grace of a pre-plotted script. It is to *Buffy*'s credit that it always presents the redemptive struggle as difficult and demanding. Andrew learns this when he agrees to wear a wire as a means of getting information on The First. When the intended sting operation fails, Andrew whines, "I never should have gone in wired. Redemption is hard" (7.14). Redemption is never easily won nor quick on *Buffy*, but always the result of a long and arduous journey.

Andrew's quest for redemption stalls because he refuses to rid his life of deceptive stories. Until he does, he remains detached from reality, an observer in his own life. Consequently, Andrew is unable to accept responsibility for his actions. By casting everything in story form, Andrew constantly manipulates the truth to his own advantage. This is why he cannot understand why Willow would try to kill him and Jonathan when, after all, "we didn't do anything" (6.21). In his story, they are innocent. This is why Andrew insists that The First "made" him kill Jonathan (7.13).

Andrew's fatal flaw is a lack of accountability that is grounded in the telling of self-deceptive stories. If the patterns of redemption on *Buffy* that we have witnessed so far hold true, then one expects Andrew's redemption to occur by breaking the deceptive hold of stories over his life. This occurs in "Storyteller" (7.16). Although I have already discussed this episode at length in chapter three, I need to tread some of the same ground again as a means of explaining the climax of Andrew's arc. The episode begins with Andrew sitting in a leather chair on a set reminiscent of Masterpiece Theater and introducing the documentary he is filming on Buffy. We quickly learn, however, that the Masterpiece Theater set exists only in Andrew's mind as he is actually sitting on a toilet seat filming himself with a camcorder. Through this beginning, the episode establishes Andrew's extensive narrative embellishments of his own life.

As mentioned in chapter three, the bookshelf behind Andrew in the Masterpiece Theater set prominently features a volume with the single word "Nietzsche" on it. Nietzsche has written that people naturally seek to avoid truths that are harmful to them. As a result, they are easily susceptible to deception through story. According to Nietzsche, a person has "an invincible tendency to let himself be deceived, and he is like one enchanted with happiness when the rhapsodist narrates to him epic romances in such a way that they appear real or when the actor on the stage makes the king appear more kingly than reality shows him."[9] Andrew craves the deception of story as a means of escaping the harsh truths of his own reality. As narrator of his documentary, he offers a revisionist tale of Buffy's exploits in which he features as a major character, either as a scientific genius plotting in a laboratory or as a powerful warlock deflecting evil Willow's every spell.

The moment of truth, so to speak, for Andrew comes when Buffy needs to close the Seal of Danzalthar, which Andrew had helped to open by shedding Jonathan's blood at the site. Despite admitting to the murder of Jonathan, Andrew has never taken true responsibility for the act. Instead, he constantly minimizes his responsibility by revising his story. When Buffy suggests to Andrew that they need him to close the seal, he says, "I'm not a part of this. I document, I don't participate. I'm a detached journalist, recording with a neutral eye." It is this very detachment from his own story that is the source of Andrew's inability to achieve redemption.

When Andrew and Buffy arrive at the Seal of Danzalthar, she calls Andrew a "murderer." Andrew protests that that is not what happened. He then tells a story in which he accidentally killed Jonathan in self-defense. Through narrative, Andrew absolves himself of responsibility. When a few moments later he tells a different version in which he was possessed by the power of the seal and so only killed Jonathan under compulsion, Buffy accuses him of changing his story. To this point, Andrew's redemptive journey has been nothing more than him playing a role. It has not yet become real.

In order to change that, Buffy deceives Andrew through a story. She tells Andrew that only the blood of the person who awoke the seal (that would be Andrew) can close it. Andrew replies, "So, this is my redemption at last? I buy back my bruised soul with the blood of my heart." He continues to romanticize the story through fictive language. Buffy, however, recognizes that this is merely another story. She tells Andrew, "You always do this. You make everything into a story so no one's responsible for anything because they're just following a script." Buffy then grabs Andrew and holds him out over the glowing seal, her knife pointed menacingly towards him.

> BUFFY: When your blood pours out, it might save the world. What do you think about that? Does it buy it all back? Are you redeemed?
> ANDREW (crying): No.
> BUFFY: Why not?
> ANDREW (sobbing): Because I killed him. Because I listened to Warren, and I pretended I thought it was him, but I knew. I knew it wasn't. And I killed Jonathan.

As Andrew's tears fall onto the seal, the glowing stops, thus revealing the deception of Buffy's story. The seal did not want Andrew's blood, but his tears. The analogy extends to Andrew himself. It is not the shedding of his blood that is required for redemption (as Andrew will later learn when he wonders why he did not die in the final battle), but the shedding of his tears in genuine repentance.

The episode ends as it began but with a vital twist. Andrew concludes the narration of his documentary as he started it — sitting on the toilet facing his camcorder. Only this time it is without any embellishment. In place of his characteristic stories is a straightforward confession of the murder of Jonathan and a full acceptance of responsibility. Only when Andrew removes the narrative facade, owns up to reality, and accepts accountability does his story truly become one of redemption. Only then does he experience the validity of Jesus' proverbial statement that "the truth will set you free" (John 8:32).

THE VAMPIRE

Spike's story of redemption is a love story. Spike, a.k.a. William the Bloody, is a character haunted, defined, motivated, and ultimately redeemed by love. Throughout his notorious career and his varied incarnations (human Spike, vampire Spike, Spike with a chip, and ensouled Spike), one thing has remained constant: he is a tortured and hopeless romantic. Spike's redemptive journey, therefore, is essentially a quest for true love.

Not Demon Enough

The first time we see Spike on *Buffy*, he shows up wearing his vampire face (2.3). Thus, we first encounter him as a monster. When he later reverts to his human face, it evokes the conflicted nature of Spike's being. Is he monster or man? Although Spike insists that he is monster through and through, he doth protest too much. The remnants of his humanity are visible from the beginning in his fondness for vampire consort Drusilla. Spike's capacity to love, even as a vampire, humanizes him.[10] The Judge tells Spike and Drusilla that they "stink of humanity" because they share "affection and jealousy" (2.13).

Spike is a slave to love as proven by his tortured melancholy in "Lovers Walk" (3.8). After Drusilla leaves him for a chaos demon, Spike returns to Sunnydale as a lovesick fool seeking solace in a bottle. The depth of his emotion increases the stench of his humanity. Two scenes reveal how Spike's ability to love causes the human in him to triumph over the demon. When he first returns to Sunnydale, Spike is drunk and distraught. He moans and weeps until suddenly realizing the humanity he has been expressing. Quickly switching to his vampire face, he starts smashing things and says out loud to the absent Drusilla, "Look what you've done to me." What she has done is made him face the human inside. In the second scene, Spike seeks out Willow in order to make her perform a love spell so that Drusilla will come back to him. After threatening to shove broken glass through Willow's face, Spike sits down next to her and speaks tenderly to her of his broken heart. He further tells Willow that Drusilla left him because she thought he had gone soft, that he "wasn't demon enough for the likes of her." Drusilla recognized that his capacity for human emotion weakened the monster's hold over him. As if just now realizing the potential truth of her statement and intending to prove it false, Spike morphs into his vampire face and threatens Willow again.

The Spike who was so forlorn and depressed at the beginning of "Lovers Walk" returns to his former self by the end, all swagger and joyful bravado. What puts the bounce back in this lover's walk is an epiphany about love. Proclaiming that "love's a funny thing," Spike vows to find Drusilla, tie her up, and "torture her until she likes me again." Such statements show that the interplay of human and monster in Spike is still hard at work.

The Heartbroken Poet

In the episode "Fool for Love" (5.7), Buffy needs information from Spike. He agrees for a monetary price, but before divulging any information demands a raise in the form of a plate of spicy Buffalo wings. When Buffy asks him if he was born such a big pain, Spike replies, "What can I tell you, baby? I've always been bad." This cuts to the heart of Spike's character. His rebel rock star look and malevolent manner is merely a pretense to hide the truth, which is that he has not always been bad.

A series of flashbacks in "Fool for Love" (5.7) and "Lies My Parents Told Me" (7.17) reveal the truth about Spike. Before his vampire days as Spike, William was a Victorian gentleman in London of the late 1800's. We first meet him at a dinner party sitting alone in a corner and composing a love poem for Cecily, the object of his affection. Unfortunately for William, who we now learn got his nickname of William the Bloody not from acts of violence but "because of his bloody awful poetry" (5.7), his poor attempts at verse fail to persuade the aristocratic Cecily. William pleads with her to look past the "bad poet" and see the "good man" that he believes he is. Cecily replies, "I do see you. That's the problem. You're nothing to me, William. You're beneath me" (5.7). Spike has been made a fool for love, and his deepest fear is that it will always be so. Later, after he becomes a vampire, Spike insists to his mother that he is no longer the man he once was. She tells him, "Darling, it's who you'll always be. A limp, sentimental fool" (7.17). That is what haunts Spike. Will he ever be anything but a lovesick poet? Can the monster in him triumph over this human weakness? When Buffy later repeats Cecily's devastating words to Spike, "You're beneath me," it arouses his fear and anger. In a defiant attempt to prove that he is nothing but a monster, Spike retrieves a shotgun and goes off to kill Buffy. Yet, when he finds her sitting on her porch weeping over the news of her mother's illness, Spike sits down next to her, the shotgun at his side in an amusing juxtaposition of the human and the monster, and comforts Buffy in her time of need (5.7). Despite all his protestations, Spike cannot kill the heartbroken poet within.[11]

All of Spike's swaggering menace and violent bravado is an attempt to hide the fact that underneath he is still the same sentimental fool. Three aspects of Spike's character serve as a continual reminder of the hopeless romantic within. The first is Spike's ability to see the truth when it comes to the love lives of others. He sees the flaws in Buffy's "relationship" with Parker Abrams long before she does (4.3) and prophetically informs Riley that he will never be able to hold on to Buffy (5.10). Spike's prescience when it comes to love enables him to shatter Buffy and Angel's illusion that they can be just friends. He tells them that they will "be in love 'till it kills you both" because "love isn't brains, children, it's blood, blood screaming inside you to work its will" (3.8). Spike's insights on love are not limited to Buffy nor is his ability to see what others miss when it comes to love, as the following conversation about Willow attests.

> GILES: She seems to be coping better with Oz's departure, don't you think?
> BUFFY: She still has a way to go, but, yeah, I think she's dealing.
> SPIKE: What, are you people blind? She's hangin' on by a thread. Any ninny can see that (4.9).

Spike's own travails in love and inner sentimentality provide him special insight into the human romantic condition.

The second manifestation of Spike's sentimentality is his passion for "Passions." Spike is a soap opera addict. Spike tells Buffy and Riley that he is tired of having to witness all the drama in their relationship because "I've got my stories on the telly for that" (4.14). Sometimes Spike's fondness for soaps and his insight into love collide as in the scene where he is in his crypt watching what appears to be "Dawson's Creek" and shouts out, "Oh Pacey, you blind idiot. Can't you see she doesn't love you?" (5.4). Third, Spike has a tendency to commiserate with others over their mutual relationship woes. He shares such love talks with Anya (4.18; 6.18), Riley (5.10), and Xander (5.11). These emotional qualities of Spike undercut his ferocity and provide a human balance to the monster within him. Spike is a tragic romantic figure — a vampire plagued by his inability to become anything more than a lovesick poet.

Selfish Love

Spike is a Mama's boy. Prior to his transformation into a vampire, he adores his mother with single-minded devotion. His love for her is selfless and giving. He devotes himself to her and vows to look after her in her elderly and sickly state (7.17). When Spike becomes a vampire, his capacity to love does not diminish, but the nature of his love changes. One of his first acts as the newly dead is to turn his mother into a vampire. He claims to do this so that she will no longer experience sickness and pain, but the truth is that he wants her with him forever. His love turns selfish and possessive. That the nature of Spike's love is so transformed immediately after his conversion to vampirism is a statement that selfish and possessive "love" is demonic.

Spike and Buffy's love story is also a story of Spike's internal struggle against the demon within him. Interestingly, the Spike who so easily recognizes the truth in other's love lives is completely blind to the truth of his own. Drusilla had left Spike because she saw his growing infatuation with the Slayer despite Spike's own obliviousness to it (5.7). In fact, Spike confuses his obsession with hatred. Just before realizing his crush on Buffy, Spike denounces her: "Everywhere I turn, she's there! That nasty little face, that bouncing shampoo-commercial hair, that whole sodding holier-than-thou attitude" (5.4). Yet once realization sets in, Spike's love quickly becomes selfish. He stalks Buffy, stealing clothes and pictures from her house so that he can possess some part of her (5.5; 5.8; 5.9).

The episode in which Spike first confesses his desire for Buffy, "Crush" (5.14), lays a foundation for understanding their relationship. The key for this is Willow and Tara's discussion of the "Hunchback of Notre Dame," which functions as a thinly veiled description of Spike and Buffy. After Willow wishes that the story had ended with Esmeralda and Quasimodo together, Tara corrects her.

> TARA: No, see, it can't, it can't end like that, 'cause all of Quasimodo's actions were selfishly motivated. He had no moral compass, no understanding of right. Everything he did, he did out of love for a woman who would never be able to love him back.

The lack of a moral compass, the inability to truly distinguish right and wrong, is what lies behind Spike's selfish love. Discussions about Spike's brain chip and the soul abound in this episode because they address the issue of the moral compass. Spike's inability to feed his monstrous nature through violence against humans allows the human emotions within him to rise to the surface. Yet without a soul, those emotions merely mask the monster beneath.

Buffy and Spike's relationship does not begin well as she is thoroughly disgusted by the thought of his feelings for her. Nevertheless, Spike believes that Buffy will eventually fall for him because he believes that she desires "some monster in her man" (5.10). Yet the irony is that it will be Spike's continued contact with Buffy that brings out more of the human within him. When Olaf the Troll threatens innocent people at The Bronze, Xander tells Spike to fight him. Spike refuses, claiming to be "paralyzed with not caring very much." Yet as soon as Buffy shows up, Spike immediately begins to help an injured woman.

> BUFFY: What are you doing?
> SPIKE: Making this woman more comfortable. I'm not sampling, I'll have you know. Just look at all these lovely blood-covered people. I could, but not a taste for Spike, not a lick. [I] know you wouldn't like it.
> BUFFY: You want credit for not feeding on bleeding disaster victims?
> SPIKE: Well, yeah.
> BUFFY: You're disgusting (5.11).

His love for Buffy has driven him to a (partly) noble act.

Further illustrating Spike's growth as a quasi-human is his involvement with the Buffybot. Spike convinces Warren to create for him a robot Buffy. The realism of this robot is so strong that it is indistinguishable from Buffy apart from its peculiar speech patterns. Spike enlists the robot as a sex toy, demonstrating again the selfishness and possessiveness of his love. Later, after Glory captures and tortures Spike in an attempt to find out who the Key is, Buffy, pretending to be the robot, comes to a severely beaten Spike to find out if he told about Dawn. Spike, believing he is speaking to the robot, says that he refused to tell "'cause Buffy . . . the other, not so pleasant Buffy . . . anything happened to Dawn, it'd destroy her. I couldn't live, her bein' in that much pain" (5.18). This is a major turning point for Spike because he demonstrates an ability to act in the interests of others. Later when the Buffybot is reactivated as a temporary replacement for the deceased Buffy, Spike is noticeably uncomfortable with and dismissive of the Buffybot, showing further growth in his concept of love (6.1).

Through season five, Spike's love for Buffy is fully unrequited. In loving Buffy, however, he is gradually learning to embrace the remnants of his humanity. Just before going off to fight Glory and knowing that he or she might not survive, Spike tells Buffy, "I know you'll never love me. I know that I'm a monster. But you treat me like a man" (5.22). By the end of season five, the man in Spike appears to be winning the battle against the monster as a result of his increasing capacity to love.

Buffy's death at the end of season five is devastating to Spike, but it is also what opens the door to their distorted romance. Buffy now shares a bond with Spike. After all both have crawled out of a grave. To her own surprise, Buffy embarks upon a sexual relationship with Spike. It is a reluctant relationship borne out of need and despair rather than out of genuine affection. When Spike asks Buffy if she even likes him, she says, "Sometimes." When he asks if she trusts him, Buffy replies, "Never" (6.13). Buffy is using Spike as a way of dealing with her depression. In this sense her involvement with Spike is just as selfish as Spike's possessive love for her. Critics of season six's sometimes envelope pushing portrayal of sexuality are correct that the graphic and adult depiction was not suitable for younger viewers. However, a critique of the moral value of this relationship is not complete without recognition that Buffy and Spike's relationship was never intended as a model to be imitated. Within the larger narrative arc of these characters, their relationship functions as a negative example that promotes a healthier view of relationships by the way it contrasts selfish and selfless love and highlights Spike's need for a soul.

As Spike's relationship with Buffy progresses, the line separating the monster and the man becomes harder to discern. The more involved in their relationship he becomes, the more human he seems. In fact, concerned that he may be softening too much, Spike decides to hunt and kill someone to prove that the monster is still in him. However, Spike's displays of affection have so doused him with the stink of humanity that he has to give himself a pep talk in order to work up the desire. He says to himself, "Creature of the night here, yeah? Some people forget that. I know what I am. I'm dangerous. I'm evil" (6.9). In the next episode, Spike tries to help Buffy locate Rack's mystical hideaway. Although he says that only those who are into "the big bad" can sense it, Spike himself is unable to do so.[12]

Despite what appears to be Spike's growing humanity, Buffy breaks off their relationship claiming that she has been "selfish" in the way she has been using Spike. That Spike is completely surprised by this turn of events demonstrates again his blindness to the truth of his own love life. After Buffy delivers the news to Spike, she says, "I'm sorry . . . William" (6.15). The deliberate use of his human name, a name Buffy rarely if ever used before, seems to be a sign of affection and an acknowledgment of his humanity; yet, it also functions as a reminder to Spike of the heartbroken poet that he once was and now is again.

Spike's attempted rape of Buffy is proof that he is still a monster (6.19). Despite all of his growth and pretenses of humanity, he remains evil. The manifestation of that evil is his attempt at the selfish and possessive act of rape. The relative nobility that Spike displayed over the course of seasons four through six humanized him in the eyes of the audience, but it was largely a facade. By making the audience experience Spike as noble, his attempted rape becomes all the more shocking as a reminder that true evil often wears a human face.

Just before his rape attempt, Spike insists to Buffy that she loves him. When she says she does not, he accuses her of lying. Whereas Spike claims that Buffy cannot see the truth, it is in fact he who is blind. Not only can he not see the truth that Buffy does not love him, he is also incapable of recognizing what love truly is. Buffy tells him that she could never love him because "I could never trust you enough for it to be love." Spike replies, "Trust is for old marrieds, Buffy. Great love is wild and passionate and dangerous. It burns and consumes" (6.19). Spike's inhumanity blinds him to the need for trust in relationship. When he then tries to force himself on Buffy, Spike becomes the rightful heir to Tara's words about Quasimodo. The selfishness of his act reveals his lack of a moral compass and his inability to distinguish right and wrong.[13] Metaphorically speaking, the monster within Spike is his incapacity to love properly. He is forever doomed to love selfishly, blindly, and without trust. Given the patterns of redemption established so far on *Buffy*, Spike's redemption cannot occur without him learning the nature of true love. For that, he will need a soul.

Selfless Love

When Spike became a vampire, his capacity for love remained, but it was distorted, twisted into a selfish parody of the real thing. In regaining his soul, Spike regains the capacity for genuine love and through that love finds his humanity. But he remains a fool for love. Love is what drove him to reacquire his soul. Love is what drove him to conquer the monster within. When Buffy asks Spike why he got his soul back, he says, "Buffy, shame on you. Why does a man do what he mustn't? For her. To be hers. To be the kind of man who would nev— (looks away) to be a kind of man" (7.2). Spike keeps insisting that he is a changed man, but the question is whether his love has changed.

The distortion of Spike's love involved three things: a selfless and possessive nature, a lack of trust, and a blindness to Buffy's true feelings for him. Each of these characteristics is reversed throughout season seven as Spike reveals a depth of love that had escaped him prior. Although he tells Buffy that "it's still all about you" (7.8), Spike now sees the truth when it comes to he and Buffy. When Buffy goes out on a date with another man, Spike confesses to a lack of jealousy because he knows that he and Buffy are not meant to be. He attributes this newfound awareness to the fact that "my eyes are clear" (7.14).

The Victorian William had begged his beloved Cecily to look past the awful poet and see the "good man" (5.7). She broke his heart by refusing to do so. What now drives Spike's love for Buffy is her fulfillment of that request. Buffy tells Giles of Spike, "He can be a good man, Giles. I feel it" (7.14). The faith that Buffy has in Spike's potential goodness is a form of trust. The same Buffy who witnessed the monster in Spike during season six and so vowed never to trust him, now trusts in his humanity. After The First captures Spike and invites him to rejoin the side of evil, Spike chooses torture instead. The First, appearing in the form of Drusilla, asks Spike, "What makes you think you will ever be any good at all in this world?" Spike says, "She does. Because she believes in me" (7.10). The desire to possess Buffy has been replaced with a desire to become in her eyes the man she thinks he can be.

The episode "Touched" (7.20) highlights the effect of a soul on this lovelorn vampire. The Spike who formerly loved selfishly, could not be trusted, and was unable to see the truth about him and Buffy is now shown to be selfless, trustworthy, and insightful. In a moment of emotional candor, Spike reveals his feelings to Buffy.

> SPIKE: A hundred plus years, and there's only one thing I've ever been sure of: you. Hey, look at me. I'm not asking you for anything. When I say, "I love you," it's not because I want you or because I can't have you. It has nothing to do with me. I love what you are, what you do, how you try. I've seen your kindness and your strength. I've seen the best and the worst of you. And I understand with perfect clarity exactly what you are. You're a hell of a woman. You're the one, Buffy.

Spike's selfless love and "perfect clarity" go hand in hand. The Spike who could always see the truth of other's love lives can now see the truth of his own. When Buffy then asks Spike to hold her, it is an act of trust. Forgetting the monster that once tried to rape her, Buffy now trusts in the man. Spike sits on the bed and holds her through the night as she sleeps. This chaste scene, contrasting as it does with the warped self-absorption of Buffy and Spike's sexual affair in season six, shows that Spike is now experiencing real love, the kind that is grounded in trust and the giving of oneself to another. It is no wonder that Spike will later say of this moment, "It was the best night of my life" (7.21).

Redemption

When Robin Wood asks Spike how having a soul is working out for him, Spike replies, "In progress" (7.15). On *Buffy*, redemption is more of a process than an act. Redemption is hard won over the course of time. It is the continual struggle of a character striving to achieve his or her moral potential. Just as in life, characters on this show do stupid, sinful, immoral, harmful, and offensive things, yet they also seek redemption for those actions through repentance, forgiveness, and through the making of amends. Singling out a specific act of violence or a specific sexual act for condemnation ignores the importance of story and is particularly misguided in a show like *Buffy* that aims for an emotional resonance that rings true to real life experience. Just as we evaluate the moral value of a person by examining their life in totality, so also should the moral evaluation of a character in a serialized narrative occur with reference to that character's entire story. The sexually irresponsible Spike of season six provides some of *Buffy*'s most morally reprehensible moments; yet, in the context of Spike's entire story arc, they serve to establish the need for and nature of his redemption.

Although Spike's redemption is a process, the climactic moment comes with Spike's sacrificial death in the series finale (7.22). The influence of the cross of Christ on Spike's redemptive story is unmistakable. In the last chapter, I examined one meaning of Spike's Crucifixion pose from "Restless" (4.22). Taken together with his smoking embrace of the cross in "Beneath You" (7.2), this scene stresses his desire for forgiveness and rest for his soul. Another interpretation of Spike's Crucifixion pose in "Restless" is the foreshadowing of his selfless sacrifice in an act of love. The cross of Christ is a symbol of unconditional and selfless love displayed through self-sacrifice. Jesus once commented that the greatest love of all (Whitney Houston notwithstanding) is when one person gives up his or her life for another (John 15:13). When Spike hugs the cross in "Beneath You," it is a plea for forgiveness, but it is also Spike's recognition that the cross is a symbol of love. Just before embracing the cross, Spike says that "everybody will forgive and love. He will be loved" (7.2).

Spike dies a sacrificial death in order to save the world, but his motivation is not strictly an altruistic concern for humanity. Spike dies for love. When Buffy shows up with the magical amulet and tells Spike that it is meant to be worn only by a champion, Spike looks down, disappointed, for he knows he is unworthy (7.22). Yet when Buffy then hands him the amulet, Spike sees in her eyes what he had longed to see in Cecily's — the reflection of a good man. Ultimately, Spike gives his life so that he can truly be the champion that Buffy sees in him.

As energy flows through both the amulet and Spike, destroying every vampire in its path and causing the hellmouth to crumble, Buffy pleads with Spike to flee with her to safety. When he declines, she looks into his eyes and says, "I love you." But this Spike, who has learned to see, replies, "No, you don't. But thanks for saying it" (7.22) Spike does not give his life in a selfish desire to win Buffy's love, but in a selfless act of sacrifice. Spike has always been seeking romantic love, whether from Cecily, Drusilla, or Buffy, but never finding it. He has remained a heartbroken poet to the last. Yet Spike has found a deeper and more powerful love. He has learned that the greatest love is not found in romance or in passion, but in the giving of oneself for others.

Considering Joss Whedon's atheistic stance, it is surprising how significant the cross of Christ is on this show, both as symbol and as idea. The most basic use of the cross, as a weapon to ward off vampires, is certainly not without Christian overtones, but is primarily grounded in folklore and tradition. Of greater importance is Buffy's cross necklace that functions early on to identify her calling and the sacrificial nature of her work (1.12). Buffy's death while stretched airborne in the shape of a cross brings that sacrificial nature to completion (5.22). Xander the carpenter's display of unconditional love, accepting Willow in an act of grace, evokes the biblical idea that Christ the carpenter came to save sinners (6.22). Spike's Crucifixion pose for photographers foreshadows both his later embrace of the cross in a plea for forgiveness and his sacrificial death (4.22). Spike's final act of selfless love saves the world by causing the hellmouth and the entire town of Sunnydale above to collapse into a giant crater (7.22). It is a testimony that sacrificial love wields more power than the gates of hell.

There is an underlying belief among many Christians and some religious critics that an atheist cannot create a product of high moral value and theological worth. The flawed assumption is that an atheist is necessarily antagonistic to Christian teaching and works with a hidden agenda designed to undermine Christian faith. With *Buffy the Vampire Slayer*, Joss Whedon has exposed the flaw in such thinking. Although he does not adhere to the Christian faith and no doubt rejects many of its claims, he demonstrates clearly the seriousness with which he takes the Christian story as story and as a cultural shaper of moral values. In *Buffy*, this self-proclaimed storyteller mines from the Christian story certain themes and ideas that provide emotional resonance for life.

Conclusion

Buffy and Moral Discourse

Although the discussion in this book has focused on *Buffy the Vampire Slayer*, this is ultimately not a book about *Buffy the Vampire Slayer*. It is a book about moral discourse in narrative television. For good or ill, television has become a significant force in the shaping of a society's moral values, and we ignore its role at our peril. When not ignored, however, assessments of the moral worth of television shows have often suffered from an overly simplified analysis that fails to appreciate the complexity of moral discourse. A reductionist approach that views all morality on television through the lenses of sex, violence, and profanity is essentially bankrupt because it does not allow for the nuances and mitigating factors that affect moral discourse. The ratings system for movies reflects a similar approach and illustrates its flaws. A movie that is rated "R" for violence and profanity may actually hold a powerful moral message for teenagers, while a "PG" movie that seems quite pristine on the surface may in fact contain a worldview or promote a philosophy that is morally unhealthy for teenagers and all the more destructive because of its subtlety.

As a case study in moral discourse, *Buffy the Vampire Slayer* is a testimony to the complexity of moral communication in televised narrative and to the need for equally sophisticated methods of analysis. *Buffy* teaches us about the complexity of communicating morality through narrative. Many moralist critics and religious viewers of television reduce the moral value of a particular show to what they see portrayed on screen. This ignores the potentially subversive nature of narrative. Narrative communicates through indirection. It is a kind of

Trojan Horse that sneaks in a message while the viewer is distracted by the pretty horse. In the case of *Buffy the Vampire Slayer*, the monsters and demons are narrative vehicles for a moral message.

Buffy teaches us that a critique of a show's moral value must occur in the context of that show's larger moral vision. When individual scenes or episodes of *Buffy* are isolated, one can easily make an argument that *Buffy* glorifies violence, irresponsible sexuality, disregard for authority, neglectful parenting, and the occult. When individual scenes or episodes are isolated, one can make the case that *Buffy* is anti-Christian and intent on undermining Judeo-Christian values and beliefs. When one looks at the larger moral vision of *Buffy*, however, another picture emerges. One sees that this is a show obsessed with the concepts of right and wrong and how moral responsibility gets defined in the context of community and in relation to other human beings. This is a show that glorifies self-sacrifice and unconditional love. This show extols the virtue of forgiveness and consistently holds out the promise of redemption from an evil life. *Buffy* employs Christian teachings as a vital piece of its moral foundation. The cross of Christ in particular strongly influences the presentation of certain characters and gives definition to the themes of sacrifice, love, redemption, and forgiveness.

Buffy teaches us that the means of communication is just as important for assessing moral value as is content. *Buffy* attempts to achieve emotional resonance through the telling of a story. As a modern fairy tale, it portrays reality through fantasy. This obsession with tapping into the emotional core of life necessitates presenting life in all its complexity and ambiguity. This includes exploration of the dark side of humanity. When understood as part of the show's means of communication, this focus on evil and the darkness within humanity becomes not a glorification of such things but an exhortation to make better moral choices.

Buffy teaches us that a show's worldview is an essential component of its moral vision. The position that a show takes with respect to cosmology, eschatology, the relationship between good and evil, human nature, and the interplay of fate and freewill affect how that show conceives of moral responsibility.

Buffy teaches us that a show's moral value should be judged in the light of a wide array of topics. Seemingly tangential topics like death, power, privilege, community, family, and identity are just as essential to a show's moral message as are presentations of sexuality or violence.

Finally, *Buffy* teaches us that the moral evaluation of a television show should involve a methodology that asks various kinds of questions. These are not exhaustive, and a study of a different television show would likely yield some different questions. Nevertheless, the following six questions recurred during my evaluation of *Buffy the Vampire Slayer*. 1) What is the manner of communication? A show may address moral issues through a variety of means (humor, satire, propositional statements, etc.). In *Buffy*'s case, the means of moral communication includes such elements as narrative development, subtext, and metaphor. 2) What is the context? As in life, a variety of contextual factors influence the moral evaluation of particular actions. 3) Where does this event or action in the life of this character fit within the character's narrative arc? Moral evaluation of a serialized narrative must allow for character evolution. The moral message contained in a character's actions may have as much to do with what comes before and after in that characters life as it does with the act itself. 4) Does this show use negative examples? Occasionally, the portrayal of immoral actions can be a highly effective method for communicating a moral message when those actions are vilified in the narrative rather than glorified. 5) Are there consequences? Often a moral message derives less from an act itself than it does from the results of that action. 6) What is the show's overall perspective? One must carefully distinguish between how an act is portrayed and what the show is ultimately attempting to say about that act.

Not every reader will agree with my conclusions about the moral value of *Buffy the Vampire Slayer*. That is perfectly acceptable because this book is less about the conclusions that one draws than it is about the questions one asks. My goal is not to convince others of the moral value of *Buffy the Vampire Slayer*, but to convince others of the complexity of moral discourse within popular culture. It is my hope that readers will take from this book a deeper understanding of the ways in which morality gets addressed in televised narrative so that they can then apply that understanding to other shows. Television has become a powerful voice in a society's moral conversation, and it is my hope that we all become more active and astute participants in that conversation.

Notes

INTRODUCTION
1. Whedon, interview, *New York Times*, Q.1.
2. Beardsmore, *Art and Morality*, 53.
3. Beardsmore, 65, 73.
4. Many of the dialogue quotations from *Buffy the Vampire Slayer* used in this book are taken from the episodes themselves, while others derive from episode transcripts available at www.buffyworld.com/.
   1. Tracy, *Girl's Got Bite,* 41.
   2. Joss Whedon, commentary on "Welcome to the Hellmouth," in *Buffy the Vampire Slayer: The Complete First Season on DVD.*
   3. Joss Whedon, interview, in *Buffy the Vampire Slayer: The Complete First Season on DVD.*
   4. Joss Whedon, commentary on "Welcome to the Hellmouth," *Buffy the Vampire Slayer: The Complete First Season on DVD.*
   5. Quoted in Havens, *Joss Whedon,* 33.
   6. Levine and Schneider claim that most scholars who undertake analysis of *Buffy the Vampire Slayer* are misguided because the value of the show and the reason for its success is due to nothing more than sex appeal and fantasy escapism, "Feeling for Buffy," 294-308. Levine and Schneider fail in their assertion, however, by not addressing several significant issues, including 1) comments by Joss Whedon and his writers to the effect that they intend for the show to evoke multiple interpretations and appeal on multiple levels besides those of sex appeal and escapism, 2) that the sheer amount of scholarly analysis of the show, even if some of it is misconstrued, is itself a testimony to *Buffy's* ability to communicate on multiple levels, and 3) that the issue in most scholarly research is not accounting for the *success* of the show (which they fixate on) but exploring the integrity of the narrative.
   7. Quoted in Nussbaum, "Must-See Metaphysics," 58.
   8. Hanks, "Deconstructing Buffy," paragraph 3.
   9. Sawyer, "Subtext is Becoming Text," paragraph 2.
   10. For representative feminist readings of *Buffy* see Playden, "'What You Are, What's To Come'," 120-147; Pender, "'I'm Buffy, and You're . . . History'," 35-44; Owen, "Vampires, Postmodernity, and Post Feminism," 24-31.
   11. Bowman, "*Buffy the Vampire Slayer*: The Greek Hero Revisited." For Campbell's presentation of the heroic monomyth, see *The Hero With A Thousand Faces.*
   12. Overbey and Preston-Matto, "Staking in Tongues," 73-84.

13. Wilson, "Laugh, Spawn of Hell, Laugh," 78-97.
14. Dechert, "'My Boyfriend's in the Band!'" 218-226.
15. Schlozman, "Vampires and Those Who Slay Them," 49-54.
16. South, "All Torment, Trouble, and Wonder," 93-102.
17. Wall and Zryd, "Vampire Dialectics," 53-77.
18. Introvigne, "God, New Religious Movements and *Buffy the Vampire Slayer.*"
19. Cordesman, "Biological Warfare and the 'Buffy Paradigm,'" 5.
20. DeCandido, "Bibliographic Good vs Evil," 44-47; Cullen, "Rupert Giles," 42.
21. Whedon, interview, *New York Times*, Q.1.
22. Whedon, online posting at *The Bronze*, December 3, 1998.
23. Whedon, online posting at *The Bronze*, January 29, 2000.
24. Throughout the book, I employ ellipses in dialogue quoted from the show. This occurs in two different ways. Three dots (. . .) represent a significant pause in speaking or a statement that is broken off in mid-sentence. Four dots (. . . .) represent the removal of dialogue.
25. Quoted in Longworth, *TV Creators*, 2.210.
26. Udovitch, "What Makes Buffy Slay?" 64.
27. Wood, *Hollywood From Vietnam to Reagan*, 47.
28. Wood, 46.
29. Whedon, online posting at *The Bronze*, May 22, 2002.

CHAPTER TWO

1. Schultze, *Redeeming Television*, 31-35.
2. Clark, "Media, Culture, and Religion," 17.
3. Martín-Barbero, "Mass Media," 111.
4. Greeley writes that although not all of popular culture is good, "some popular culture is excellent and, therefore, given pop culture's propensity to search for meaning, possibly theological," *God in Popular Culture*, 13; see also 9-12.
5. Hoover, "Introduction," 2. Romanowski points out that the concern among American churches over cultural competitors for the "time, money, and souls of its members" did not develop with television, but goes back to the early American theater, *Pop Culture Wars*, 41-43.
6. Romanowski, 35.
7. Fore, *Television and Religion*, 24-25.
8. Baehr, *Media-Wise Family*, 57-84; Wildmon, "Religious Bigotry," 3-6.
9. Medved, *Hollywood vs America*, 3.
10. The Parents Television Council (www.parentstv.org/) for instance, keeps track on their website of the number of times sex, violence, and profanity are portrayed during the family hour each week.
11. Schultze, 15, 130.
12. See Romanowski, 328.
13. Schultze, 133-34.
14. The Parents Television Council is a Los Angeles based organization that attempts to change television content through economic pressure on advertisers. Each year they rank the top ten best and worst shows on television on their website (www.parentstv.org/).
15. This is my own informal survey. The percentages may not be fully accurate but do reflect ballpark figures.

16. Quoted in Nussbaum, 59.
17. Joss Whedon, commentary on "The Harvest," in *Buffy the Vampire Slayer: The Complete First Season on DVD*.
18. Brody, "'Buffy the Vampire Slayer' Mocks Christianity."
19. Quoted in Jensen, "To Hell and Back," 61.
20. Hertz, "Don't Let Your Kids Watch *Buffy the Vampire Slayer*," pargraph 18.
21. Rosenberger, "Morality Tale," paragraph 5.
22. Skippy R., "*The Door* Theologian of the Year."
23. Hanks, paragraph 10.
24. Graeber, "Rebel Without a God," 29-30.
25. Udovitch, 66.
26. "VQT Endorses 'Sopranos,' 'Buffy,'" 12; Havens, 1.
27. Romanowski, 309-312; Bryant, "Cinema, Religion, and Popular Culture," 114. Miles argues that the assumption that discussions about morality can only occur under the umbrella of religion must be replaced by an awareness that "value conflicts do not always occur in the context of religion." Thus, it is important for television to depict "confrontations of values" outside the boundaries of religion, "What You See Is What You Get," 43.
28. Whedon told the Houston Chronicle, "I make up every story, with the writers, for every show. I look at every single script, and I either punch it up or give specific notes about it." See McDaniel, "TV's Cult Hero," paragraph 12.
29. Whedon, interview by Tasha Robinson, *The Onion*.
30. Nussbaum, 58.
31. "'Buffy' Creator on Show, Final Episode," *CNN.com*; Longworth, 216.
32. Udovitch, 66.
33. Beardsmore, 73.
34. See Suman, "Religion on Fiction Television?" 76-78.
35. For example, see Romanowski, 330.
36. Whedon, interview by Tasha Robinson, *The Onion*.
37. Whedon, online posting at *The Bronze*, May 22, 2002.
38. Joss Whedon, interview on "Innocence," in *Buffy the Vampire Slayer: The Complete Second Season on DVD*.
39. Quoted in Mazor, "Marti Noxon."
40. Quoted in Golden, Bissette and Sniegoski, *The Monster Book*, 4.
41. Whedon, online posting at *The Bronze*, Dec. 15, 1998. I have made a few minor alterations to correct typographical errors.
42. Simpson, "Myth Versus Faux Myth," B16.

CHAPTER 3

1. Greeley, 177, 185. Greeley argues that fantasy stories are primarily about religion, not morality, because they embrace a dualistic world of good and evil with little moral complexity. This distinction is invalid with respect to *Buffy* which contains a great deal of moral complexity.
2. Whedon, interview by Tasha Robinson, *The Onion*; Nussbaum, 59.
3. Whedon, online posting at *The Bronze*, Jan. 3, 1998 and Dec. 15, 1998.
4. Petrie, *BBC Cult Interviews*, n.d.
5 Quoted in Havens, 81.
6. Quoted in Havens, 5.
7. Quoted in Havens, 158.
8. Quoted in Golden, Holder, with DeCandido, *Watcher's Guide*, 1.241.

266 Notes

9. Campbell with Moyers, *Power of Myth*, 2, 10, 39.
10. Whedon, interview, *New York Times*, Q.3.
11. Whedon, online posting at *The Bronze*, May 22, 2002.
12. Quoted in Longworth, 213.
13. Campbell, *Power of Myth*, 183.
14. Schultze, 44, 48.
15. Nussbaum, 58.
16. Quoted in Bellafante, "Bewitching Teen Heroines," 84.
17. For instance, see Whedon, online posting at *The Bronze*, January 29, 2000; Tracy, 32.
18. Nietzsche, "Truth and Falsity," 634-39. I am indebted to Jennifer Hamilton both for calling my attention to the Nietzsche reference in this scene and for pointing me towards this essay.
19. Longworth, 208.
20. Golden, Bissette, and Sniegoski, ix; Holder, with Mariotte and Hart, *Watcher's Guide*, 2.338.
21. Black, "More About Metaphor," 38-39; Foss, *Rhetorical Criticism*, 188-89.
22. Lakoff and Johnson, *Metaphors We Live By*, ix, 3.
23. Denham, *Metaphor and Moral Experience*, 309.
24. Lakoff and Johnson, 7-8.
25. Denham, 229-230.
26. Denham, 339.
27. Denham, 352.
28. Lakoff and Johnson, 5, 158; Foss, 189.
29. Whittock, *Metaphor and Film*, 37, 116.
30. Whittock, 42-44.
31. Whittock, 131.
32. Gordon and Hollinger, "Introduction," 5.
33. Quoted in Golden, Bissette, and Sniegoski, 39.
34. Auerbach, *Our Vampires, Ourselves*.
35. See Zanger, "Metaphor into Metonymy," 17-26; Carter, "The Vampire as Alien," 27-44; Nixon, "When Hollywood Sucks," 115-128.
36. Wood, 75.
37. Joss Whedon, interview on "Angel" and "The Puppet Show," in *Buffy the Vampire Slayer: The Complete First Season on DVD*.
38. Golden, Bissette, and Sniegoski, 166.
39. Quoted in Tracy, 33.
40. Joss Whedon, interview on "Welcome to the Hellmouth" and "The Harvest," in *Buffy the Vampire Slayer: The Complete First Season on DVD*.
41. Whedon, interview by Tasha Robinson, *The Onion*.
42. Joss Whedon, commentary on "Welcome to the Hellmouth," in *Buffy the Vampire Slayer: The Complete First Season on DVD*.
43. David Greenwalt, commentary on "Reptile Boy," in *Buffy the Vampire Slayer: The Complete Second Season on DVD*.
44. Joss Whedon, interview on "Witch," in *Buffy the Vampire Slayer: The Complete First Season on DVD*.
45. Quoted in Longworth, 207.
46. Little, "High School Is Hell," 287.
47. Golden, Bissette, and Sniegoski, 330, 362.

CHAPTER 4
1. Quoted in Havens, 8.
2. Campbell, *Power of Myth*, 14.
3. Quoted in Havens, 8.
4. Sutherland, *BBC Cult Interviews*. Gellar, *BBC Cult Interviews*.
5. Jensen, 65.

CHAPTER 5
1. Golden, Bissette, and Sniegoski, 2-3, 93.
2. Wall and Zryd, 59.
3. Anderson, "Prophecy Girl," 221.
4. Quoted in Golden and Holder, 242.
5. Zanger, 18-19; Carter, 33.
6. Abbott, "'A Little Less Ritual'," 6; Playden, 134-35.
7. Whedon, online posting at *The Bronze*, January 2, 1998.
8. Sakal, "No Big Win," 239-241.
9. Erickson, "'Sometimes You Need a Story'," 114; Introvigne.
10. Shuttleworth, "They Always Mistake Me for the Character I Play!" 236.
11. Marinucci, "Feminism and the Ethics of Violence," 64.

CHAPTER 6
1. Zanger, 23.
2. Charnas, "Meditations in Red," 59.
3. Noxon, *BBC Cult Interviews*.
4. One could object that any connection between this episode and Willow's later descent into evil was unintentional, but given that Sarah Michelle Gellar has commented that Joss Whedon always intended for Willow to go bad, the connection seems valid; see Jensen, "The Good-Bye Girl," 21.
5. Fossey, "'Never Hurt the Feelings of a Brutal Killer'," 10.
6. Fury, *BBC Cult Interviews*.
7. Espenson, *BBC Cult Interviews*.
8. Quoted in Mazor.
9. Fossey, 10.
10. Wilcox, "'Every Night I Save You'," 16.
11. Whedon, interview, *New York Times*, Q.5.
12. Whedon, interview, *New York Times*, Q.5.

CHAPTER 7
1. Joss Whedon, commentary on "The Harvest," in *Buffy the Vampire Slayer: The Complete First Season on DVD*.
2. Shuttleworth, 228.
3. Noxon, *BBC Cult Interviews*.

CHAPTER 8
1. Joss Whedon, commentary on "The Harvest," in *Buffy the Vampire Slayer: The Complete First Season on DVD*.
2. Joss Whedon, commentary on "The Harvest," in *Buffy the Vampire Slayer: The Complete First Season on DVD*.
3. Quoted in Udovitch, 66.

4. For a discussion of this idea in the teachings of Immanuel Kant and in *Buffy* see Lawler, "Between Heavens and Hells," 107-8
5. Joss Whedon, commentary on "The Harvest," in *Buffy the Vampire Slayer: The Complete First Season on DVD*.
6. Abbott, 17.
7. Nussbaum, 59.
8. Wilcox, "T.S. Eliot Comes to Television," 13.
9. Anderson, "What Would Buffy Do?" 43.
10. Dumars, "*Buffy the Vampire Slayer*: Writer-Producer David Fury."
11. Quoted in Golden, Bissette, and Sniegoski, 369.
12. Quoted in Golden, Bissette, and Sniegoski, 108-9.
13. Joss Whedon, interview on "Bad Girls," in *Buffy the Vampire Slayer: The Complete Third Season on DVD*.
14. Joss Whedon, interview on "Bad Girls," in *Buffy the Vampire Slayer: The Complete Third Season on DVD*.

CHAPTER 9

1. For some of the dissimilarities between Wicca and *Buffy*'s portrayal see Winslade, "Teen Witches, Wiccans, and 'Wanna-Blessed-Be's'."
2. Quoted in Golden, Bissette, and Sniegoski, 163.
3. Quoted in Golden, Bissette, and Sniegoski, 166.
4. Quoted in Golden, Bissette, and Sniegoski, 166.
5. For a few representative examples see Clark and Miller, "Buffy, the Scooby Gang, and Monstrous Authority"; Wall and Zryd, 53-77; Playden, 120-147; Graeber, 30.
6. Buinicki and Enns, "Buffy the Vampire Disciplinarian"; King, "Brownskirts," 197-211.
7. Buinicki and Enns, 1.
8. Wall and Zryd, 56.
9. Rose, "Of Creatures and Creators," 135.
10. Alessio, "'Things Are Different Now?'" 737.

CHAPTER 10

1. Wilcox makes the same observation in connection with her analysis of Faith, "'Who Died and Made Her the Boss?'" 8-9.
2. I add italics throughout this section for emphasis.
3. Interesting exceptions are "Empty Places" (7.19) and "Touched" (7.20). Buffy's solo mission to the vineyard where she finds the scythe is a success, while the community's mission ends in total failure. The vital distinction here is that Buffy did not reject her community, rather the community rejected her. They broke the trust and they suffered for it.
4. Wilcox, "'Who Died and Made Her the Boss?'" 7.
5. On the flip side, Forrest accuses Buffy of tearing apart the "family" of the Initiative, thus identifying her as their Yoko.
6. Money, "Undemonization of Supporting Characters," 101.
7. Quoted in Havens, 75.
8. Whedon, interview, *New York Times*, Q.4.
9. Joss Whedon, commentary on "Welcome to the Hellmouth," in *Buffy the Vampire Slayer: The Complete First Season on DVD*.
10. This, however, should not be taken as a rejection of the traditional family unit because, in a later episode, Buffy politely rejects Giles' offer to help

with Dawn by stating, "This is a family thing" (5.13). There remains a distinction on *Buffy* between a community that functions as a family and a more traditionally-rendered family unit.
  11. Quoted in Havens, 75.
  12. Quoted in Golden, Bissette, and Sniegoski, 363.
  13. For this argument see Bowers, "Generation Lapse," 2.
  14. Bowers, 3.
  15. Bowers, 9.
  16. Bowers, 25.
  17. Note also that Willow's fall occurs after Tara leaves (the adult voice in her life).
  18. This quote comes from Frank Furedi, author of *Paranoid Parenting*. For the quote and a concise discussion of his book see Peterson, "For Parents, Advice Overkill," 6D.

CHAPTER 11
  1. Hanson, "Apocalypticism," 29-30.
  2. Quoted in Havens, 76.
  3. Campbell, *Hero With A Thousand Faces*, 36-37; Bowman.
  4. Kaveney, "She Saved the World," 16.

CHAPTER 12
  1. Baehr, 77.
  2. Udovitch, 64.
  3. Hertz, paragraph 7.
  4. Espenson, *BBC Cult Interviews*.
  5. Quoted in Havens, 92-93.
  6. Whedon, interview, *New York Times*, Q.7.
  7. Quoted in Longworth, 214.
  8. "Growing Up," *Buffy the Vampire Slayer Official Magazine*, 15.
  9. Whedon, as quoted in Longworth, 209.
  10. Wilcox makes a similar point with respect to Giles' comment about the town's tendency to rationalize and forget their occasional encounters with vampires. She says that "his words apply to the social problems of the real world just as emphatically as they do to monsters," "'There Will Never Be a 'Very Special' Buffy'," 19.
  11. Whedon, interview, *New York Times*, Q.7.
  12. Quoted in Rosenthal, "'Buffy' Boss."
  13. "'Buffy' Creator on Show, Final Episode," *CNN.com*.

CHAPTER 13
  1. Medved, 96, 107-8. For his full discussion of Hollywood's promotion of promiscuity see 95-121.
  2. Wildmon, 5.
  3. Godawa, *Hollywood Worldviews*, 201.
  4. Joss Whedon, commentary on "Innocence," in *Buffy the Vampire Slayer: The Complete Second Season on DVD*.
  5. Petrie, *BBC Cult Interviews*, August 21, 2001.
  6. "A Buffy Bestiary," in *Buffy the Vampire Slayer: The Complete Second Season on DVD*.

7. Joss Whedon, interview on "Surprise," in *Buffy the Vampire Slayer: The Complete Second Season on DVD.*
8. Braun says, "It is notable that Angel's shift from good to evil occurred because of sex. This emotionally and physically charged event — and Buffy's concurrent loss of virginity — thus had extremely traumatic results for the slayer," "Ambiguity of Evil," 90.
9. Joss Whedon, interview on "Innocence," in *Buffy the Vampire Slayer: The Complete Second Season on DVD.*
10. Jarvis, "School is Hell," 262.
11. Joss Whedon, commentary on "Innocence," in *Buffy the Vampire Slayer: The Complete Second Season on DVD.*
12. Rosenberger.
13. "Top 10 Worst Anti-Family Shows on Television," *Human Events*, 12.
14. Krzywinska's statement that it is the sexual repression of orphans that triggers the haunting and not sex itself is an imprecise distinction, "Hubble-Bubble," 191. The sexual repression of orphans is the source of the poltergeist, but it is distinctly the sex acts of Buffy and Riley that cause the poltergeist to manifest.
15. Longworth, 214.
16. Bernstein, "Raising the Stakes," 15-16.
17. "*Buffy* Getting Darker," *Sci-Fi Wire.*
18. Quoted in Havens, 84.
19. Petrie, *BBC Cult Interviews*, n.d.
20. See the discussion on incoherence in chapter one.
21. Quoted in Longworth, 214.

CHAPTER 14
1. For a brief history of the relationship between television and violence see Fore, 131-139.
2. See Schultze, 105; Romanowski, 315.
3. Romanowski, 315.
4. Godawa, 196.
5. Marinucci, 67.
6. Marinucci, 67.
7. Nussbaum, 59.
8. Quoted in Longworth, 213.
9. Joss Whedon, commentary on "Welcome to the Hellmouth" and interview on "Angel" and "Puppet Show," in *Buffy the Vampire Slayer: The Complete First Season on DVD.*
10. Longworth, 212.
11. McConnell, "Chaos at the Mouth of Hell," 128.
12. Quoted in Longworth, 213.
13. Golden, Bissette, and Sniegoski, 330.
14. Quoted in Havens, 128.
15. Lakoff and Johnson, 4.
16. Marinucci, 69.

CHAPTER 15
1. Joss Whedon, interview on "I Only Have Eyes For You," in *Buffy the Vampire Slayer: The Complete Second Season on DVD.*

2. Quoted in Longworth, 220.
3. Author's own translation. Italics mine.
4. It is never made clear why Spike and Angel feel guilt since one could argue that they are not responsible for acts committed without a soul.
5. Whedon, interview, *New York Times*, Q.7.
6. Alessio describes and documents several of these criticisms in "'Things are Different Now?'" 731-740.
7. Alessio, 732-36.
8. Alessio, 739.
9. Alessio, 738.

CHAPTER 16

1. Whedon, interview, *New York Times*, Q.7.
2. Godawa, 51.
3. Krzywinska, 184.
4. I have altered the order of the characters for the sake of logical progression and ease of discussion.
5. South discusses these components of Willow's personality as a means of identifying the irrationality of her actions; see "'My God, It's Like a Greek Tragedy'," 131-145.
6. I am indebted to Ron Cox for filling in some of the gaps in my knowledge of C. S. Lewis.
7. Whedon, interview, *New York Times*, Q.7.
8. Golden, Bissette, and Sniegoski, 166.
9. Nietzsche, 638.
10. See also Boyette, "The Comic Anti-Hero," 10; DeKelb-Rittenhouse, "Sex and the Single Vampire," 151.
11. *Buffy* writer Douglas Petrie says that the writers wanted to show that Spike had not changed in 125 years. Petrie says, "He's a heartbroken poet, he'll never be anything else," *BBC Cult Interviews*, August 21, 2001.
12. Wilcox, "'Every Night I Save You'," 16.
13. Marti Noxon says that the writers of *Buffy* included the rape scene in order to remind people that even though Spike has made great progress, he is still evil and "doesn't quite know the difference between right and wrong." Quoted in Havens, 89.

Episode Guide

SEASON ONE

Episode	Title	Writer(s)
1.1	*Welcome to the Hellmouth*	Joss Whedon
1.2	*The Harvest*	Joss Whedon
1.3	*Witch*	Dana Reston
1.4	*Teacher's Pet*	David Greenwalt
1.5	*Never Kill A Boy On the First Date*	Rob Des Hotel / Dean Batali
1.6	*The Pack*	Matt Kiene / Joe Reinkemeyer
1.7	*Angel*	David Greenwalt
1.8	*I, Robot . . . You Jane*	Ashley Gable / Thomas A. Swyden
1.9	*The Puppet Show*	Dean Batali / Rob Des Hotel
1.10	*Nightmares*	Joss Whedon / David Greenwalt
1.11	*Out of Mind, Out of Sight*	Joss Whedon / Ashley Gable / Thomas A. Swyden
1.12	*Prophecy Girl*	Joss Whedon (D)

SEASON TWO

Episode	Title	Writer(s)
2.1	*When She Was Bad*	Joss Whedon (D)

2.2	*Some Assembly Required*	Ty King
2.3	*School Hard*	Joss Whedon
		David Greenwalt
2.4	*Inca Mummy Girl*	Matt Kiene
		Joe Reinkemeyer
2.5	*Reptile Boy*	David Greenwalt (D)
2.6	*Halloween*	Carl Ellsworth
2.7	*Lie To Me*	Joss Whedon (D)
2.8	*The Dark Age*	Dean Batali
		Rob Des Hotel
2.9	*What's My Line? - Part One*	Howard Gordon
		Marti Noxon
2.10	*What's My Line? - Part Two*	Marti Noxon
2.11	*Ted*	David Greenwalt
		Joss Whedon
2.12	*Bad Eggs*	Marti Noxon
2.13	*Surprise*	Marti Noxon
2.14	*Innocence*	Joss Whedon (D)
2.15	*Phases*	Rob Des Hotel
		Dean Batali
2.16	*Bewitched, Bothered and Bewildered*	Marti Noxon
2.17	*Passion*	Ty King
2.18	*Killed By Death*	Rob Des Hotel
		Dean Batali
2.19	*I Only Have Eyes For You*	Marti Noxon
2.20	*Go Fish*	David Fury
		Elin Hampton
2.21	*Becoming - Part One*	Joss Whedon (D)
2.22	*Becoming - Part Two*	Joss Whedon (D)

SEASON THREE

Episode	*Title*	*Writer(s)*
3.1	*Anne*	Joss Whedon (D)
3.2	*Dead Man's Party*	Marti Noxon
3.3	*Faith, Hope and Trick*	David Greenwalt
3.4	*Beauty and the Beasts*	Marti Noxon
3.5	*Homecoming*	David Greenwalt (D)

3.6	*Band Candy*	Jane Espenson
3.7	*Revelations*	Douglas Petrie
3.8	*Lovers Walk*	Dan Vebber
3.9	*The Wish*	Marti Noxon
3.10	*Amends*	Joss Whedon (D)
3.11	*Gingerbread*	Jane Espenson
		Thania St. John
3.12	*Helpless*	David Fury
3.13	*The Zeppo*	Dan Vebber
3.14	*Bad Girls*	Douglas Petrie
3.15	*Consequences*	Marti Noxon
3.16	*Dopplegangland*	Joss Whedon (D)
3.17	*Enemies*	Douglas Petrie
3.18	*Earshot*	Jane Espenson
3.19	*Choices*	David Fury
3.20	*The Prom*	Marti Noxon
3.21	*Graduation Day - Part One*	Joss Whedon (D)
3.22	*Graduation Day - Part Two*	Joss Whedon (D)

SEASON FOUR

Episode	*Title*	*Writer(s)*
4.1	*The Freshman*	Joss Whedon (D)
4.2	*Living Conditions*	Marti Noxon
4.3	*The Harsh Light of Day*	Jane Espenson
4.4	*Fear Itself*	David Fury
4.5	*Beer Bad*	Tracey Forbes
4.6	*Wild at Heart*	Marti Noxon
4.7	*The Initiative*	Douglas Petrie
4.8	*Pangs*	Jane Espenson
4.9	*Something Blue*	Tracey Forbes
4.10	*Hush*	Joss Whedon (D)
4.11	*Doomed*	Marti Noxon
		David Fury
		Jane Espenson
4.12	*A New Man*	Jane Espenson
4.13	*The I in Team*	David Fury
4.14	*Goodbye Iowa*	Marti Noxon
4.15	*This Year's Girl*	Douglas Petrie

4.16	*Who Are You?*	Joss Whedon (D)
4.17	*Superstar*	Jane Espenson
4.18	*Where the Wild Things Are*	Tracey Forbes
4.19	*New Moon Rising*	Marti Noxon
4.20	*The Yoko Factor*	Douglas Petrie
4.21	*Primeval*	David Fury
4.22	*Restless*	Joss Whedon (D)

SEASON FIVE

Episode	Title	Writer(s)
5.1	*Buffy vs. Dracula*	Marti Noxon
5.2	*The Real Me*	David Fury
5.3	*The Replacement*	Jane Espenson
5.4	*Out of My Mind*	Rebecca Rand Kirshner
5.5	*No Place Like Home*	Douglas Petrie
5.6	*Family*	Joss Whedon (D)
5.7	*Fool for Love*	Douglas Petrie
5.8	*Shadow*	David Fury
5.9	*Listening to Fear*	Rebecca Rand Kirshner
5.10	*Into the Woods*	Marti Noxon (D)
5.11	*Triangle*	Jane Espenson
5.12	*Checkpoint*	Douglas Petrie / Jane Espenson
5.13	*Blood Ties*	Steven S. DeKnight
5.14	*Crush*	David Fury
5.15	*I Was Made to Love You*	Jane Espenson
5.16	*The Body*	Joss Whedon (D)
5.17	*Forever*	Marti Noxon (D)
5.18	*Intervention*	Jane Espenson
5.19	*Tough Love*	Rebecca Rand Kirshner
5.20	*Spiral*	Steven S. DeKnight
5.21	*The Weight of the World*	Douglas Petrie
5.22	*The Gift*	Joss Whedon (D)

SEASON SIX

Episode	Title	Writer(s)
6.1	*Bargaining - Part One*	Marti Noxon
6.2	*Bargaining - Part Two*	David Fury
6.3	*After Life*	Jane Espenson
6.4	*Flooded*	Douglas Petrie (D)
		Jane Espenson
6.5	*Life Serial*	David Fury
		Jane Espenson
6.6	*All the Way*	Steven S. DeKnight
6.7	*Once More, With Feeling*	Joss Whedon (D)
6.8	*Tabula Rasa*	Rebecca Rand Kirshner
6.9	*Smashed*	Drew Z. Greenberg
6.10	*Wrecked*	Marti Noxon
6.11	*Gone*	David Fury (D)
6.12	*Doublemeat Palace*	Jane Espenson
6.13	*Dead Things*	Steven S. DeKnight
6.14	*Older and Far Away*	Drew Z. Greenberg
6.15	*As You Were*	Douglas Petrie (D)
6.16	*Hell's Bells*	Rebecca Rand Kirshner
6.17	*Normal Again*	Diego Gutierrez
6.18	*Entropy*	Drew Z. Greenberg
6.19	*Seeing Red*	Steven S. DeKnight
6.20	*Villains*	Marti Noxon
6.21	*Two To Go*	Douglas Petrie
6.22	*Grave*	David Fury

SEASON SEVEN

Episode	Title	Writer(s)
7.1	*Lessons*	Joss Whedon
7.2	*Beneath You*	Douglas Petrie
7.3	*Same Time, Same Place*	Jane Espenson
7.4	*Help*	Rebecca Rand Kirshner
7.5	*Selfless*	Drew Goddard
7.6	*Him*	Drew Z. Greenberg
7.7	*Conversations Wtih Dead*	Jane Espenson

	People	Drew Goddard
7.8	*Sleeper*	David Fury
		Jane Espenson
7.9	*Never Leave Me*	Drew Goddard
7.10	*Bring On the Night*	Marti Noxon
		Douglas Petrie
7.11	*Show Time*	David Fury
7.12	*Potential*	Rebecca Rand Kirshner
7.13	*The Killer In Me*	Drew Z. Greenberg
7.14	*First Date*	Jane Espenson
7.15	*Get It Done*	Douglas Petrie (D)
7.16	*Storyteller*	Jane Espenson
7.17	*Lies My Parents Told Me*	David Fury (D)
		Drew Goddard
7.18	*Dirty Girls*	Drew Goddard
7.19	*Empty Places*	Drew Z. Greenberg
7.20	*Touched*	Rebecca Rand Kirshner
7.21	*End of Days*	Jane Espenson
		Douglas Petrie
7.22	*Chosen*	Joss Whedon (D)

"D" = directed also

Bibliography

Abbott, Stacey. "'A Little Less Ritual and a Little More Fun': The Modern Vampire in *Buffy the Vampire Slayer*." *Slayage: The On-Line International Journal of Buffy Studies* 3 (June 2001), http://www.slayage.tv/essays/slayage3/sabbott.htm.

Alessio, Dominic. "'Things are Different Now'?: A Postcolonial Analysis of *Buffy the Vampire Slayer*." *The European Legacy* 6 (2001): 731-740.

Anderson, Wendy Love. "Prophecy Girl and The Powers That Be: The Philosophy of Religion in the Buffyverse." In *Buffy the Vampire Slayer and Philosophy: Fear and Trembling in Sunnydale*, edited by James B. South, 212-226. Popular Culture and Philosophy 4. Chicago and La Salle, Ill.: Open Court, 2003.

―――. "What Would Buffy Do?" *Christian Century*, May 17, 2003, 43.

Auerbach, Nina. *Our Vampires, Ourselves*. Chicago: University of Chicago Press, 1995.

Baehr, Ted. *The Media-Wise Family*. Colorado Springs, CO: Chariot Victor Publishing, 1998.

Beardsmore, R. W. *Art and Morality*. London: Macmillan, 1971.

Bellafante, Ginia. "Bewitching Teen Heroines." *Time*, May 5, 1997, 82-84.

Bernstein, Abbie. "Raising the Stakes." *Buffy the Vampire Slayer Official Magazine*, May 2002, 14-16.

Black, Max. "More About Metaphor." In *Metaphor and Thought*, edited by Andrew Ortony, 2nd ed., 19-41. Cambridge: Cambridge University Press, 1993.

Bowers, Cynthia. "Generation Lapse: The Problematic Parenting of Joyce Summers and Rupert Giles." *Slayage: The On-Line*

International Journal of Buffy Studies 2 (March 2001), http://www.slayage.tv/essays/slayage2/bowers.htm.
Bowman, Laurel. "*Buffy the Vampire Slayer*: The Greek Hero Revisited." Paper from the Department of Greek and Roman Studies, University of Victoria, 2002. http://web.uvic.ca/~lbowman/buffy/buffythehero.html.
Boyette, Michele. "The Comic Anti-Hero in *Buffy the Vampire Slayer*, or Silly Villain: Spike is for Kicks." *Slayage: The On-Line International Journal of Buffy Studies* 4 (December 2001), http://www.slayage.tv/essays/slayage4/boyette.htm.
Braun, Beth. "The *X-Files* and *Buffy the Vampire Slayer*: The Ambiguity of Evil in Supernatural Representations." *Journal of Popular Film and Television* 28 (Summer 2000): 88-94.
Brody, David. "'Buffy the Vampire Slayer' Mocks Christianity." *Family News in Focus*, April 22, 2003, http://www.family.org/cforum/fnif/news/a0025634.html.
The Bronze. December 3, 1998. http://www.cise.ufl.edu/cgi-bin/cgiwrap/hsiao/buffy/get-archive?date=19981203.
_____. December 15, 1998. http://www.cise.ufl.edu/cgi-bin/cgiwrap/hsiao/buffy/get-archive?date=19981215.
_____. January 2, 1998. http://www.cise.ufl.edu/cgi-bin/cgiwrap/hsiao/buffy/get-archive?date=19980102.
_____. January 3, 1998. http://www.cise.ufl.edu/cgi-bin/cgiwrap/hsiao/buffy/get-archive?date=19980103.
_____. January 29, 2000. http://www.cise.ufl.edu/cgi-bin/cgiwrap/hsiao/buffy/get-archive?date=20000129.
_____. May 22, 2002. http://www.cise.ufl.edu/cgi-bin/cgiwrap/hsiao/buffy/get-archive?date=20020522.
Bryant, M. Darrol. "Cinema, Religion, and Popular Culture." In *Religion in Film*, edited by John R. May and Michael Bird, 101-114. Knoxville: University of Tennessee Press, 1982.
"'Buffy' Creator on Show, Final Episode." *CNN.com*, May 16, 2003. http://www.cnn.com/.
"*Buffy* Getting Darker." *Sci-Fi Wire*, January 18, 2002. http://www.scifi.com/scifiwire/art-tv.html?2002-01/18/13.00.tv.
Buffy the Vampire Slayer: The Complete First Season on DVD. Twentieth Century Fox Home Entertainment, 2001.
Buffy the Vampire Slayer: The Complete Second Season on DVD. Twentieth Century Fox Home Entertainment, 2002.

Buffy the Vampire Slayer: The Complete Third Season on DVD. Twentieth Century Fox Home Entertainment, Inc., 2002.

Buffy the Vampire Slayer: The Complete Fourth Season on DVD. Twentieth Century Fox Home Entertainment, Inc., 2003.

Buinicki, Martin and Anthony Enns. "Buffy the Vampire Disciplinarian: Institutional Excess and the New Economy of Power." *Slayage: The On-Line International Journal of Buffy Studies* 4 (December 2001), http://www.slayage.tv/essays/slayage4/buinicki-enns.htm.

Campbell, Joseph. *The Hero With A Thousand Faces*. 2nd ed. Bollingen Series 17. Princeton: Princeton University Press, 1968.

Campbell, Joseph with Bill Moyers. *The Power of Myth*. New York: Anchor Books, 1991.

Carter, Margaret L. "The Vampire as Alien in Contemporary Fiction." In *Blood Read: The Vampire as Metaphor in Contemporary Culture*, edited by Joan Gordon and Veronica Hollinger, 27-44. Philadelphia: University of Pennsylvania Press, 1997.

Charnas, Suzy McKee. "Meditations in Red: On Writing *The Vampire Tapestry*." In *Blood Read: The Vampire as Metaphor in Contemporary Culture*, edited by Joan Gordon and Veronica Hollinger, 59-67. Philadelphia: University of Pennsylvania Press, 1997.

Clark, Daniel A. and P. Andrew Miller. "Buffy, the Scooby Gang, and Monstrous Authority: Buffy the Vampire Slayer and the Subversion of Authority." *Slayage: The On-Line International Journal of Buffy Studies* 3 (June 2001), http://www.slayage.tv/essays/slayage3/clarkmiller.htm.

Clark, Lynn Schofield. "At the Intersection of Media, Culture, and Religion: A Bibliographic Essay." In *Rethinking Media, Religion, and Culture*, edited by Stewart M. Hoover and Knut Lundby, 15-36. Thousand Oaks, CA: Sage Publications, 1997.

Cordesman, Anthony H. "Biological Warfare and the 'Buffy Paradigm.'" Paper for the Center for Strategic and International Studies, September 29, 2001, 1-41. http://www.csis.org/burke/hd/reports/Buffy012902.pdf.

Cullen, John. "Rupert Giles, The Professional Image Slayer." *American Libraries* 31 (May 2000): 42.

DeCandido, GraceAnne A. "Bibliographic Good vs. Evil in *Buffy the Vampire Slayer*." *American Libraries* 30 (September 1999): 44-47.

Bibliography

Dechert, S. Renee. "'My Boyfriend's in the Band!' *Buffy* and the Rhetoric of Music." In *Fighting the Forces: What's At Stake in Buffy the Vampire Slayer,* edited by Rhonda V. Wilcox and David Lavery, 218-226. Lanham, MD: Rowman and Littlefield, 2002.

DeKelb-Rittenhouse, Diane. "Sex and the Single Vampire: The Evolution of the Vampire Lothario and It's Representation in *Buffy*." In *Fighting the Forces: What's At Stake in Buffy the Vampire Slayer,* edited by Rhonda V. Wilcox and David Lavery, 143-152. Lanham, MD: Rowman and Littlefield, 2002.

Denham, A. E. *Metaphor and Moral Experience*. Oxford: Clarendon Press, 2000.

Dumars, Denise. "*Buffy the Vampire Slayer*: Writer-Producer David Fury." *Cinescape Online*, April 20, 2000. http://www.cinescape.com/.

Erickson, Gregory. "'Sometimes You Need a Story': American Christianity, Vampires, and Buffy," In *Fighting the Forces: What's At Stake in Buffy the Vampire Slayer,* edited by Rhonda V. Wilcox and David Lavery, 108-119. Lanham, MD: Rowman and Littlefield, 2002.

Espenson, Jane. *BBC Cult Interviews*, August 23, 2001. http://www.bbc.co.uk/cult/buffy/interviews.

Fore, William F. *Television and Religion: The Shaping of Faith, Values, and Culture*. Minneapolis: Augsburg, 1987.

Foss, Sonja K. *Rhetorical Criticism: Exploration and Practice*. Prospect Heights, Ill.: Waveland Press, 1989.

Fossey, Claire. "'Never Hurt the Feelings of a Brutal Killer': Spike and the Underground Man." *Slayage: The On-Line International Journal of Buffy Studies* 8 (March 2003), http://www.slayage.tv/essays/slayage8/Fossey.htm.

Fury, David. *BBC Cult Interviews*, August 23, 2001. http://www.bbc.co.uk/cult/buffy/interviews.

Gellar, Sarah Michelle. *BBC Cult Interviews*, 2001. http://www.bbc.co.uk/cult/buffy/interviews.

Godawa, Brian. *Hollywood Worldviews: Watching Films with Wisdom and Discernment*. Downers Grove, Ill.: InterVarsity Press, 2002.

Golden, Christopher and Nancy Holder with Keith R. A. DeCandido. *Buffy the Vampire Slayer: The Watcher's Guide*. Vol. 1. New York: Pocket Books, 1998.

Golden, Christopher, Stephen R. Bissette and Thomas E. Sniegoski. *Buffy the Vampire Slayer: The Monster Book*. 2nd ed. New York: Simon Pulse, 2002.

Gordon, Joan and Veronica Hollinger. "Introduction: The Shape of Vampires." In *Blood Read: The Vampire as Metaphor in Contemporary Culture*, edited by Joan Gordon and Veronica Hollinger, 1-16. Philadelphia: University of Pennsylvania Press, 1997.

Graeber, David. "Rebel Without a God." *In These Times*, December 27, 1998, 29-30.

Greeley, Andrew. *God in Popular Culture*. Chicago: Thomas More, 1988.

"Growing Up." *Buffy the Vampire Slayer Official Magazine*, April 2002, 12-16.

Hanks, Robert. "Deconstructing Buffy." *Independent*, July 1, 2002. http://www.independent.co.uk/story.jsp?story=310937.

Hanson, P. D. "Apocalypticism." In *Interpreter's Dictionary of the Bible Supplement*, edited by Keith Crim et al, 28-34. Nashville: Abingdon, 1976.

Havens, Candace. *Joss Whedon: The Genius Behind Buffy*. Dallas: Benbella Books, 2003.

Hertz, Todd. "Don't Let Your Kids Watch *Buffy the Vampire Slayer*. But You Can Tape It and Watch After They Go To Bed." *Christianity Today*, September 16, 2002. http://www.christianitytoday.com/ct/2002/136/31.0.html.

Holder, Nancy with Jeff Mariotte and Mary Elizabeth Hart. *Buffy the Vampire Slayer: The Watcher's Guide*. Vol. 2. New York: Pocket Books, 2000.

Hoover, Stewart M. "Introduction: The Cultural Construction of Religion in the Media Age." In *Practicing Religion in the Age of Media*, edited by Stewart M. Hoover and Lynn Schofield Clark, 1-6. New York: Columbia University Press, 2002.

Introvigne, Massimo. "God, New Religious Movements and *Buffy the Vampire Slayer*." Paper for *CESNUR: Center for Studies on New Religions*, April 2000. http://www.cesnur.org/2001/buffy_march01.htm.

Jarvis, Christine. "School is Hell: Gendered Fears in Teenage Horror." *Educational Studies* 27 (2001): 257-267.

Jensen, Jeff. "The Good-Bye Girl." *Entertainment Weekly*, March 7, 2003, 14-21.

_____. "To Hell and Back." *Entertainment Weekly*, September 7, 2001, 58-65.

Kaveney, Roz. "She Saved the World. A Lot: An Introduction to the Themes and Structures of *Buffy* and *Angel*." In *Reading the Vampire Slayer: An Unofficial Critical Companion to "Buffy" and "Angel*," edited by Roz Kaveney, 1-36. London: Tauris Parke, 2001; reprint, 2003.

King, Neal. "Brownskirts: Fascism, Christianity, and the Eternal Demon." In *Buffy the Vampire Slayer and Philosophy: Fear and Trembling in Sunnydale*, edited by James B. South, 197-211. Popular Culture and Philosophy 4. Chicago and La Salle, Ill.: Open Court, 2003.

Krzywinska, Tanya. "Hubble-Bubble, Herbs, and Grimoires: Magic, Manichaeanism, and Witchcraft in *Buffy*." In *Fighting the Forces: What's At Stake in Buffy the Vampire Slayer,* edited by Rhonda V. Wilcox and David Lavery, 178-194. Lanham, MD: Rowman and Littlefield, 2002.

Lakoff, George and Mark Johnson. *Metaphors We Live By*. Chicago: University of Chicago Press, 1980.

Lawler, James. "Between Heavens and Hells: The Multi-Dimensional Universe in Kant and *Buffy the Vampire Slayer*." In *Buffy the Vampire Slayer and Philosophy: Fear and Trembling in Sunnydale*, edited by James B. South, 103-116. Popular Culture and Philosophy 4. Chicago and La Salle, Ill.: Open Court, 2003.

Levine, Michael P. and Steven Jay Schneider. "Feeling for Buffy: The Girl Next Door." In *Buffy the Vampire Slayer and Philosophy: Fear and Trembling in Sunnydale*, edited by James B. South, 294-308. Popular Culture and Philosophy 4. Chicago and La Salle, Ill.: Open Court, 2003.

Little, Tracy. "High School Is Hell: Metaphor Made Literal in *Buffy the Vampire Slayer*." In *Buffy the Vampire Slayer and Philosophy: Fear and Trembling in Sunnydale*, edited by James B. South, Popular Culture and Philosophy 4., 282-293. Chicago and La Salle, Ill.: Open Court, 2003.

Longworth, James L., Jr. *TV Creators: Conversations with America's Top Producers of Television Drama*, Vol. 2. Syracuse, New York: Syracuse University Press, 2002.

Marinucci, Mimi. "Feminism and the Ethics of Violence: Why Buffy Kicks Ass." In *Buffy the Vampire Slayer and Philosophy: Fear and

Trembling in Sunnydale, edited by James B. South, 61-75. Popular Culture and Philosophy 4. Chicago and La Salle, Ill.: Open Court, 2003.

Martín-Barbero, Jesús. "Mass Media as a Site of Resacralization of Contemporary Culture." In *Rethinking Media, Religion, and Culture*, edited by Stewart M. Hoover and Knut Lundby, 102-116. Thousand Oaks, CA: Sage Publications, 1997.

Mazor, David. "Marti Noxon on the Future of *Buffy the Vampire Slayer*." *Preview Magazine*, 2002. http://www.prevuemagazine.com/Articles/Flash/540.

McConnell, Kathleen. "Chaos at the Mouth of Hell: Why the Columbine High School Massacre Had Repercussions for *Buffy the Vampire Slayer*." *Gothic Studies* 2 (April 2000): 119-135.

McDaniel, Mike. "TV's Cult Hero." *HoustonChronicle.com*, Nov. 10, 2002. http://www.HoustonChronicle.com/.

Medved, Michael. *Hollywood vs America*. New York: HarperPerennial, 1993.

Miles, Margaret R. "What You See Is What You Get: Religion on Prime Time Fiction Television." In *Religion and Prime Time Television*, edited by Michael Suman, 37-46. Westport, CT: Praeger, 1997.

Money, Mary Alice. "The Undemonization of Supporting Characters in *Buffy*." In *Fighting the Forces: What's At Stake in Buffy the Vampire Slayer,* edited by Rhonda V. Wilcox and David Lavery, 98-107. Lanham, MD: Rowman and Littlefield, 2002.

Nietzsche, Friedrich. "Truth and Falsity in an Ultramoral Sense." In *Critical Theory Since Plato*, edited by Hazard Adams, 634-39. Rev. ed. Heinle and Heinle, 1992.

Nixon, Nicola. "When Hollywood Sucks, or, Hungry Girls, Lost Boys, and Vampirism in the Age of Reagan." In *Blood Read: The Vampire as Metaphor in Contemporary Culture*, edited by Joan Gordon and Veronica Hollinger, 115-128. Philadelphia: University of Pennsylvania Press, 1997.

Noxon, Marti. *BBC Cult Interviews*, August 23, 2001. http://www.bbc.co.uk/cult/buffy/interviews.

Nussbaum, Emily. "Must-See Metaphysics." *New York Times Magazine*, September 22, 2002, 56-59.

Overbey, Karen Eileen and Lahney Preston-Matto. "Staking in Tongues: Speech Act as Weapon in *Buffy*." In *Fighting the Forces: What's At Stake in Buffy the Vampire Slayer,* edited by Rhonda V.

Wilcox and David Lavery, 73-84. Lanham, MD: Rowman and Littlefield, 2002.

Owen, Susan A. "'Buffy the Vampire Slayer': Vampires, Postmodernity, and Post Feminism." *Journal of Popular Film and Television* 27 (1999): 24-31.

The Parents Television Council Website. http://www.parentstv.org/.

Pender, Patricia. "'I'm Buffy, and You're . . . History': The Postmodern Politics of *Buffy*." In *Fighting the Forces: What's At Stake in Buffy the Vampire Slayer,* edited by Rhonda V. Wilcox and David Lavery, 35-44. Lanham, MD: Rowman and Littlefield, 2002.

Peterson, Karen S. "For Parents, Advice Overkill." *USA Today*, October 30, 2002, 6D.

Petrie, Doug. *BBC Cult Interviews*, August 21, 2001. http://www.bbc.co.uk/cult/buffy/interviews.

———. *BBC Cult Interviews*, n.d. http://www.bbc.co.uk/cult/buffy/interviews.

Playden, Zoe-Jane. "'What You Are, What's To Come': Feminisms, Citizenship and the Divine." In *Reading the Vampire Slayer: An Unofficial Critical Companion to "Buffy" and "Angel*," edited by Roz Kaveney, 120-147. London: Tauris Parke, 2001; reprint, 2003.

R., Skippy. "*The Door* Theologian of the Year." *TheDoorMagazine*, Sept./Oct. 2002. http://www.thedoormagazine.com/archives/buffy.html.

Romanowski, William. *Pop Culture Wars: Religion and the Role of Entertainment in American Life*. Downers Grove, Ill.: InterVarsity Press, 1996.

Rose, Anita. "Of Creatures and Creators: Buffy Does Frankenstein." In *Fighting the Forces: What's At Stake in Buffy the Vampire Slayer,* edited by Rhonda V. Wilcox and David Lavery, 133-142. Lanham, MD: Rowman and Littlefield, 2002.

Rosenberger, Chandler. "Morality Tale . . . From the Crypt." *National Review Online*, May 26-28, 2001. http://www.nationalreview.com/weekend/television/television-rosenberger052601.shtml.

Rosenthal, Phil. "'Buffy' Boss: It's Not Over When It's Over." *Chicago Sun-Times*, April 29, 2003. http://www.suntimes.com/.

Sakal, Gregory J. "No Big Win: Themes of Sacrifice, Salvation, and Redemption." In *Buffy the Vampire Slayer and Philosophy: Fear and Trembling in Sunnydale,* edited by James B. South, 239-253.

Popular Culture and Philosophy 4. Chicago and La Salle, Ill.: Open Court, 2003.

Sawyer, Andy. "In a Small Town in California . . . the Subtext is Becoming Text." *The Alien Online*, June 2002. http://www.the alienonline.net/features/buffy_jun02.asp?tid=3&scid=26&iid=722.

Schlozman, Steven C. "Vampires and Those Who Slay Them: Using the Television Program *Buffy the Vampire Slayer* in Adolescent Therapy and Psychodynamic Education." *Academic Psychiatry Online* 24 (March 2000): 49-54. http://ap.psychiatyronline.org/.

Schultze, Quentin J. *Redeeming Television: How TV Changes Christians — How Christians Can Change TV*. Downers Grove, Ill.: InterVarsity Press, 1992.

Shuttleworth, Ian. "They Always Mistake Me for the Character I Play!: Transformation, Identity and Role-Playing in the Buffyverse (and a defence of fine acting)." In *Reading the Vampire Slayer: An Unofficial Critical Companion to "Buffy" and "Angel,"* edited by Roz Kaveney, 211-236. London: Tauris Parke, 2001; reprint, 2003.

Simpson, Craig S. "Myth Versus Faux Myth." *Chronicle of Higher Education* 47 (May 25, 2001): B15-16.

South, James B. "'All Torment, Trouble, and Wonder, and Amazement Inhabits Here': The Vicissitudes of Technology in *Buffy the Vampire Slayer*." *Journal of American & Comparative Cultures* 24 (2001): 93-102.

_____. "'My God, It's Like a Greek Tragedy': Willow Rosenberg and Human Irrationality." In *Buffy the Vampire Slayer and Philosophy: Fear and Trembling in Sunnydale*, edited by James B. South, Popular Culture and Philosophy 4, 131-145. Chicago and La Salle, IL: Open Court, 2003.

Suman, Michael. "Do We Really Need More Religion on Fiction Television?" In *Religion and Prime Time Television*, edited by Michael Suman, 69-83. Westport, CT: Praeger, 1997.

Sutherland, Kristine. *BBC Cult Interviews*, January 10, 2002. http://www.bbc.co.uk/cult/buffy/interviews.

"Top 10 Worst Anti-Family Shows on Television." *Human Events*, August 25, 2000, 12.

Tracy, Kathleen. *The Girl's Got Bite: The Unofficial Guide to Buffy's World*. Los Angeles: Renaissance Books, 1998.

Udovitch, Mim. "What Makes Buffy Slay?" *Rolling Stone*, May 11, 2000, 60-66.

"VQT Endorses 'Sopranos,' 'Buffy.'" *Electronic Media*, April 5, 1999, 12.

Wall, Brian and Michael Zryd. "Vampire Dialectics: Knowledge, Institutions and Labour." In *Reading the Vampire Slayer: An Unofficial Critical Companion to "Buffy" and "Angel,"* edited by Roz Kaveney, 53-77. London: Tauris Parke, 2001; reprint, 2003.

Whedon, Joss. Interview by Tasha Robinson. *The Onion A.V. Club*, Sept. 5, 2001. http://www.theonionavclub.com/avclub3731/av feature-3731.html.

———. Interview with *New York Times*, May 16, 2003. http://www.nytimes.com/2003/05/16/readersopinions/16WHED.html?ex=1054435756&ei=1&en=4611982269e71ecf.

Whittock, Trevor. *Metaphor and Film*. Cambridge: Cambridge University Press, 1990.

Wilcox, Rhonda V. "'Every Night I Save You': Buffy, Spike, Sex and Redemption." *Slayage: The On-Line International Journal of Buffy Studies* 5 (May 2002, http://www.slayage.tv/essays/slayage 5/wilcox.htm.

———. "'There Will Never Be a 'Very Special' Buffy': *Buffy* and the Monsters of Teen Life." *The Journal of Popular Film and Television* 27 (1999): 16-23.

———. "T.S. Eliot Comes to Television: *Buffy*'s 'Restless'." *Slayage: The On-Line International Journal of Buffy Studies* 7 (December 2002), http://www.slayage.tv/essays/slayage7/Wilcox.htm.

———. "'Who Died and Made her the Boss?' Patterns of Mortality in *Buffy*." In *Fighting the Forces: What's At Stake in Buffy the Vampire Slayer,* edited by Rhonda V. Wilcox and David Lavery, 3-17. Lanham, MD: Rowman and Littlefield, 2002.

Wildmon, Donald E. "It Is Time to End Religious Bigotry." In *Religion and Prime Time Television*, edited by Michael Suman, 3-6. Westport, CT: Praeger, 1997.

Wilson, Steven. "Laugh, Spawn of Hell, Laugh." In *Reading the Vampire Slayer: An Unofficial Critical Companion to "Buffy" and "Angel,"* edited by Roz Kaveney, 78-97. London: Tauris Parke, 2001; reprint, 2003.

Winslade, J. Lawton. "Teen Witches, Wiccans, and 'Wanna-Blessed-Be's': Pop-Culture Magic in *Buffy the Vampire Slayer*." *Slayage: The On-Line International Journal of Buffy Studies* 1 (2001), http://www.slayage.tv/essays/slayage1/winslade.htm.

Wood, Robin. *Hollywood From Vietnam to Reagan.* New York: Columbia University Press, 1986.

www.buffyworld.com/.

Zanger, Jules. "Metaphor into Metonymy: The Vampire Next Door." In *Blood Read: The Vampire as Metaphor in Contemporary Culture*, edited by Joan Gordon and Veronica Hollinger, 17-26. Philadelphia: University of Pennsylvania Press, 1997.

Index

Abrams, Parker, 195, 196, 201,
Adam, 27, 28, 54, 94, 133, 147
addiction: drug, 154, 172, 181-83; magic, 176, 239, 241
adoption, 150-51
After Life, 164, 168-170, 175
alcohol, 14, 39, 85, 89, 174, 181-83
alcoholism, 157, 180
All the Way, 178, 182, 238
Amends, 21, 66, 69, 85, 97, 192, 226-29
Andrew, 30-32, 57, 72-73, 145, 175, 209, 246-47
A New Man, 67, 85, 86, 132, 137, 159
Angel, 48; Angelus, 48, 78, 112, 151, 192: and Buffy, 48, 100, 177-178, 191-93; as metaphor, 180; murder of Jenny, 218-19; redemption, 63, 69, 226-29; soul, 72, 78, 82, 84, 85, 192, 226-27
Angel, 48, 82, 84, 85, 111, 114, 226
anger, 58, 97, 129, 150, 185, 221
Anne, 15, 67, 112
Anya (Anyanka): and community, 145; death, 167, 213; sex, 195-97, 200, 202; socialization, 51, 126, 143, 162-63, 166-67; vengeance, 36, 78, 137, 176, 211-13; and Xander, 53, 78, 98, 164
apocalypse, 63, 100, 108, 159, 161-67 *passim*; definition, 160
apocalyptic eschatology, 160, 169
apocalyptic traditions, 68, 114, 160
Aquinas, Thomas, 14
As You Were, 88, 207, 253
atheism, 14, 17, 20, 21, 24, 61, 89
atonement, 51
Bad Eggs, 82, 110, 191
Bad Girls, 119, 221
Band Candy, 52, 97, 108, 153-54
Bargaining - Part One, 148, 170, 175, 212, 241, 252
Bargaining - Part Two, 170
Beauty and the Beasts, 81, 82, 194
Becoming - Part One, 47, 71-72, 84, 91, 106, 108, 226
Becoming - Part Two, 63, 71, 91, 99, 112, 137, 139, 166
Beer Bad, 14, 180-81
Ben, 84, 165-66, 182
Beneath You, 66, 69, 88, 200, 204, 213, 225, 254, 256

betrayal, 52, 74, 178
Bewitched, Bothered and Bewildered, 47, 186, 191, 193
Bible, 12, 33, 66, 73, 189, 203-5; Isaiah, 14; Job, 112; John, 115, 117; Mark, 116; Revelation, 115, 160, 167, 204; 2 Thessalonians, 115
Blood Ties, 134, 150
The Body, 134, 162, 206
Bring On the Night, 30, 139, 149, 204, 244, 255
Buchanan, Ted, 73, 137, 152-53, 176-77
Buffybot, 252
Buffy the Vampire Slayer: academic interest, 3-4; Christian criticism of, xiii, 12-13, 14-15, 20, 128, 134, 175, 195, 201; feminist agenda, xiii, 4, 18, 26, 43, 150; moral vision, xiii, xiv, 16, 17-21, 33, 123, 125, 259-261; and narrative, 27-32, 198
Buffy vs. Dracula, 23, 94-95
Caleb, 15, 59, 62, 66, 67, 73, 135, 194
Calendar, Jenny, 49, 50, 126, 127, 142, 178, 193
Campbell, Joseph, 4, 25-26, 43
Cecily, 248-49, 254
Chase, Cordelia, 48, 92, 107; social justice, 184-86; truthteller, 178; and Xander, 50, 97, 100, 101, 191, 196
Checkpoint, 136
Choices, 142, 157, 165
Chosen, 60, 64, 89, 130, 167, 187, 213, 256-57
Christianity, 62, 63, 64, 117, 136; abuse of power, 135, 153; anti-institutional, 14; and *Buffy*, 13, 14, 20-21, 65-71, 114, 115, 134, 174, 224, 227, 257, 260; individualism, 140; and metaphor, 33; prophecy, 160; redemption, 235-36, 240
christology, 16, 69, 101-2, 114-18, 224-26, 242-43, 256-57
church(es), 13, 67-68, 114, 132; abandoned, 13, 16, 68; metaphor, 13-14; places of redemption, 16, 66, 68, 122, 209, 225-26
Clem, 90
Columbine, 206
community, 67, 139-140, 145-49; ethics, 141-144; redemption, 144-45
consequences, 58, 174-76, 190-201 *passim*, 215, 261
Consequences, 74, 75, 120, 136, 142, 174, 221
context, 16, 71, 176-179, 189, 203, 204, 214, 261
Conversations With Dead People, 64, 66, 161, 223, 244
cosmology, 13, 14, 15, 20, 169
Creation, 62, 135
cross: crucifix, 16, 45, 68-69, 82, 109, 112, 199; of Christ, 101, 117, 208, 225, 256-57, 260; symbol of forgiveness, 226; symbol of love, 256; symbol of sacrifice, 69, 115-16, 118
Crucifixion, 16, 66, 116, 224-26, 256; *see also* cross
Crusades, 134
Crush, 86, 87, 180, 251
The Dark Age, 141, 153, 182

Darla, 82
Dead Man's Party, 15, 40, 52, 174, 209
Dead Things, 88, 95, 108, 119, 137, 222, 222, 244, 252
death, 117, 160-61; and appreciation of life, 161-63; and clarification, 165-68; fantasy vs. "real", 206-7; and prioritization, 163-65; social death, 109, 127; source of enlightenment, 161
dependence, 140, 143-44, 145, 147, 155, 172
D'Hoffryn, 212, 213
Dirty Girls, 15, 32, 47, 52, 62, 66, 73, 75, 123, 135
Doomed, 86, 147, 171-72
Dopplegangland, 47, 64, 83, 173, 196, 237, 238
Doublemeat Palace, 37, 211
Dracula, 54, 94-95
drug abuse, 153-54
Drusilla, 49, 50, 71, 87, 89, 151, 177
dualism, 65, 74, 81-88 *passim*, 99, 107, 109, 167, 168, 229
Earshot, 191, 206, 237
Empty Places, 66, 90, 96, 142, 209
End of Days, 139, 167, 256
Entropy, 86, 200, 213, 224, 250
eschatology, 16, 159-173
Espenson, Jane, 35, 87, 119, 129, 176
Eyghon, 153, 182
Faith, 51; accountability, 221-22; and Buffy, 105, 118; corruption of power, 118-120, 184; fall, 83, 118-120; marginalization, 118, 142, 148; moral responsibility, 118-123, 157; murder of Allan Finch, 119, 174, 208; redemption, 68, 120-23, 145, 194-95, 209; sex, 194-95, 200; trust, 142; violence, 209
Faith, Hope and Trick, 129
family, 97, 149-151, 164; source of strength, 112, 118, 123, 148
Family, 73, 151, 180
fate, 71-73
Father Gabriel, 134
Fear Itself, 97, 239
feminism, 4, 130
Finn, Riley: and Buffy, 53, 249; churchgoer, 67, 132; educator, 132; moral character, 92-93; moral code, 76-77; sex, 194, 196, 197; soldier, 54, 92-93, 132
First Date, 59, 88, 162, 168, 244, 254
First, The, 58-60, 62-64, 74, 211, 244
Flooded, 75, 95, 209-210
Flutie, Principal, 39, 110, 131, 132, 136
Fool for Love, 117, 162, 248, 249, 250, 254
Ford (Billy Fordham), 74, 165, 166, 177
Forever, 66, 164, 197, 217, 240
forgiveness, 215-219, 227; community, 141, 223-24; and the cross, 225; rejection of, 222-23
Forrest, 93, 133
Frankenstein, 35, 133, 208
freewill, 65, 71-73, 84, 125
The Freshman, 15, 53, 94, 184

friendship, 53, 118-120, 123, 141-149
Fury, David, 87, 116
Gellar, Sarah Michelle, 15, 44
Gethsemane, 116
Get It Done, 85, 96, 115, 164, 209, 255
The Gift, 16, 65, 79, 84, 116-18, 159, 166, 179, 224, 239, 252, 257
Giles, Rupert, 46; as father figure, 46, 150-51, 154-56; forgiveness, 227; Fyarl demon, 85; guilt, 141; murder of Ben, 79; imperialism, 230-31; Watcher, 45, 115
Gingerbread, 52, 63, 82, 129, 139, 154, 184, 208, 238
Glorificus (Glory), 54-55, 84, 166, 182, 215
God, 13, 18, 21, 24, 62, 63, 65, 72, 108, 112, 133, 134, 136, 167, 169, 177, 226, 227; absence, 13, 14, 16, 20; existence, 65-66; immanence, 70; transcendence, 70; and violence, 203-5
Go Fish, 50, 97, 181, 185, 186
Gone, 183, 222, 238
Goodbye Iowa, 45, 72, 76, 85, 133-34, 250
grace, 223, 224, 224-25, 227
Graduation Day - Part One, 78, 136, 143, 164, 166
Graduation Day - Part Two, 51, 94, 131, 172, 207
Grave, 58, 101, 129, 130, 155-56, 170, 208, 242-43, 257
Greenwalt, David, 37, 153
guilt, 141, 176, 209, 213, 215-229;

cultural guilt, 229-34
Halfrek, 154, 211, 212, 213
Halloween, 46, 97, 237
Harmony, 78, 195, 196
Harris, Xander, 47; as Christ figure, 69, 101-2, 242-43, 257; moral character, 96-103
The Harsh Light of Day, 89, 164, 195, 249
The Harvest, 14, 62, 110, 114, 143, 165, 171
heaven, 64, 169, 170; Buffy in, 56, 65, 168-69; existence of, 20, 64; television depictions, 168
hell, 20, 51, 56, 64, 82, 169-170, 226; absence of hope, 113; torment, 65
Hell's Bells, 66, 212
Help, 71, 164
Helpless, 52
Him, 85, 88, 145, 216, 225
holy water, 16, 69, 109
Homecoming, 50, 52, 106, 110
homelessness, 113-14
homosexuality, xiii, 6, 13, 83, 189, 201
hope, 113-14, 204, 228
Hus, 229-32 *passim*
Hush, 132
The I in Team, 79, 132, 133, 238
immanence, 14, 70-71
Inca Mummy Girl, 97, 99, 109, 166, 204
incoherent text, 7, 16-17, 173, 204, 205, 213-14
individualism, 140, 144, 145
The Initiative, 136, 204
Innocence, 126, 142, 151, 192, 193, 211
institutional authority, 4, 14, 125,

136-37; education, 130-32, 136; government, 132-34; law enforcement, 108, 111, 112, 119, 123, 136, 137; religion, 134-36
Internet, 14, 38, 40, 68, 126, 127, 128
Intervention, 115, 117, 164, 252
Into the Woods, 141, 179, 249, 250, 251
I Only Have Eyes For You, 129, 218-19
I, Robot . . . You Jane, 14, 38, 45, 46, 126-128
I Was Made to Love You, 126, 178, 197
Jesus, 13, 15, 66, 112-17 *passim*, 140, 203, 225, 226, 247, 256
Jonathan, 27-28, 57, 111, 175-77
Judaism, 65, 66, 69
Judeo-Christian values, 12, 107-8, 197, 201, 260
Kendra, 49, 50, 51, 77, 108, 111, 112, 141, 148
Killed By Death, 99, 111, 178, 204, 218
The Killer In Me, 217, 245
Knights of Byzantium, 134
Lessons, 62, 183, 212, 242
Lewis, C. S., 67, 240
Lies My Parents Told Me, 79, 80, 82, 139, 210, 248, 249, 250
Lie To Me, 25, 74, 85, 113, 165, 177-178
Life Serial, 57, 95, 155
Lily (Chanterelle), 112-113
Listening to Fear, 250
Living Conditions, 141
love, 49, 127-28, 169; and sex, 198, 201; tough love, 141-42; unconditional, 58, 101-2, 242-43, 256, 260
Lovers Walk, 39, 40, 89, 134, 179, 196, 217, 237, 247, 249
lying, 123, 174, 176-179
Maclay, Tara, 151, 251; death, 57, 72, 79, 137, 208, 213, 217, 241; as moral voice, 241; and Willow, 6, 53, 55, 129, 182-83
magic (witchcraft), xiii, 13, 38, 128-130, 238, 240-42; as metaphor, 38, 40, 129, 175, 182-83
Master, The, 48, 71, 74, 172, 209; religiosity, 49, 67-68, 114
Mayor, The, 51-52, 74, 131, 145
media watchdogs, 9, 10, 15, 19, 135, 174, 195, 202
metaphor, 2, 5-6, 13, 52, 77, 95, 144, 170, 191, 193, 196, 198-199, 254; adoption, 150; apocalypses, 170-72; beer, 180-81; and *Buffy*, 35-41, 261; class warfare, 184; drug use, 153, 181-83; embodied metaphor, 34, 40; family, 150-51; homelessness, 113; root metaphor, 33, 36, 37, 57; race, 77, 231; Slayer as, 43, 94, 96, 107, 109; technology, 127-28; vampire as, 35, 81-2, 180, 231, 234; Watcher as, 155; werewolf as, 191-92; *see also* magic, morality, sex, violence, Whedon
Moloch the Corruptor, 127, 128
moral responsibility, 74, 96, 105-114, 118, 120, 122, 123, 125, 136, 155, 184, 260
morality: absolutism, 73-74; and

art, xii, 17, 18; ambiguity, 20, 74-80, 85, 177, 202; and metaphor, 32-34; and narrative, 20, 21, 24-26, 32, 202, 205-7; and redemption, 235-36; relativism, 73; and television, xii, xiv, 8-12, 17, 92, 123, 259
murder, 58, 63, 67, 79, 82, 108, 134, 218, 244, 246; of Allan Finch, 52, 208; of Ben, 79; of Father Gabriel, 134-35; of Jenny Calendar, 193, 218, 227; of Jonathan, 72, 244, 246, 247; of Katrina, 244; of Tara, 72, 79, 241; of Warren, 176, 208
mythology, 9, 18, 21, 25-26, 43, 187, 206; *Buffy* and, 17, 20, 36, 63, 192; classical, 4, 64, 129, 170; religious, 10, 20-21; and television, 10
narrative arc, 123, 201, 214, 241, 256, 261
negative example, 123, 221-22, 223, 253, 261
Never Kill A Boy On the First Date, 108, 162
Never Leave Me, 225
New Moon Rising, 76, 77
Newton, Cassie, 71, 164
Nietzsche, Friedrich, 31, 245
Nightmares, 40, 208, 217, 237
No Place Like Home, 134, 212, 250
Normal Again, 27, 28-30, 89, 224
Noxon, Marti, 7, 81, 95, 182; on Satan, 20; on Spike, 87; on Spike and Buffy, 199; on werewolves, 191-92; on witches, 129-130

Older and Far Away, 154, 176, 183, 211, 212
Once More, With Feeling, 143
O'Toole, Jack, 100-101
Out of Mind, Out of Sight, 185
Out of My Mind, 209, 241, 250, 250
Owen, 108-9, 162
Oz: as metaphor, 191-92; werewolf, 39, 49, 76-77; and Willow, 49
The Pack, 38, 66, 184
Palmer, Billy, 208
Pangs, 135, 144, 229-34
parenting, 151-57
Parents Television Council, 12, 13, 15, 16, 175, 195
Passion, 69, 178, 193, 209, 218
perspective, 11-12, 123, 149, 179-181, 189, 201-2, 205, 214, 261
Petrie, Douglas, 23, 118, 190, 199
Phases, 39, 46, 78, 85
polytheism, 13, 61, 64, 65
Potential, 30, 99, 102, 108, 162, 179
Potentials, 59, 60, 179, 211
Primeval, 133, 147
profanity, 11, 12, 13, 51, 140, 187
The Prom, 52, 111, 133, 162, 178
prophecy, 48, 49, 71, 116
Prophecy Girl, 14, 61, 69, 71, 115-16, 148, 163, 166, 257
The Puppet Show, 2-3, 131, 208, 237
Quasimodo, 251, 254
racism, 77
Rack, 183, 253
rape, 57, 59, 88, 182, 194, 204, 209, 253-54
Rayne, Ethan, 67, 153

The Real Me, 55, 240
redemption: Andrew, 243-47; Angel, 63, 69, 226-29, 236; Anya, 211-13, 236; Faith, 68, 120-23, 145, 194-95, 209; Spike, 68-69, 87, 88-89, 247-257; through violence, 208-9; Willow, 236-43; *see also*, Christianity, church, community, Whedon
religion, 9, 10, 16, 19, 23, 24, 61-67 *passim*, 113, 114, 140, 153
repentance, 224-26, 247
The Replacement, 98, 99, 163, 201
Reptile Boy, 47, 67, 174, 178, 180, 181, 184
Restless, 94, 96, 98, 101, 115, 147, 175, 224, 239-240, 256, 257
Revelations, 52, 77, 118, 142, 178, 194
Rosenberg, Willow, 46-47; addiction, 154, 175-77, 181-83; emotional control, 238-39, 241; forgiveness, 224; guilt, 222; homosexuality, 6, 201; impatience, 238-39; insecurity, 237-38, 239-41; and magic, 128-130; pride, 75; as vampire, 64, 78, 83
Ross, Marcie, 185
sacrifice, 69, 88, 99, 101, 105-123 *passim*, 143, 145, 256-57, 260; of Christ, 101-2, 224-26, 242
Same Time, Same Place, 144, 212, 213, 224
Satan, 20, 62, 112, 114, 167
School Hard, 16, 47, 49, 66, 85, 111, 142, 148, 247
science, 25, 53, 133
Seeing Red, 87, 88, 200, 209, 253, 254
Selfless, 78, 137, 212, 213
sex, 7, 23, 189-202, 253; consequences, 174, 191, 193-99; criticism of *Buffy*, 12-13, 195, 198; defense of *Buffy*, 15; metaphor, 129, 192-93; necessity of, 19, 25; perspective on, 201-2; predators, 38, 43; repression, 135, 197; and violence, 199-200
Shadow, 250
Show Time, 30, 63, 74, 128, 205
Sineya, 147, 175
Sleeper, 178, 200, 225, 254
Smashed, 183, 199, 238, 253
Snyder, Principal, 131, 132, 136
social justice, 183-87
Some Assembly Required, 208
Something Blue, 149, 151, 222, 238-39, 249
soul, 61, 84-90; conscience, 226-27; free will, 128; guilt, 216, 225-26; moral compass, 251; redemption, 200, 209, 246; restlessness, 224-26
Spider-Man, 105
Spike (a.k.a. William the Bloody): and Buffy, 29, 87, 175-76, 198-201, 222, 251-56; chip, 53, 77, 85-88, 144, 251; as Christ figure, 69, 257; and community, 144; death, 256-57; guilt, 225; identity, 86-88; imperialism, 230, 232-33; as metaphor, 82, 234; poet, 248-250; redemption, 68-69, 87, 88-89; repentance, 224-26; soul, 66, 85-90, 128, 224-26,

256; violence, 209
Spiral, 219
Storyteller, 27, 30-32, 167, 208, 210, 245-47
subtext, 3, 5, 6, 7, 12, 31, 181, 261
Summers, Buffy, 6, 43, 45-46; as Christ figure, 16, 69, 114-118, 257; death, 16, 71, 168-170, 252; forgiveness, 218-24; guilt, 217-24; identity, 105-114; moral responsibility, 74, 78, 80, 107-114, 120, 122; as parent figure, 154-56; power, 93-96, 133, 187; and religion, 66-67; sex, 190, 191, 192-200, 252; solitude, 139, 146-48; view of authority, 136-37; violence, 204, 210-11
Summers, Dawn: adoption metaphor, 150; and Buffy, 154-56; insecurity, 102; shoplifting, 175, 176; and Spike, 86, 204
Summers, Joyce, 121; death, 162, 206; as parent, 139, 152
Superstar, 27-28, 29, 30, 63
Surprise, 97, 162, 178, 192, 247
Sutherland, Kristine, 44
Tabula Rasa, 65, 129, 182, 238
Teacher's Pet, 191
technology, 4, 9, 25, 53, 125, 126-28, 130, 133
Ted, 6, 37, 73, 137, 152, 176
temptation, 199
This Year's Girl, 76, 93, 120, 151
Touched, 200, 210, 255
Tough Love, 182, 239
transcendence, 14, 21, 69, 70-71
Triangle, 46, 64, 170-71, 182, 250, 251

trust, 49, 74, 118, 142-43, 146, 178, 253-54
Two To Go, 58, 176, 213, 237, 242, 245
vengeance, 211-14, 232; Anya, 57, 78, 145, 176, 211-13; Hus, 232; Robin Wood, 59; Willow, 72, 129
Villains, 72, 79, 83, 137
violence, 7, 11-12, 203-211; criticism, 13; incoherence, 204-5; as metaphor, 209-11; and narrative, 19, 24-25, 205-7; redemptive, 208-9; and sex, 199-201
Walsh, Maggie, 54, 72, 79, 132, 133, 136, 180
warfare, 167-68, 210-11
Warren, 57, 101, 137, 175, 176, 197, 208, 217
Webster, Holden, 66, 111, 161
The Weight of the World, 164, 166, 216, 220
Welcome to the Hellmouth, 37, 46, 71, 106, 115, 131, 162
What's My Line? - Part One, 14, 66, 111
What's My Line? - Part Two, 68, 77, 111, 141
Whedon, Joss, xi, 1, 186; and Andrew, 31; atheism, 14, 20, 21, 24, 61, 89; Christian influence, 20-21, 61, 62, 65-66, 67, 69, 115, 257; feminism, 18, 26, 43, 150, 187; and metaphor, 37, 38, 107, 199; and mythology, 4, 20, 36; and narrative, 23-25; narrative responsibility, 19, 205-7; on addiction, 180; on

Buffy's morality, 107, 110, 119-120; on culture, 17-18, 187; on death, 162; on family, 149-150; on genre, 2-3; on incoherence, 7; on power, 186; on realism, 19, 25, 32, 40, 190; on season six, 56, 176; on sensationalism, 24; on sex, 193, 202; on soul, 89-90; on subtext, 5-6; on vampires, 35; redemption, 208, 219, 227, 235, 241; writing process, 17, 44
When She Was Bad, 146, 209, 223
Where the Wild Things Are, 135, 144, 196-97, 250
Whistler, 63, 72, 84, 91, 99, 112, 139
Who Are You?, 15, 121, 194, 196, 209
Wicca, xiii, 65, 128
Wild at Heart, 81, 196, 216
Wile E. Coyote, 133
The Wish, 63, 64, 148, 217
Witch, 38, 47, 106, 129, 152
witchcraft: *see* magic
Wood, Robin (film theorist), 7, 35
Wood, Robin (Principal), 59, 79, 80, 82, 84, 132, 164, 194-95, 200
Wrecked, 183, 199, 241
The Yoko Factor, 147, 151
The Zeppo, 100, 204

About the Author

Gregory Stevenson has been teaching in the Religion department at Rochester College since 1999. Among his course load are classes on the New Testament, ancient Greek, and religion and popular culture. In addition to *Buffy*, he has a particular interest in archaeology and apocalyptic literature and is the author of *Power and Place: Temple and Identity in the Book of Revelation*. He currently lives in Michigan with his wife and three young children.